# IN FRANKENSTEIN'S SHADOW

# In Frankenstein's Shadow

### Myth, Monstrosity, and
### Nineteenth-century Writing

CHRIS BALDICK

CLARENDON PRESS · OXFORD
1987

Oxford University Press, Walton Street, Oxford OX2 6DP
Oxford New York Toronto
Delhi Bombay Calcutta Madras Karachi
Petaling Jaya Singapore Hong Kong Tokyo
Nairobi Dar es Salaam Cape Town
Melbourne Auckland
and associated companies in
Beirut Berlin Ibadan Nicosia

Oxford is a trade mark of Oxford University Press

Published in the United States
by Oxford University Press, New York

British Library Cataloguing in Publication Data
Baldick, Chris
In Frankenstein's shadow: myth, monstrosity,
and nineteenth-century writing.
1. English literature—19th century—
History and criticism   2. Monsters in
literature
I. Title
820.9′375   PR469.M6
ISBN 0-19-811726-4

Library of Congress Cataloging-in-Publication Data
Baldick, Chris.
In Frankenstein's shadow.
includes index.
1. Shelley, Mary Wollstonecraft, 1797–1851.
Frankenstein.   2. Shelley, Mary Wollstonecraft, 1797–
1851—. Influence.   3. Frankenstein (Fictitious
character).   4. Monsters in literature.   5. Myth in
literature.   6. Fiction—19th century—History and
criticism.   7. France—History—Revolution, 1789–1799—
Literature and the revolution.   8. Politics and
literature.   9. Literature and technology.   I. Title.
PR5397.F73B3   1987   823′.7   87–12573
ISBN 0-19-811726-4

Set by Dobbie Typesetting Service, Plymouth
Printed in Great Britain
at the University Printing House, Oxford
by David Stanford
Printer to the University

*To my sister in the South*

# Acknowledgements

THE immediate incitement to pursue the research embodied in this book came from reading the stimulating contributions by George Levine and Lee Sterrenburg to a collection of essays entitled *The Endurance of 'Frankenstein'*, edited by George Levine and U. C. Knoepflmacher (Berkeley, 1979). My work differs in approach from the one and in scale from the other, but should rightly begin with this salute to two pioneering students of things Frankensteinian.

Among the colleagues and friends who have offered me helpful hints, suggestions, and corrections, I am happy to thank here Alan Bird, Penny Boumelha, Chris Brooks, Peter Currie, Steven Peet, and John Simons.

C.B.

# Contents

# Illustrations

# 1

## Introduction

The story of Frankenstein and his monster enjoys a status which appears to literary criticism as an anomaly, a scandal: it is a modern myth. Such a thing simply should not exist, according to the most influential accounts of what 'myth' is. In anthropology and in Jungian psychology as in literary myth criticism from T. S. Eliot to Northrop Frye and beyond, the consensus in discussion of myths is that they are defined by their exclusive anteriority to literate and especially to modern culture. 'Myth'—the singular state posited in these discussions—is a lost world, to which modern writers may distantly and ironically allude, but in which they can no longer directly participate. Myth is, so the argument goes, exclusively a product of pre-literate cultures, from which the alienated and fragmented modern world of money, books, politics, and above all, scientific rationality is by definition cut off. People belonging to pre-literate, mythopoeic cultures, on the other hand, are to be regarded as being at one with themselves and with the timeless rhythms of the natural and cosmic cycle. The more this argument rejects the possibility of modern myths, the more, ironically, it becomes one itself (in the derogatory sense, that is): a modern, and specifically Romantic, 'myth of myth'. Looking beyond actual myths, it seeks to establish a state of mind, a 'mythic consciousness' as a prelapsarian condition whose wholeness can readily be contrasted with the impoverished and self-divided mentality which is the modern.

In certain diluted forms, this position may be respected: Claude Lévi-Strauss's defence of mythological thinking has its virtues as a rebuke to the arrogance (and worse) of the imperial metropolis towards 'primitive' peoples, although he shares some blame for keeping myth and history too sharply distinct. In its stronger forms, as in the tradition founded by C. G. Jung, the myth of myth becomes a substitute religion which offers a tempting refuge from the calamities of known history. If alcohol is the quickest way out of Manchester, myth is the quickest way out of the twentieth century, allowing instant access to a transcendent timeless order outside or

1

behind this age of anxiety. The result has been the setting up of an
impassable division between myth, which is integrative and redeeming,
and history, which is chaotic and fallen. So powerful has this ideology
been in twentieth-century culture, that the existence of actual modern
myths has been denied serious attention, and passed over as a
contradiction in terms.

To argue for the existence of modern myths should not involve
any claim that they have the same importance or quite the same
nature that myths have in pre-literate cultures; this would be just
as anti-historical as the position we have just reviewed. Modern
myths are marginalized by rational discourses, they do not command
the same sorts of assent as 'primitive' myths; their status bears,
in short, the scars and handicaps imposed upon it by successive
cultural transformations. They would hardly be *modern* myths
if they failed to suffer this depletion. That these myths exist,
though, in forms much stronger than the everyday sense of myth
as mere fallacy, seems undeniable if we consider the lasting significance
in Western culture of the stories of Faust, Don Quixote, Robinson
Crusoe, Frankenstein, Jekyll, and Dracula. If there remain any
problems in according mythic status to these tales, they resolve
themselves into problems of distinguishing myths from literary
texts.

A literary text will usually, since the advent of printing, be fixed
in its form but may be complex and multivocal in its meaning. A
myth, on the other hand, is open to all kinds of adaptation and
elaboration, but it will preserve at the same time a basic stability
of meaning. As Lévi-Strauss argues, poetry cannot be translated
without serious distortion, 'whereas the mythic value of the myth
remains preserved, even through the worst translation'.[1] (This
applies, we could add, to translations not just from one language
but from one medium to another, although distortion is more likely
here.) The reason for this openness to translation is that a myth's
true substance as myth 'does not lie in its style, its original music,
or its syntax, but in the *story* which it tells'.[2] The grand style and
original music of Shelley's *Prometheus Unbound* or of Blake's *Vala*
could not, for all their mythopoeic pretensions, give us more than

---

[1] Claude Lévi-Strauss, 'The Structural Study of Myth', in Thomas A. Sebeok (ed.),
*Myth: A Symposium* (Bloomington, Ind., 1958), 85.
[2] Ibid., 86.

old myths warmed up, whereas the clumsily-written *Frankenstein* created a living myth because it contained more fruitful possibilities in its story.

In myths, this essential 'story'—corresponding to Aristotle's *mythos*, or basic action—is a more economical and malleable thing than the elaborately plotted and sub-plotted narrative which we expect to find in a novel. Most myths, in literate societies at least, prolong their lives not by being retold at great length, but by being alluded to, thereby finding fresh contexts and applications. This process strips down the longer stories from which they may be derived, reducing them to the simplest memorable patterns. Thus the story of Victor Frankenstein and his monster first published in Mary Shelley's novel *Frankenstein; or, The Modern Prometheus* in 1818, appears within an elaborate framework of concentric narratives and is filled out with digressions, dialogues, scenic descriptions, and minor characters.[3] The myth, however, carries a skeleton story which requires only two sentences:

(a) Frankenstein makes a living creature out of bits of corpses.
(b) The creature turns against him and runs amok.

The process of myth-making violates the multiplicity and interplay of meanings which the novel's narrative complexity sustains, and sets its radically foreshortened story free to attract new narrative or interpretative elaborations around it.

For an introductory glimpse at the kind of revision which this process brings about, we can consult a reference book to find out how the mythically condensed Frankenstein story was formulated in the late nineteenth century. The Revd Ebenezer Cobham Brewer in his often reprinted *Dictionary of Phrase and Fable*, defined 'Frankenstein' as

A young student, who made a soulless monster out of fragments of men picked up from churchyards and dissecting-rooms, and endued it with life by galvanism. The tale, written by Mrs. Shelley, shows how the creature longed for sympathy, but was shunned by every one. It was only animal life, a parody on the creature man, powerful for evil, and the instrument of dreadful retribution on the student who usurped the prerogative of the creator.[4]

[3] For readers who do not recall these details, a plot-summary of *Frankenstein* is provided as an appendix to this book.
[4] E. Cobham Brewer, *Dictionary of Phrase and Fable* (London, 1870), 315. Brewer

As a summary of Mary Shelley's novel this is not just inadequate but plainly inaccurate in some respects: her monster is not 'soulless' nor merely animal, and the means by which he is created are never revealed in the novel (only in Mary Shelley's 1831 Introduction is galvanism mentioned as one of the topics discussed at the time of the ghost-story competition which prompted her story). Even in Brewer's very short account of the story, then, we have a new set of interpolations and revisions which are specifically Christian and conservative in character. In the novel the problem of the monster's soul simply does not arise, nor (except again in the 1831 Introduction) is there any sign of a God whose creative monopoly Frankenstein has infringed. These interpolations became accepted later, as we shall see, as a way of accommodating a disturbing and impiously secular tale into a Christian culture by simplifying it according to a received dichotomy of flesh and spirit. They belong to the development of the myth, not to the novel.

The point here is not to lament the corruption and distortion of an authentic literary original, nor to correct erroneous departures from the truth of a 'real' Frankenstein story. There may be Shelleyan purists for whom the development of the myth is all a huge mistake, but I shall prefer in this study to avoid giving any final authority to the novel. The truth of a myth, as Lévi-Strauss rightly insists, is not to be established by authorizing its earliest version, but by considering all its versions. The vitality of myths lies precisely in their capacity for change, their adaptability and openness to new combinations of meaning. That series of adaptations, allusions, accretions, analogues, parodies, and plain misreadings which follows upon Mary Shelley's novel is not just a supplementary component of the myth; it *is* the myth.

The one preliminary qualification I should enter here, since it helps to define the limits of this study, is that the openness or adaptability of myths is not a question of infinite variety: myths are also susceptible to 'closure', or to adaptations which constrain their further development into fixed channels. In the case of the Frankenstein myth, this moment of closure arrived in 1931 in the shape of William

seems to have borrowed from William A. Wheeler's *Dictionary of the Noted Names of Fiction* (London, 1866), misquoting a speech by the American politician Charles Sumner in which the Southern Confederacy is likened to 'the soulless monster of Frankenstein', although Brewer avoids repeating Wheeler's erroneous ascription of the name 'Frankenstein' to the monster.

Henry Pratt (better known as Boris Karloff), whose rectangular face and bolt-adorned neck have fixed our idea of the monster into a universally-known image from which it is hard to see further revisions breaking free. The film versions and their offspring are of course now very much part of the myth, but they dominate a phase of it in which the story's several possibilities have been narrowed and reduced by the sheer visual impact of Karloff's performance. There are incidental features of the Universal Pictures film which aggravate the narrowing process: the business of Fritz's mistake with the criminal's pickled brain, for instance, offers a crudely simple 'explanation' for the monster's motives, and kills off at a stroke one of the most fruitful enigmas of the myth's earlier phase. But the central problem, as I shall try to explain in Chapters 2 and 3, has to do with the difference between visible and invisible monsters, a contrast which goes back to the earliest stage versions of *Frankenstein* in the 1820s, and beyond that to earlier conceptions of monstrosity. The openness of the Frankenstein myth before its now authoritative cinematic representation was very largely the openness of literary revisions and allusions, in which no visible monster figured.

In this book I shall examine the development of the Frankenstein myth in the nineteenth century (that is—in human rather than calendar terms—between 1789 and 1917), and attempt to show not just that there was life before Karloff, but that the myth's vitality in this earlier period drew upon and in turn imaginatively embraced some of the central and most pressing problems of modern history. Some modern myths are more modern than others: those of Faust and Don Quixote arise from the decomposition of feudal religious and chivalric codes, that of Robinson Crusoe corresponds to a later mercantile bourgeois individualism, while the myth of Frankenstein registers the anxieties of the period inaugurated in the twin social and industrial revolutions in France and Britain. Unlike most of the Gothic novels of its time, which carry on safely retrospective flirtations with feudal and Papal power, Mary Shelley's novel is set in the Age of Reason itself (in the late eighteenth century, although with some anachronisms which would place its action even later), and it explores the godless world of specifically modern freedoms and responsibilities. The myth which develops out of it turns repeatedly upon these new problems of an age in which humanity seizes responsibility for re-creating the world, for violently reshaping its natural environment and its inherited social and political forms, for remaking itself.

In order to pursue and substantiate this claim, I shall need first to set aside the two most readily available kinds of interpretation of this myth, both of them anti-historical and both tending to narrow and close prematurely the range of meanings which the Frankenstein story has suggested. The first, which is a lazy equivalent of the 'archetypal' approach discussed above, simply ignores the historical conditions in which the Frankenstein story arose, and is content to explain its appeal by reference to 'our deepest fears': a handy enough cliché for the blurb-writer, perhaps, but one which refuses to recognize that fears are themselves subject to history (we are not usually afraid of bubonic plague or devils today, but then Chaucer did not spend any sleepless nights worrying about nuclear fall-out). Even if there are some deep fears which undergo little historical change, we are still left with the problem of explaining why humanity should have waited until the nineteenth century before revealing them in the form of the Frankenstein myth. By assuming that all myths belong in some timeless psychic plane, this first kind of reading reduces the story of Frankenstein to a parable about the eternal dilemmas of the human condition—the curse of innate evil, or the agony of self-consciousness. Lowry Nelson Jr., for instance, interprets *Frankenstein* as a 'model of the mind' representing 'the intimate good and bad struggle in the human personality', and draws this banal liberal moral from the tale:

Human nature being what it is . . . some sort of compromise must be made between the good and evil instincts of human nature in order to survive, since human nature deeply drives toward both good and evil; or at least some sort of modus vivendi must be found, most hopefully through full self-knowledge and self-discipline.[5]

Nelson goes on to define the developing myth as 'a mythology of the mind',[6] and he is followed by L. J. Swingle, who reads the story as a 'purely mental drama of damnation'.[7] In what are usually genuine, if misguided, efforts to persuade us that the story of Frankenstein is not outdated, such readings discard history in favour of perennial psychic truths, asserting, with Pope, that

[5] Lowry Nelson Jr., 'Night Thoughts on the Gothic Novel', *Yale Review*, lii (1963), 247–8.
[6] Ibid., 251.
[7] L. J. Swingle, 'Frankenstein's Monster and Its Romantic Relatives: Problems of Knowledge in English Romanticism', *Texas Studies in Literature*, xv (1973), 63.

. . . what thou seek'st is in thee! Look, and find
Each Monster meets his likeness in thy mind.[8]

The myth does indeed have its important psychological dimension,
and could not exist without mobilizing powerful fears. *Frankenstein*
itself is a novel which cannot be understood fully if psychological
interpretations are not brought into play. But it is of little help to
reduce the story of Frankenstein and his monster to a conflict of
psychic structures if this means abstracting it from the world outside
the psyche, with which the myth engages.

The second, and now more popular, interpretation of the
myth appears to take the opposite course, but ends up collapsing
back into the first error. What I shall call the technological
reduction sees the story chiefly as an uncanny prophecy of dangerous
scientific inventions. Its heyday came during the technological
euphoria of the 1960s, when, for instance, the true greatness of
Leonardo da Vinci was found to lie in his nearly inventing the
helicopter, thereby showing himself to be almost as clever as us.
Within the same self-regarding perspective, the true significance of
*Frankenstein* was seen to be its foreshadowing of robots, 'test-tube'
babies, and the heart-transplant surgery of Dr Christiaan Barnard.
Announcing a breakthrough in genetic engineering, the *New York
Times Magazine* proclaimed 'The *Frankenstein* Myth Becomes a
Reality: We Have The Awful Knowledge to Make Exact Copies of
Human Beings'.[9]

These were only the sillier and more trivial versions, though, of
a more general tendency to bind the myth to a restricted technological
meaning. The more intelligent, like Martin Tropp in his book *Mary
Shelley's Monster*, look further back to the mechanical and electrical
discoveries of the Industrial Revolution, but still insist on interpreting
the monster as a 'technological double', a symbol of 'the ambiguous
nature of the machine', or as 'the first and most enduring symbol
of modern technology'.[10] Tropp's description of the monster as 'half
human, half machine'[11] may bear some relation to the post-Karloff
myth, but is quite inapplicable to Mary Shelley's creature, who is

---

[8] Alexander Pope, *The Dunciad*, iii. 251–2.
[9] Willard Gaylen, *New York Times Magazine*, 5 Mar. 1972, cited by Martin
Tropp, *Mary Shelley's Monster* (Boston, 1977), 65.
[10] Tropp, *Mary Shelley's Monster*, 63, 65, 66.
[11] Ibid., 67.

not in the least mechanical; the most disturbing thing about him, indeed, is that he has fully human feelings. The technological interpretation of the myth resembles many influential diagnoses of 'the machine age' in that its isolation of the machine as the root evil of modern civilization merely reinforces the very fetishism of mechanical power which it sets out to deplore. Ignoring the relationships between people, within which technology operates, it can link the mechanical with the human only by absorbing it back into the timeless categories of 'the self'. Mary Shelley understood, claims Tropp, 'that technology can never be any more than a magnified image of the self'.[12] This brings us right back to the cosy idealism of Nelson, as we are reassured that

> our technology reflects ourselves and our motives; if we replace repression, fear, arrogance, and the desire for control with acceptance, love, humility, and the capacity for understanding, our machines can become a well-adjusted part of our culture.[13]

This might be a plausible happy ending to the Frankenstein story of modern civilization if the problem were really as simple and identifiable as a domestication of machines or a cultivation of the better side of 'the self'. The endurance and importance of the Frankenstein myth, however, derives largely from its capacity to refer beyond adjustments of the self or of the machine, to problems of greater scope.

   Although the Frankenstein myth did, in one of its possible metaphoric uses, come to be applied to technological development, its great powers of suggestion and connotation have always centred primarily on relations between people, and between people and nature. The relationship between Frankenstein and his monster is modelled ultimately upon that between parent and child, and its mythic development embraces the relations between men and women, rulers and ruled, masters and servants, propertied and propertyless. Within the myth, the inhuman—whether mechanical or demonic—has figured very strikingly, but usually as a metaphor of distortion in these relationships. The range of mythic applications here, and within it the possibilities for overlapping metaphoric connections, is far greater than the narrowly psychological or technological interpretations of the myth recognize. It is these often

[12] Ibid., 55.
[13] Ibid., 155.

neglected dimensions of the Frankenstein myth that I shall be trying
to recover in the following chapters. I shall explore the work of
several writers, most of them British or American, examining the
different uses to which they put this myth, and the ways in which
its major historical concerns are reworked in their writings. This will
not be an exercise in tracing Mary Shelley's literary 'influence' (as
far as prose style is concerned, it is just as well she had none), but
a study of that process of adaptation, allusion, and revision by which
a modern myth is born and sustains its life. The kind of connection
which I shall be looking for, then, is often not one between a given
writer and a literary 'source' in Mary Shelley, but rather the sharing
of a concern for the problems which the later development of the
myth comes to formulate.

Because myths exist in a latent state of subterranean and invisible
diffusion in the cultures which adopt them, it is possible after the
event to catch them only at those moments when they have surfaced
in some documentary form, and so I have not been able to gather
more than the most visible and memorable traces of the nineteenth-
century Frankenstein. My account will appear even more broken than
this implies, though, because the writers who used and adapted the
myth did so in such various ways: one will play upon the idea
of constructing people artificially from fragments, another will
investigate the self-destructive consequences of the solitary quest for
knowledge, yet another will be fascinated by creations which turn
against their creators, and all will dabble in strange conjunctions of
the scientific and the ghoulish. It would be easier merely to salute
the versatility of the myth, but I shall try as well to indicate how
its various facets refer back to common and continuous anxieties,
to genuine causes for alarm in the monstrous and uncontrollable
tendencies of the modern world.

# 2

# The Politics of Monstrosity

Vice is a monster of so frightful mien
As, to be hated, needs but to be seen.

Pope, *Essay on Man*

For the reader of Mary Shelley's novel, there is some uncertainty whether best to define the being created by Victor Frankenstein as 'monster', 'wretch', 'daemon', 'creature', or 'fiend'.[1] The myth, however, has evolved a consensus that the unnamed hominoid deserves at least the name of 'the monster'. In order to clarify the particular historical significance of the myth in its early stages, it will be worth assessing this term in its various meanings and associations. In modern usage 'monster' means something frighteningly unnatural or of huge dimensions. But in earlier usages, which persist into the nineteenth century, the word carries further connotations essential to the development of the Frankenstein myth, the essence of which is that they are not physiological but moral in their reference.

As Michel Foucault reminded us in his discussion of the public performances put on by the inmates of lunatic asylums until the early nineteenth century, a 'monster' is something or someone to be *shown*.[2] (Cf. Latin, *monstrare*; French, *montrer*; English, demonstrate.) In a world created by a reasonable God, the freak or lunatic must have a purpose: to reveal visibly the results of vice, folly, and unreason, as a warning (Latin, *monere*: to warn) to erring humanity. Theological interpretation of monsters and prodigies goes back to Augustine, who argued in his *De civitate Dei* that monsters reveal the will of God. By the time of the Reformation we find Martin Luther himself indulging in monster-interpretation, explaining the birth of a freakish 'monk-calf' as a warning from God about the

---

[1] A simple word-tally shows 'monster', with 27 appearances, to have won by a short head from 'fiend' (25), followed by 'daemon' (18), 'creature' (16), 'wretch' (15), and 'devil' (8); 'being' (4) and 'ogre' (1) also ran.

[2] Michel Foucault, *Madness and Civilization: A History of Insanity in the Age of Reason*, trans. Richard Howard (London, 1967), 68–70.

10

corruption of Rome.[3] Not satisfied with the explicitness of this divine message, Luther and Melanchthon invented their own 'pope-ass' monster to supplement it. Popular broadsheets of this period would carry woodcuts of deformed children or animals, together with extended teratoscopic analyses of the divine message contained in these prodigious births.

It is with a similar, if more secular, sense of monstrous *display* that Shakespeare has Antony address Cleopatra, referring to her expected surrender to Octavian:

> Let him take thee
> And hoist thee up to the shouting plebeians,
> Follow his chariot, like the greatest spot
> Of all thy sex. Most monster-like be shown
> For poor'st diminutives, for dolts . . .
>
> (*Antony and Cleopatra*, IV. xii. 33–7)

There is nothing monstrous in the modern sense about Cleopatra (whatever the length of her nose); her anticipated 'monstrosity' here will be her position in Caesar's triumphal procession as a demonstration that resistance to his power is futile. The same sense is employed in the closing scenes of *Macbeth*, as Macduff (regarded by Macbeth as the product of a monstrously unnatural birth) triumphs over the usurper, shifting on to him the stigma of monstrosity:

> Then yield thee, coward,
> And live to be the show and gaze o'the time:
> We'll have thee, as our rarer monsters are,
> Painted upon a pole, and underwrit,
> 'Here may you see the tyrant'.
>
> (V. viii. 23–7)

More clearly than in Cleopatra's case, the final defining tag here brings out a particular characteristic of this meaning of monstrosity: its habitual use as an illustration of a particular vice or transgression. Monstrosity, for Shakespeare, is less a matter of physiological prodigies and freaks than a way of defining moral aberrations; as Antonio remarks in *Twelfth Night*:

---

[3] See Lorraine J. Daston and Katherine Park, 'Unnatural Conceptions: The Study of Monsters in Sixteenth- and Seventeenth-Century France and England', *Past and Present*, xcii (1981), 20–54.

In nature there's no blemish but the mind;
None can be call'd deform'd but the unkind.

(III. iv. 376-7)

This moral sense of monstrosity is very common in Renaissance literature generally, but to continue with Shakespearian instances alone, we find that in *Othello* Emilia characterizes jealousy as a monster; Gower in the prologue and epilogue to *Pericles* refers to the 'monster envy' and 'monstrous lust'; Petruchio in *The Taming of the Shrew* complains of 'monstrous arrogance', and Gloucester in *Henry the Sixth, Part One* of 'monstrous treachery', while Holofernes in *Love's Labour's Lost* exclaims: 'O thou monster Ignorance, how deformed dost thou look.'[4] When Celia seals her promise to Rosalind by swearing 'and when I break that oath let me turn monster' (*As You Like It*, I. ii. 22), she means 'let me be displayed publicly as the very emblem of disloyalty'. In these uses, monstrosity is employed not just as an intensifier, highlighting the degree or extent of the vice, but as a special kind of superlative which indicates that the particular case has revealed the essence of the vice in question, and can be displayed as its very model and type. In Hegelian terms we can say that this usage shows degree or quantity transforming itself into quality. When the Poet in *Timon of Athens*, referring to Timon's friends, speaks of 'The monstrous bulk of this ingratitude' (V. i. 65), he appears merely to be measuring its scale, but in fact is announcing its fully representative status as the clearest possible display of the vice—which on the stage, of course, is just what it is. The same goes for the King of France's view of Cordelia's alleged crime: 'her offence must be of such unnatural degree / That monsters it' (*King Lear*, I. i. 219-20). The monster is one who has so far transgressed the bounds of nature as to become a moral advertisement.

*Timon* and *Lear* highlight the most important class within this usage: the representation of ingratitude. Leaving aside the rather special case of Caliban, a literal monster and (in Prospero's eyes) ingrate, Shakespeare's most powerful and memorable representations of moral monstrosity are concentrated upon this vice. (It is not, for our purposes, important that the protagonists of these plays are blind or indiscriminate in their accusations—their sense alone

---

[4] *Othello*, III. iv. 161; *Pericles*, Prologue, 12, V. iii. 86; *Taming of the Shrew*, IV. iii. 107; *I Henry VI*, IV. i. 61; *Love's Labour's Lost*, IV. ii. 23.

concerns us.) Timon, who has 'flung in rage from this ingrateful
seat / Of monstrous friends' ( *Timon of Athens*, IV. ii. 45-6), is
moved to exclaim:

> And yet, O! see the monstrousness of man
> When he looks out in an ungrateful shape
>
> (III. ii. 72-3)

The 'monster of ingratitude' (as even Time itself is described by
Ulysses in *Troilus and Cressida*) is so prominent among monstrous
representations of vice that, especially in cases of children's behaviour
towards parents, the offence need not even be specified. So in *Lear*,
Gloucester, incredulous at Edmund's accusations against Edgar, can
say 'He cannot be such a monster . . . to his father' (I. ii. 94-6).
Lear is more specific in complaining of Goneril's 'monster ingratitude',
but Albany can simply describe her behaviour as 'most monstrous'
(I. v. 39; V. iii. 160). It is the vices of ingratitude, rebellion, and
disobedience, particularly towards parents, that most commonly
attract the appellation 'monstrous': to be a monster is to break the
natural bonds of obligation towards friends and especially towards
blood-relations. The crime may even be extended to cover contractual
obligations: Milton writes in his *Tenure of Kings and Magistrates* that
'If I make a voluntary Covnant as with a man, to doe him good, and he
prove afterward a monster to me, I should conceave a disobligement.'[5]
Long before the monster of Frankenstein, monstrosity already
implied rebellion, or an unexpected turning against one's parent
or benefactor.

A further characteristic of the monstrous needs to be noted: it is
an almost obligatory feature of the monsters in classical mythology
that they should be composed of ill-assorted parts, sometimes
combined from different creatures (centaurs, satyrs, the Minotaur,
the Sphinx), sometimes merely multiplied to excess (Argus, the
Hydra). This feature has two kinds of consequence in the history
of monstrosity, one aesthetic, the other political, and both have a
bearing on the Frankenstein myth. The aesthetic discussion of
monstrosity does not at first proceed from the moral dimension of
the concept we have discussed above, but uses instead the directly
physical notion of deformity to illustrate certain problems of the

---

[5] John Milton, *Selected Prose*, ed. C. A. Patrides (Harmondsworth, 1974),
276.

relation of parts to the whole in works of art. Horace begins his *Ars Poetica* with just this problem:

> Suppose a painter chose to put a human head on a horse's neck, or to spread feathers of various colours over the limbs of several different creatures, or to make what in the upper part is a beautiful woman tail off into a hideous fish, could you help laughing when he showed you his efforts?[6]

This injunction against ridiculous and unnatural combinations became, in the Age of Reason, a sacred text within the neo-classical Rules for the decorous imitation of Nature. Transgression of Horace's rule in fanciful and disturbing compounds of images constitutes the category of the 'grotesque', which unlike the 'picturesque' is an artificially contrived violation of Nature. The problem of wilful and unnatural assembly comes to be discussed as a major problem in the new aesthetics of Romanticism, notably in Coleridge's famous distinction between the organic fusion of parts achieved by the Imagination, and the merely mechanical combinations produced by Fancy. In Victor Frankenstein's assembly of his creature this aspect of monstrosity, too, is clearly present, and is a factor in the subsequent uses of the myth. The most important connection in which this issue presents itself is in the contribution of the image of the hybrid or hydra-monster to the political senses of monstrosity, which we should now review.

The representation of fearful transgressions in the figure of physical deformity arises as a variant of that venerable cliché of political discourse, the 'body politic'. When political discord and rebellion appear, this 'body' is said to be not just diseased, but misshapen, abortive, monstrous. Once the state is threatened to the point where it can no longer be safely identified (according to the medieval theory) with 'the King's body'—that is, with an integral and sacred whole— then the humanly recognizable form of the body politic is lost, dispersed into a chaos of dismembered and contending organs. The *OED*, under 'Monstrous', cites Starkey writing in 1538 that 'The partys in proportyon not agreyng . . . make in this polityke body grete and monstrose deformyte'. Like very many of the writers who use this figure, Sir Thomas Browne in *Religio Medici* (1643) locates this 'deformyte' in the debased nature of the popular rabble,

---

[6] Horace, 'On the Art of Poetry', trans. E. T. Dorsch, in Aristotle, Longinus, Horace, *Classical Literary Criticism* (Harmondsworth, 1965), 79.

'the multitude, that numerous piece of monstrosity, which taken asunder seeme men, and the reasonable creatures of God; but confused together, make but one great beast & a monstrosity more prodigious than Hydra'.[7] A similar image of 'the blunt monster with uncounted heads, / The still-discordant wavering multitude' appears in Shakespeare's *Henry the Fourth, Part Two* (Induction, 18). A glance at Shakespeare's more celebrated use of the body politic figure in *Coriolanus* may help to amplify the senses in which the multitude is seen as monstrous:

Ingratitude is monstrous; and for the multitude to be ingrateful, were to make a monster of the multitude; of the which, we being members, should bring ourselves to be monstrous members. (II. iii. 9–12)

The Third Citizen's quibble here incorporates the familiar moral vice of ingratitude into the image of disorganized members, making the multitude doubly monstrous: hydra-headed and therefore irrepressible, and at the same time an ingrate, rebelling against its political parent.

In the shadow of this monster, the founding of modern political theory during the years of Revolution in the seventeenth century had to replace the integrity of the medieval 'King's body' with a fearfully inhuman substitute. This problem of the body politic and the relations of its organs is the central preoccupation of Thomas Hobbes in his *De Corpore Politico* (1640) and *Leviathan* (1651), the latter work announcing from the start its new sense of the political 'body':

For by Art is created that great LEVIATHAN, called a COMMON-WEALTH, or STATE, (in latine, CIVITAS) which is but an Artificiall Man; though of greater stature and strength than the Naturall . . . Lastly, the *Pacts* and *Covenants* by which the parts of this Body Politique were first made, set together, and united, resemble that *Fiat*, or the *Let us make man*, pronounced by God in the Creation.[8]

There is an uneasy feeling of human responsibility involved in this conception, fully in accord with subsequent uses of 'monstrosity' since, like Horace's mermaids, the monsters both of poetic fancy and of political organization are made not by nature but by fallible human arts. From the perception of such a gulf between nature and culture

---

[7] Sir Thomas Browne, *The Major Works*, ed. C. A. Patrides (Harmondsworth, 1977), 134.

[8] Thomas Hobbes, *Leviathan*, ed. C. B. Macpherson (Harmondsworth, 1968), 81–2.

the fear that human society may itself be producing monsters emerges as early as 1697, as the *OED* records from South's *Sermons*: 'We sometimes read of Monstrous Births, but we may often see a greater Monstrosity in Educations.' This artificial man is a monster closely related to Hobbes's gigantic creature; both need to be kept in mind when we come to examine the development of the Frankenstein myth. They both reflect the dismemberment of the old body politic as incarnated in the personal authority of late feudal and absolutist rule. They signal the growing awareness, hastened in the heat of regicide and revolution, of destinies no longer continuous with nature but shaped by art, by 'policy'—the prospect in politics and in broader cultural life of the 'artificial man'. When revolution and regicide reappear on the agenda of European history, this spectre will be re-animated.

In Britain the first decade of the French Revolution witnessed the prodigious proliferation of two bodies of writing: a boom in 'Gothic' novels led by Ann Radcliffe, and a flurry of books and pamphlets provoked by Edmund Burke's *Reflections on the Revolution in France* (1790). The one is typically preoccupied with feudal forms of unlimited personal power and its tyrannical abuse: imprisonment, rape, persecution, and the victim's claustrophobia. The other is concerned with the very new 'monster' (as Burke saw it) of the French Revolution itself; with the novelty, the rationality, and the irrationality in the consciously artificial order of revolutionary France, and with the Terrors of both the new and the old regimes. Bridging these two bodies of work there is an intermediary category of writings which constitutes what Gary Kelly calls the 'Jacobin Novel'[9]—the fictional works of Robert Bage, Elizabeth Inchbald, Thomas Holcroft, Mary Wollstonecraft, and William Godwin. If the flourishing of the Gothic novel is a sure but unconscious and remote reverberation of the events in France,[10] the works of this group are more openly addressed to the social and political issues highlighted by the revolutionary process. Politico-philosophical novels (in some respects the muted British equivalents of the works of Sade), these writings bring together the terrors of the Gothic novel and the topical social criticism of

---

[9] Gary, Kelly, *The English Jacobin Novel 1780–1805* (Oxford, 1976).

[10] In his 'Idée sur les romans' (1800), the Marquis de Sade wrote of the Gothic novels of Lewis and Radcliffe as 'the inevitable result of the revolutionary shocks which all of Europe has suffered'. *The 120 Days of Sodom and Other Writings*, trans. A. Wainhouse and R. Seaver (New York, 1966), 109.

*Things as They Are*—the original title of Godwin's *Adventures of Caleb Williams* (1794). It was from the area marked out by this overlapping of literary and political discourses that the Frankenstein myth was born, as a late product of the controversy generated in Britain by the French Revolution.

The controversy begins with Burke's extravagantly rhetorical attack on the French revolutionaries. What was even more shocking than Burke's apparent change of loyalties since his earlier championing of liberal causes was the ferocity of his imagery, the sheer violence of his tropes. In the *Reflections* Burke's conservative faith is tied to a powerful emotional investment in a 'natural' policy which antedates Hobbes's artificial man. Above all, he identifies the political status quo so insistently with the sanctities of familial feelings that his account becomes an Oedipal drama. 'Ingratitude to benefactors is the first of revolutionary virtues', Burke later wrote, and went on to describe the revolutionaries as 'miscreant parricides'.[11] Burke mobilizes, and intensifies, a Shakespearian sense of monstrosity as rebellion against the father:

[We] should approach to the faults of the state as to the wounds of a father, with pious awe and trembling solicitude. By this wise prejudice we are taught to look with horror on those children of their country who are prompt rashly to hack that aged parent in pieces, and put him in the kettle of magicians, in hopes that by their poisonous weeds, and wild incantations, they may regenerate the paternal constitution, and renovate their father's life.[12]

Monstrous ingratitude to the father is combined here, as in *Coriolanus*, with a monstrous dismemberment, a castratory hacking which precedes the reassembly of limbs into an abortive body politic. Even before the Terror, the French Revolution is to Burke a monstrous jumble of elements, 'out of nature' (*RRF*, 92), producing a 'monster of a constitution' (*RRF*, 313). More important than this rehearsal of horrors is Burke's attempt to turn the events into a species of cautionary tale. His explanation of the fall of the *ancien régime*

---

[11] *The Works of the Rt Hon Edmund Burke*, 6 vols. (Oxford, 1907), vi. 67, 78. Subsequent page references in the text are to this edition, abbreviated as *Works*. On Burke's Oedipal version of the Revolution, see Ronald Paulson, *Representations of Revolution (1789–1820)* (New Haven, 1983), ch. 6.

[12] Edmund Burke, *Reflections on the Revolution in France, and on the Proceedings in Certain Societies in London Relative to that Event*, ed. Conor Cruise O'Brien (Harmondsworth, 1968), 194. Subsequent page references in the text are to this edition, abbreviated as *RRF*.

includes the following criticism of its last ministries: 'Rather too much countenance was given to the spirit of innovation, which soon was turned against those who fostered it, and ended in their ruin.' (*RRF*, 237.) The proverbial wisdom here is not in itself original, but in its application to the understanding of the Revolution's bewildering events, it helped to formulate a very influential narrative logic. Its pattern reappears in the long quotation from the Comte de la Tour du Pin's report to the Assembly on military affairs, which was later to take on the status of a prophecy:

'*The nature of things requires*, that the army should never act but as *an instrument*. The moment that, erecting itself into a deliberative body, it shall act according to its own resolutions, the *government, be it what it may*, will immediately degenerate into a military democracy; a species of political monster, which has always ended by devouring those who have produced it.' (*RRF*, 333)

Burke goes on, in his own words, to complain of the municipal army of the Paris district that 'considered in a view to any coherence or connection between its parts, it seems a monster, and can hardly fail to terminate its perplexed movements in some great national calamity' (*RRF*, 350).

The monster image is a powerful means of organizing, understanding, and at the same time preserving the chaotic and confused nature of the revolutionary events in Burke's account. Burke had first adopted this approach in a letter to his son in October 1789, writing of 'the portentous State of France—where the Elements which compose Human Society seem all to be dissolved, and a world of Monsters to be produc'd in the place of it.'[13] After the Terror of 1793 had borne out his prophecy, the revolutionary Monster in his writings returns in even more lurid colours. Burke's *Letters on the Proposals for Peace with the Regicide Directory of France* (1796–7) repeat this kind of imagery with hysterical insistence: France is a 'monster of a state', it is 'the mother of monsters', a 'monstrous compound', and a 'cannibal republic' (*Works*, vi. 95, 127, 161, 188). In his *Letter to a Noble Lord* (1796) Burke plays upon the strong interest in scientific experiment among the radicals of his age (Paine, Franklin, and Marat, for example), attacking the French revolutionaries not just as cannibals, but as sorcerers, alchemists, and fanatical chemists.

---

[13] *The Correspondence of Edmund Burke*, ed. Alfred Cobban and Robert A. Smith (Cambridge, 1967), vi. 30.

Dwelling often on stories of graves being robbed to provide materials for arms, he extends this ghoulishness into a wider accusation against the radical *philosophes* and their inhuman lust for desecration. The manufacture of saltpetre from the rubble of aristocratic houses strikes him as another such horror: 'There is nothing, on which the leaders of the republic, one and indivisible, value themselves, more than on the chemical operations by which, through science, they convert the pride of aristocracy to an instrument of its own destruction.' (*Works*, vi. 73 n.) The unfeeling *philosophes* are so fanatically devoted to scientific pride that 'they would sacrifice the whole human race to the slightest of their experiments' (*Works*, vi. 70). From this rhetorical riot of ghoulish scientists and ransacked graves looms Burke's most ominous image of the Revolution as a whole:

. . . out of the tomb of the murdered monarchy in France has arisen a vast, tremendous unformed spectre, in a far more terrifick guise than any which ever yet have overpowered the imagination, and subdued the fortitude of man. (*Works*, vi. 88)

As Conor Cruise O'Brien points out, the spectre haunting Europe in the opening sentence of *The Communist Manifesto* 'walks for the first time in the pages of Burke' (*RRF*, 9), although, as we have seen, the figure has a certain tradition behind it in political metaphors of the state and the multitude.

The spate of Anti-Jacobin writings inaugurated by Burke took up the same themes, regularly depicting the Parisian mob as a monster. Augustin de Barruel, whose writings were later devoured by Percy Shelley, wrote of 'that disastrous monster Jacobin', which he believed had been 'engendered' by a conspiracy of Enlightenment intellectuals (the 'Illuminati') originating in Ingolstadt.[14] The basis of the monstrous imagery used in these diatribes is a sketchy explanation of events in France: that godless *philosophes* had consciously desecrated traditional sanctities and produced from the resulting chaos a monster which, according to mythic logic, was sure to devour its creators. As J. M. Roberts has shown in his fascinating study of the masonic and Illuminati scares of this period, conscious design

---

[14] Abbé Barruel, *Memoirs Illustrating the History of Jacobinism*, trans. R. Clifford (London, 1798), iii. 414; cited by Lee Sterrenburg, 'Mary Shelley's Monster: Politics and Psyche in *Frankenstein*', in George Levine and U. C. Knoepflmacher (eds.), *The Endurance of 'Frankenstein'* (Berkeley, 1979), 156. On the Illuminati scare, see J. M. Roberts, *The Mythology of the Secret Societies* (London, 1972), chs. 5-6.

and conspiracy was the only kind of causal logic available to most people at the time as an explanation for the French events. Percy Shelley himself, whose idealism stretched so far as to claim that poets were the unacknowledged legislators of the world, must have found Barruel's conspiracy theory so attractive because of the enormous influence it attributed to a determined and enlightened élite. And for all his deep commitment to traditional continuities, prejudices, and unexamined loyalties, even Burke shared the age's belief in the limitless power of conscious human will, for he concedes that 'Man' is 'in a great degree a creature of his own making' (*RRF*, 189). Burke observed that self-making capacity at work on the grandest and most momentous scale: a parricidal dismemberment of the old body politic, an unprecedented reassembling of its disjointed parts, and the armed multitude conjured up by the propertied and educated classes, but no longer under their control. Burke first recognized and named the great political 'monster' of the modern age.

Burke's opponents rarely resort to such lurid figures; much of their criticism, indeed, is levelled at these extravagances of his rhetoric as well as at his arguments. But the charge of monstrosity had to be answered. In the most important of the responses to Burke, Tom Paine in *Rights of Man* attempts to turn the tables on him. Singling out Burke's phrase 'out of nature', he castigates the system of monarchy and aristocracy as itself a monstrous regime: 'It is by distortedly exalting some men, that others are distortedly debased, till the whole is out of nature.'[15] If the actions of the 'mob' appear unnatural, then the cause is to be found in the artificial exaggerations of wealth, rank, and privilege. Paine picks up on Burke's parricidal imagery and turns the accusation of unnatural child–parent relations back upon the aristocratic system itself:

By the aristocratical law of primogenitureship, in a family of six children, five are exposed. Aristocracy has never more than *one* child. The rest are begotten to be devoured. They are thrown to the cannibal for prey, and the natural parent prepares the unnatural repast.

As everything which is out of nature in man, affects, more or less, the interests of society, so does this. . . . To restore, therefore, parents to their children, and children to their parents—relations to each other, and man

---

[15] Thomas Paine, *Rights of Man*, ed. Henry Collins (Harmondsworth, 1969), 81 (cf. 95, 104). Subsequent page references in the text are to this edition, abbreviated as *RM*.

to society—and to exterminate the monster Aristocracy, root and branch—the French constitution has destroyed the law of PRIMOGENITURESHIP. Here then lies the monster; and Mr Burke, if he pleases, may write its epitaph. (*RM*, 104)

Paine has aimed his blow astutely at the parental callousness of primogeniture, thereby establishing aristocracy as a monstrous parent to counter Burke's monster child. Burke announces the birth of the monster child Democracy, while Paine records the death of the monster parent Aristocracy.[16] The 'sort of breathing automaton' (*RM*, 196) which is Monarchy is laid to rest, giving way to a remade humanity: 'the present generation will appear to the future as the Adam of a new world' (*RM*, 290), declares Paine, heralding the new rational Creation.

Paine's purpose in *Rights of Man* goes beyond the desire to trade monstrous countercharge against charge. It is to identify not merely the true monster but the true *parent* of the Revolution: the aristocracy, rather than any innovators or Illuminati, is to blame for exposing not just its younger sons but its whole people to cannibalism. In the darker years of the Revolution the importance of this argument to the radical cause increases noticeably, as can be seen in a second major reply to Burke, that of Mary Wollstonecraft in her *Historical and Moral View of the Origin and Progress of the French Revolution* (1794). Wollstonecraft traces the causes of the Revolution to the negligence of the decadent and over-refined French court. The widening gulf between court luxury and popular starvation has made French life inhospitable to the 'healthy beams' of the human soul:

But, by the habitual slothfulness of rusty intellects, or the depravity of the heart, lulled into hardness on the lascivious couch of pleasure, those heavenly beams are obscured, and man appears either an hideous monster, a devouring beast; or a spiritless reptile, without dignity or humanity.[17]

Wollstonecraft's Nonconformist distaste for court luxuries here identifies the source of monstrosity less in primogeniture than in the dehumanizing callousness of a life of lascivious pleasure. To Burke's picture of the revolutionaries as a 'race of monsters', Wollstonecraft

[16] Paine had already challenged England's right to be regarded as a natural 'parent' in his *Common Sense* pamphlets: Americans have fled, he claims, 'not from the tender embraces of the mother, but from the cruelty of the monster'. *The Writings of Thomas Paine*, ed. Moncure Daniel Conway, 4 vols. (New York, 1894–6), i. 87.

[17] Mary Wollstonecraft, *An Historical and Moral View of the Origin and Progress of the French Revolution; and the Effect it has Produced in Europe* (London, 1794), 513–14. Subsequent page references in the text are to this edition, abbreviated as *HMV*.

responds with a reminder of the cruelty and despotism practised by Europe's aristocratic governments:

Sanguinary tortures, insidious poisonings, and dark assassinations, have alternately exhibited a race of monsters in human shape, the contemplation of whose ferocity chills the blood, and darkens every enlivening expectation of humanity: but we ought to observe, to reanimate the hopes of benevolence, that the perpetration of these horrid deeds has arisen from a despotism in the government, which reason is teaching us to remedy. (*HMV*, 515)

Wollstonecraft does not deny that elements of the Parisian crowd deserve to be regarded as monstrous (*HMV*, 258, 447), but these are, in the first place, 'a set of monsters, distinct from the people' (*HMV*, 450), and moreover, their bloody actions are engendered by despotism, as retaliation. The actions of the people are compared with those of a blind elephant lashing out indiscriminately under provocation (*HMV*, 32): in these circumstances 'the retaliation of slaves is always terrible' (*HMV*, 520). Identifying, like Paine, the aristocracy as the parent of the revolutionary violence, Wollstonecraft adapts Burke's model of poetic justice to them: 'whilst despotism and superstition exist, the convulsions, which the regeneration of man occasions, will always bring forward the vices they have engendered, to devour their parents' (*HMV*, 259). Wollstonecraft is prepared to extend the same logic to the fate of the Jacobins too, in what looks more like a Burkean argument: they brought about 'public misery, involving these short-sighted men in the very ruin they had themselves produced by their mean intrigues' (*HMV*, 465–6). The inhumanity of the court or of the Montagne recoils upon itself, but Wollstonecraft insists that the same process cannot be imputed to rational innovation and enlightenment, as Burke has suggested. Wollstonecraft's purpose is to refute all attempts to use the Terror as an illustration of the consequences of political change:

We must get entirely clear of all the notions drawn from the wild traditions of original sin: the eating of the apple, the theft of Prometheus, the opening of Pandora's box, and the other fables, too tedious to enumerate, on which priests have erected their tremendous structures of imposition, to persuade us, that we are naturally inclined to evil . . . (*HMV*, 17)

The apparently monstrous actions of the French people show not the evils of change, but the reflected evils of government tyranny, the retaliation of slaves. It is provocation rather than innate wickedness that engenders them: 'People are rendered ferocious by misery; and

1. The French Revolution as Monster: 'The Nightmare', from the *Anti-Jacobin Review*, 1799. The sleeper has been reading Godwin's *Political Justice*, a copy of which protrudes from his coat pocket.

misanthropy is ever the offspring of discontent.' (*HMV*, 71.) This is the essence of the radical explanation of the Revolution as a product of insufferable circumstances rather than of monstrous designs.

The most intellectually prestigious of the English radical responses to Burke, and to the Revolution, came from Mary Shelley's other parent, William Godwin, whose *Enquiry Concerning Political Justice* (1793) enjoyed for a while an influential stature as the theoretical cornerstone of English 'Jacobinism', inspiring the early thinking of Wordsworth, Coleridge, and Percy Shelley. Godwin's measured tones are a distinct contrast to the rhetorical extremes of Burke or even of Paine, and he rarely ventures into a figurative rendition of political principles. Indeed, Godwin takes some care to parody the colourful style of the reactionaries when introducing their hypothetical objections to his arguments.[18] One such imaginary opponent is made to assert that 'Democracy is a monstrous and unwieldy vessel, launched upon the sea of human passions, without ballast.'[19] Godwin recognizes and mimics the characteristic tropes of Burkean discourse, to reply along with Paine that it is the institutions of monarchy and aristocracy that are monstrous. 'The feudal system', writes Godwin, 'was a ferocious monster, devouring, wherever it came, all that the friend of humanity regards with attachment and love.' (*EPJ*, 476.)

*Political Justice*, though, is concerned less with supporting Paine's kind of direct riposte to Burke than with conducting a general critique of Government from a standpoint of rationalist anarchism. Godwin finds that Government itself, since it is a Hobbesian 'artificial man' with too many heads, is monstrous in its actions:

A multitude of men may be feigned to be an individual, but they cannot become a real individual. The acts which go under the name of the society are really the acts now of one single person and now of another. The men who by turns usurp the name of the whole perpetually act under the pressure of incumbrances that deprive them of their true energy. They are fettered by the prejudices, the humours, the weakness and vice of those with whom they act; and, after a thousand sacrifices to these contemptible interests,

---

[18] On the politics of Godwin's style see James T. Boulton, *The Language of Politics in the Age of Wilkes and Burke* (London, 1963), ch. 11.

[19] William Godwin, *Enquiry Concerning Political Justice and its Influence on Modern Morals and Happiness*, ed. Isaac Kramnick (Harmondsworth, 1976), 487–8. Subsequent page references in the text are to this edition, abbreviated as *EPJ*.

their project comes out at last, distorted in every joint, abortive and monstrous. (*EPJ*, 558)

From the standpoint of Godwin's atomized individualism, the monstrosity of Government is a perversion, not of any organic 'King's body', but of the integrity of responsible individual action. That gulf between project and abortive outcome, in which we can already read the outlines of the Frankenstein story, was a crucial discrepancy which English radicalism had to explain to itself in the 1790s. For the basic doctrine of the radical group, proclaimed in *Political Justice*, is the invincibility of Reason's progress in eliminating the injustices and superstitions of the old feudal heritage. Mary Wollstonecraft had described the principles embodied in the Declaration of the Rights of Man as 'truths, the existence of which had been eternal; and which required only to be made known to be generally acknowledged' (*HMV*, 489). The eternal truths of reason had only to be announced in order that the structures of despotism and priestcraft should fade painlessly away. It is in this conviction that Godwin devotes the fourth Book of *Political Justice* to an attack upon what he sees as the hot-headed impatience of more genuinely Jacobinical radicals like Thelwall, who advocated practical political action to secure reforms. The contemplation and propagation of Reason, Godwin felt, would suffice. And yet, in the mid-1790s, Godwin's circle was to find that the diffusion of truth and reason had encountered unforeseen obstacles: Britain, far from embracing enlightenment, was in the grip of war and reaction, with the radicals besieged by legal persecution or by 'Church and King' rioters, and the Revolution itself taking a far from rational course. How, then, could Reason so miscarry?

Mary Wollstonecraft's attempts at an answer place their emphasis on the corrupting tendency of aristocratic institutions, which debase their victims to the point either of servility or of unthinking retaliation. Her work usually looks for answers in the realm of education and reformed upbringing, while William Hazlitt was later to reflect upon the slave mentality as an explanation. Godwin's brief consideration of the abortive projects of Government begins to offer a mode of explanation far removed from the world of Illuminati plots and conscious orchestration, which tries to account for the *inadvertent* distortion of a purpose as it is filtered through a welter of contradictory and competing pressures. The kind of monstrosity produced in such a process will no longer be the old emblem of vice or caricature of the mob, but a new and puzzling image of humanity's loss of control over its world.

Godwin's new-found sense of the obstacles to rational progress was to be presented and explored in his novel *Things as They Are, or The Adventures of Caleb Williams*. This novel is, as its title implies, very much an attempt to explain the actual conditions of British society in the 1790s; an examination of the entrenched mechanisms and wide extent of established power, in the field of what Godwin calls 'domestic tyranny'. A powerful study of persecution and fear, it embraces a range of political issues from crime and imprisonment to servitude, chivalry, honour, and of course justice. Behind its action can be detected allegories of the English Revolution, of Edmund Burke's career, and of the radical philosopher's remorse for attacking a culture to whose values he is ultimately still committed.[20] In its central incident the novel's narrator-protagonist Caleb Williams is overpowered by his ruling passion, 'a mistaken thirst of knowledge'.[21] Gripped by this epistemophilia, Caleb breaks into his master Falkland's private box, the dark secret of which is never fully disclosed. Apprehended by the proud Falkland, who is now incriminated by this glimpse at his secret, Caleb is to be pursued with the full rigour of class injustice. Falkland is able, because of his social position, to track his potential accuser across the length and breadth of the country and purchase the means of unremitting legal persecution, driving Caleb into outlawry and prison. Through Caleb's ordeal we are shown the capacity for persecution and injustice available to the English ruling class by virtue of its control over the legal machine; we are given the point of view of the complete outcast, as Caleb disguises himself successively as gipsy, Jew, and Irishman, encountering the higher morality of outlaws and convicts. The dynamic principle of the narrative is one of endless flight and ineluctable pursuit, as the roles of accuser and accused exchange between 'father' and 'son' figures. Falkland and Williams, master and servant, are recognizable examples of the 'double', locked into a guilty duel in which they

---

[20] See Kelly, *Jacobin Novel*, ch. 4; Boulton, *Language of Politics*, ch. 11; and Kelvin Everest and Gavin Edwards, 'William Godwin's *Caleb Williams*: Truth and "Things as They Are"', in Francis Barker *et al.* (eds.), *1789: Reading Writing Revolution* (Colchester, 1982), 129–46.

[21] William Godwin, *Caleb Williams*, ed. David McCracken (Oxford, 1970), 133. Subsequent page references in the text are to this edition, abbreviated as *CW*.

constantly mirror one another. Yet the field of action expands beyond the private struggle of master and servant into the arena of 'legal despotism' (*CW*, 184), to the point at which Caleb can regard 'the whole human species as so many hangmen and torturers' (*CW*, 183). Caleb, like both Victor Frankenstein and his monster, has to endure the intolerable injustice of suffering for the misdeeds of another. Falkland brings about his own ruin by persisting in his persecution: Caleb had not intended to betray his master's secret, but is driven at last to take this course of revenge, the emptiness of which finally spoils his success in having Falkland convicted of murder.

Apart from its concern with curiosity and mutual destruction, *Caleb Williams* prefigures *Frankenstein* in its unsettling of stable identities and values. The unreliable first-person narrative and the undisclosed secrets place all moral certainties in a state of suspension, leaving us only a terrible power-struggle in which the injustices of contemporary society are (as in the sub-plots of *Frankenstein*) brought into the open. In the confusion of identities and moral bearings which is brought about by the mutual mirroring of Caleb and Falkland, what is lost is that clear shape of vice which traditionally distinguishes the monstrous from the human. Even Caleb himself comes to doubt whether he is morally superior to the murderer Falkland, and we find that robbers and outlaws have a surer sense of honour and justice than magistrates have. It is from this new species of politico-philosophical novel that Mary Shelley's *Frankenstein* derives many of its preoccupations, while its story of the creation of a monster emerges from her parents' debate with Burke over the great monstrosity of the modern age, the French Revolution.

Before we leave Godwin, a final point needs to be made about the place of *Political Justice* in the Frankenstein myth. There is one interpretation of *Frankenstein* which takes the figure of Victor Frankenstein to be a satirical representation of William Godwin himself. Now there are some biographical connections here in Mary Shelley's experience of parental neglect, but the principal basis for this identification, insisted upon by D. H. Lawrence,[22] is the unreliable legend of Godwin's supposed doctrine of human 'perfectibility'. According to the repeated misconception of his stated views on this question, Godwin believed that rational enlightenment would

---

[22] D. H. Lawrence, *The Symbolic Meaning: The Uncollected Versions of 'Studies in Classic American Literature'* ed. Armin Arnold (Arundel, 1962), 36. See also below, ch. 8.

produce a new 'perfect' kind of human being. Not surprisingly, then, he is taken as the original of the similarly deluded Victor Frankenstein. But although it is true that Godwin did entertain some bizarre notions about the future possibilities open to the species, his doctrine of 'perfectibility' is in fact the precise opposite of the delusion so often attributed to him. Godwin's own explanation could hardly be clearer:

Lastly, man is perfectible. This proposition needs some explanation.

By perfectible, it is not meant that he is capable of being brought to perfection. But the word seems sufficiently adapted to express the faculty of being continually made better and receiving perpetual improvement; and in this sense it is here to be understood. The term perfectible, thus explained, not only does not imply the capacity of being brought to perfection, but stands in express opposition to it. If we could arrive at perfection, there would be an end to our improvement. (*EPJ*, 144–5)

The idea of absolute human perfection is, Godwin insists, 'pregnant with absurdity and contradiction' (*EPJ*, 145). His quite distinct claim is that 'man' is always *im*perfect, and therefore always open to improvement, and that he has a capacity for such improvement, which (again contrary to the legend) is not an inevitable prospect, as he explains in his critique of optimism in Book IV of *Political Justice*. Godwin was of course mistaken in believing that the word 'perfectible' was sufficiently clear to convey this view; on the contrary, it has done much mischief with his reputation.

In the genuine weaknesses of Godwin's Romantic idealism, however, faint traces of a Frankensteinian mentality can be detected. The final and least convincing chapters of *Political Justice* introduce some dizzying extrapolations from the 'sublime conjecture', attributed to Benjamin Franklin, that 'the term of human life may be prolonged, and that by the immediate operation of the intellect, beyond any limits we are able to assign' (*EPJ*, 776). The men of the future (given the nature of the prediction, it is hard to tell whether Godwin includes women here) 'will probably cease to propagate. The whole will be a people of men, and not of children.' (*EPJ*, 776.) It is a chillingly disembodied extension of Godwin's often rarefied rationalism, but if it smacks of Frankensteinian irresponsibility, this is not a consistent feature of Godwin's outlook. His anarchist individualism, which prohibits marriage, procreation, and even collaborative work, is qualified by important warnings against the detachment of science from social ties: 'science and abstraction will soon become cold,'

Godwin argues, 'unless they derive new attractions from ideas of society.' (*EPJ*, 300.) Elsewhere he asserts that little good can be done by solitaries, a principle illustrated by his disciple Percy Shelley in *Alastor, or The Spirit of Solitude* (1816). This doctrine supplies the moral of *Frankenstein* too; Mary Shelley dedicated it to Godwin less because she was a dutiful daughter (her elopement lost her that title) than because Godwin was in so many ways the novel's intellectual begetter.

# 3

## The Monster Speaks: Mary Shelley's Novel

Literary history is the great morgue where everyone seeks
out his dead, those whom he loves or to whom he is related.

Heinrich Heine, *The Romantic School*

### (i) *'Hideous progeny'*: the book as monster

Books themselves behave monstrously towards their creators,
running loose from authorial intention and turning to mock their
begetters by displaying a vitality of their own. 'Unluckily', writes
Freud, 'an author's creative power does not always obey his will:
the work proceeds as it can, and often presents itself to the author
as something independent or even alien.'[1] There is a sense in which
all writing must do this, but with Mary Shelley's *Frankenstein* the
process goes much further. This novel manages to achieve a double
feat of self-referentiality, both its composition and its subsequent
cultural status miming the central moments of its own story. Like
the monster it contains, the novel is assembled from dead fragments
to make a living whole; and as a published work, it escapes Mary
Shelley's textual frame and acquires its independent life outside it,
as a myth. These peculiarities of *Frankenstein* arise not because (as
dogmatic versions of critical Deconstruction would have it) literary
texts can refer to nothing beyond themselves, but because Romantic
writing typically selects the creative labour of the artist as itself the
adumbrating figure and symbol for all human engagement with the
world, thereby making out of its apparently circular self-reference
a wider domain of significance which aspires to the universal. There
is even a case for reading *Frankenstein* as a dramatization of just
this perversity in the Romantics' self-referring quest for universal
meanings—which would make the novel self-referential to the second
power. Rather than get lost in this kind of infinite regression, though,

---

[1] Sigmund Freud, 'Moses and Monotheism II', *The Origins of Religion*, trans.
Angela Richards (Harmondsworth, 1985), 350.

let us look more closely at the kinds of meaning which the textual monstrosity of Mary Shelley's work generates.

Her own description of the novel as 'my hideous progeny'[2] has been one of the most suggestive starting-points for recent interpretation. Since Ellen Moers pointed out that *Frankenstein* could be read as a 'birth myth'[3] concerned with the anxieties of maternity, the tissue of connections between the horror-story of Mary Shelley's own early life and the events of the novel has become more noticeable. Others have drawn connections beyond these events to the very 'textuality' of the work: Sandra M. Gilbert and Susan Gubar stress in *The Madwoman in the Attic* the extraordinary bookishness both of the novel and of the personal anxieties which produced it. In their reading, the 'birth' of *Frankenstein* is no longer a straightforward case of Art imitating Life; now, Life imitates Art in what Gilbert and Gubar call 'bibliogenesis'.[4]

Just as the creature and the creator tend to merge their identities in the novel, so in Mary Shelley's own role the categories of author, creator, and mother mirror and overlap one another. Both her parents were authors, but her mother Mary Wollstonecraft died as a result of giving birth to her. Mary Godwin was, then, the unwitting agent of her own creator's death, and—again like the monster and like several other characters in the novel—a motherless orphan. Her relationship with her mother had then to become a *textual* one, in rather morbid ways: she took to reading her mother's works at her graveside, and it was here that she kept her trysts with Percy Shelley prior to their elopement in 1814. Marc A. Rubenstein has speculated that she may also have read her parents' love-letters, in a textual quest for her own origins—a form of research which reappears in the novel in the monster's perusal of (and disgust with) Frankenstein's

[2] Mary Shelley, *Frankenstein; or The Modern Prometheus*, ed. M. K. Joseph (Oxford, 1969), 10. Like most modern editions, Joseph's is based on Mary Shelley's third edition of 1831. Since part of my argument will involve discussion of differences between this text and the first edition of 1818 (see pp. 61–2 below), subsequent page references to *Frankenstein*, abbreviated as *F*, will be given in pairs, the first reference being to Mary Wollstonecraft Shelley, *Frankenstein; or The Modern Prometheus: The 1818 Text*, ed. James Reiger (Indianapolis, 1974; rev. edn. Chicago 1982), and the second to the corresponding page in Joseph's edition. Where the material quoted appears only in the 1831 text, the first page reference (in parentheses) will be to the 1831 variants as printed in the appendix to Reiger's edition.

[3] Ellen Moers, *Literary Women* (London, 1978), 92.

[4] Sandra M. Gilbert and Susan Gubar, *The Madwoman in the Attic: The Woman Writer and the Nineteenth-Century Literary Imagination* (New Haven, 1979), 224.

laboratory notes.[5] Rubenstein observes too that *Frankenstein* is 'a book constructed like a pregnancy',[6] in that the concentric Russian-doll structure of the narrative 'contains' the monster's story within that of its 'parent'. It has even been pointed out that the novel itself had a nine-month 'gestation' between the beginning of the first draft chapter and its acceptance for publication.[7]

If some of these bibliogenetic connections between textual and sexual generation appear far-fetched, we do have some confirmation from her other writings that the links are indeed a repeated feature of Mary Shelley's thinking. The hero of her later novel *The Last Man*, for example, observes of his own experience of authorship: 'Suddenly I became as it were the father of all mankind. Posterity became my heirs.'[8] The metaphor is perhaps a hackneyed one, but there are strong reasons why Mary Shelley in particular should so firmly identify the anxieties of parenthood with what Harold Bloom (and following him, Gilbert and Gubar) understands as the anxieties of authorship. For Mary Shelley such a double anxiety is overdetermined in the first place by her literary parentage and her association with Percy Shelley and Lord Byron. The competitive pressures which she records in her famous account of the ghost-story contest bring these anxieties to a head, so that the daring transgression of Victor Frankenstein can itself be read as a projection of Mary Shelley's own ambitions in aspiring to authorship, her hero's struggles amplifying the mixed feelings, both assertive and guilty, of the adolescent for whom fully adult identity means both motherhood and (in her circle) authorship too. Barbara Johnson has shown how in these terms, '*Frankenstein* . . . can be read as the story of the experience of writing *Frankenstein*', and has diagnosed a 'frustrated female pen-envy'[9] in Mary Shelley's attitude to Byron and Percy Shelley, which in the novel becomes transposed into a tale of Victor's male womb-envy. Following the connections of authorship and parenthood still further, Johnson argues that Victor's narrative itself is, like all autobiography, a kind of self-reproduction, the creation of a 'life' after his own image,

[5] Marc A. Rubenstein, '"My Accurs'd Origin": The Search for the Mother in *Frankenstein*', *Studies in Romanticism*, xv (1976), 172.

[6] Ibid., 194.

[7] Gay Clifford, '*Caleb Williams* and *Frankenstein*: First-Person Narratives and "Things as They Are"', *Genre*, x (1977), 615.

[8] Mary Shelley, *The Last Man* (London, 1985), 113.

[9] Barbara Johnson, 'My Monster/My Self', *Diacritics*, 12 (Summer 1982), 8.

so that he ends up with two monstrous offspring, the creature and the story. He is acknowledged by the monster as both his 'father' and the 'author' of his being (*F*, 135/139; 217/220).

Even if we stop short of Johnson's conclusion, which sees the monster as 'a figure for autobiography as such',[10] we can recognize that there is a peculiarly concentrated series of identifications between Frankenstein's creation of the monster and Mary Shelley's creation of the novel. Not just to some shocked readers in the early nineteenth century, but to Mary Shelley herself, the book appeared as a monster. She had unwittingly endowed it with a quality even more monstrously ungovernable than the deadly strength, size, and agility given to his creation by Frankenstein: an abundant excess of meanings which the novel cannot stably accommodate, a surplus of significance which overruns the enclosure of the novel's form to attract new and competing mythic revisions. My examination of *Frankenstein* will be less concerned with providing any new or improved interpretation than with surveying (as I have begun to do already) the range of readings which the novel has stimulated in modern criticism, in order to build up a picture of its special kind of mythopoeic 'productivity' as a generator of mythic possibilities.

(ii) *It is assembled*

That Victor Frankenstein assembles his monster from parts of corpses collected from charnel-houses and dissecting rooms is one of the most memorable and enduring features of the story, even to those who have never read Mary Shelley's novel. The monstrosity of the creature is clearly enough the consequence of its assembly from different parts, but it still sets us a puzzle, which James Whale's 1931 film version evades by introducing a faulty component, the Abnormal Brain: why should a creature constructed from parts which Victor selects as perfect and indeed beautiful specimens turn out to be hideously repulsive? The novel provides no explanation for the creature's ugliness, and if we are tempted to account for it psychologically as a mere projection of Frankenstein's guilty revulsion from his deed, we run up against the evidence of the other characters' reactions. The monster appears frighteningly ugly not just to his creator but to all who see him, even to himself as he studies his reflection in

[10] Ibid., 4.

water. By stressing clearly the beauty of the component parts and the ugliness of the finished combination, Mary Shelley is isolating and dramatizing a problem which was in her time central to philosophical, and by extension to aesthetic and political discussion; namely the question of the relation of parts to wholes.

Just as for Kant the mind had to be more than the sum of its sense-impressions, so for Coleridge, the British avatar of German Idealism, any living 'whole'—whether a plant, a poem, or a nation—was always more than a mere aggregation of its constituent parts. It was upon this principle that Romantic Idealism founded its critique of the empiricist thought of the preceding century and set the terms of that central opposition between the mechanical and the organic which was to define so many of the conflicts within nineteenth-century culture.

In aesthetic theory, this opposition appears most clearly in Coleridge's own distinction between the Fancy, which merely re-assembles ready-made memories and impressions, and the Imagination, which fuses and harmonizes into a new living entity not just images and sensations but the different faculties of the mind itself. In politics, a similar conviction is at work in the insistently organic imagery of Burke's writings, in which the organic integrity of the state is contrasted with the ridiculous and deadly artificial concoctions of the *philosophes*. And combining the political with the aesthetic, Friedrich Schiller's response to the French Revolution and the social fragmentation it threatened is to offer the harmonizing properties of art as a cure for the disintegrating tendencies of the age. Schiller's celebrated Sixth Letter in *The Aesthetic Education of Man* asserts that the development of human society has necessarily left behind it the noble simplicity of ancient Greek culture, 'but instead of rising to a higher form of organic existence it degenerated into a crude and clumsy mechanism'. Modern society is but 'an ingenious mechanism' made from 'the piecing together of innumerable but lifeless parts'.[11] In Schiller's diagnosis an advanced division of labour has dismembered the human personality so completely into distinct faculties that 'one has to go the rounds from one individual to another in order to piece together a complete image of the species'.[12] Now that the individual

---

[11] Friedrich Schiller, *On The Aesthetic Eduction of Man*, ed. and trans. Elizabeth M. Wilkinson and L. A. Willoughby (Oxford, 1967), 35.
[12] Ibid., 23.

has become just a stunted fragment, society can be little more than a monstrous aggregation of incomplete parts.

From such diagnoses of the disorganization of European society, a whole tradition of culture-criticism was to develop in the nineteenth century. The fragmented society, the patchwork or clockwork individual—these become the themes of Romantic social analysis from Schiller through Carlyle and beyond. Mary Shelley's *Frankenstein* takes its place within this pattern of Romantic contrasts between lifeless parts and living wholes, partly as a dramatization of that principle of inorganic aggregation which Schiller saw as the modern disease. Viewed in this light, Victor Frankenstein's error is to have confused the beauty of the dead limbs he has collected with the beauty of a whole organism. According to the Idealist philosophy of the Romantics, the beauty of the whole can arise only from a pure vital principle within, to which all subordinate parts and limbs will then conform. The parts, in a living being, can only be as beautiful as the animating principle which organizes them, and if this 'spark of life' proceeds, as it does in Victor's creation, from tormented isolation and guilty secrecy, the resulting assembly will only animate and body forth that condition and display its moral ugliness.

Among the self-reflexive peculiarities of *Frankenstein* which I have mentioned is the fact that the novel is part of the same problem. As Mary Shelley herself recognized in her Introduction of 1831, what we too often call literary 'creation' is really a process of assembling and combining pre-existing elements:

Invention, it must be humbly admitted, does not consist in creating out of void, but out of chaos; the materials must, in the first place, be afforded: it can give form to dark, shapeless substances, but cannot bring into being the substance itself. (*F*, (226)/8)

From here she goes on to reveal as her raw materials the conversations at the Villa Diodati about galvanism and Erasmus Darwin's wriggling vermicelli. These conversations are, however, only a small part of the stock of materials from which *Frankenstein* was assembled. In addition to—and in odd intimacy with—the distressing problems of Mary Shelley's own life, of which some elements go into the book, there is a fund of literary sources upon which *Frankenstein* cannibalistically feeds. To form an idea of the range of both kinds of constituent material, we should begin with Mary Shelley's immediate circle and proceed outwards from there.

To begin with, the names and status of some of the novel's characters are drawn from Mary Shelley's acquaintance: Elizabeth was the name of Percy Shelley's sister and his mother, and Victor was a name adopted in boyhood by Percy himself—a fact which has encouraged some commentators to identify him too hastily with Victor Frankenstein, when his portrait is given more clearly in the character of Henry Clerval. William was the name not just of Mary Shelley's father but also of her half-brother and of the son she was raising while writing the novel. The killing of William Frankenstein dramatizes perhaps some hidden sibling rivalries, while the recurrence of orphaned (in particular, of motherless) characters more clearly echoes the facts of her own childhood: Safie, indeed, is given a deceased mother who has championed the rights of women (*F*, 119/123-4), and the monster's sense of neglect seems to derive partly from William Godwin's paternal remoteness. Closer still to the author's own feelings at the time when the novel was written lies the trauma of her own motherhood, as Ellen Moers has established. The fantasy of reanimating the dead occurred to Mary Godwin not just as a second-hand scientific speculation overheard from Byron, but as a most disturbing dream recorded in her journal of March 1815, in which her first dead child was brought back to life by being rubbed before a fire. The Alpine setting of the novel draws, obviously enough, upon the 1816 holiday which also inspired Percy Shelley's 'Mont Blanc' and Byron's *Manfred*; and the University of Ingolstadt appears as a result of Percy's interest in the alleged Illuminati conspiracy which Barruel traced to that town. Such lived 'sources' should not be forgotten, particularly those closest to Mary Shelley's personal troubles, but as a literary composition *Frankenstein* is constituted more fully by its written sources.

Mary Godwin kept quite extensive records of her reading from 1814 onwards, so the identification of literary borrowings has plentiful possibilities, ranging from the German ghost stories mentioned in the 1831 Introduction, through the novels of the American Godwinian Charles Brockden Brown, to William Beckford's *Vathek* (1786), whose hero is driven by his restless curiosity to 'penetrate the secrets of heaven'.[13] The major influences, though, can be reduced to a handful, among them being the works of the author's own parents.

---

[13] William Beckford, *Vathek*, ed. Roger Lonsdale (Oxford, 1970), 4.

The Frankensteinian elements latent in some of their political writings and in Godwin's *Caleb Williams* have been touched on above; but in some ways just as suggestive a source is another of Godwin's novels, *St. Leon, A Tale of the Sixteenth Century* (1799). The hero of this tale discovers the secrets of the philosopher's stone and the elixir of life, only to be disappointed in his fruitless efforts to benefit mankind by their means. As his project inadvertently brings about the deaths of his loved ones and other innocents, he exclaims:

Fatal legacy! Atrocious secrets of medicine and chemistry! Every day opened to my astonished and terrified sight a wider prospect of their wasteful effects! A common degree of penetration might have shown me, that secrets of this character cut off their possessor from the dearest ties of human existence, and render him a solitary, cold, self-centered individual; his heart no longer able to pour itself into the bosom of a mistress or a friend; his bosom no longer qualified to receive upon equal terms the overflowing of a kindred heart. But no mere exercise of imagination . . . could have adequately represented the mischiefs of a thousand various names, that issued from this Pandora's box, this extract of a universal panacea. . . . I felt as truly haunted with the ghosts of those I had murdered, as Nero or Caligula might have been; my wife, my son, my faithful negro; and now, in addition to these, the tender Julia and her unalterable admirer. I possessed the gift of immortal life, but I looked on myself as a monster that did not deserve to exist.[14]

St. Leon's bafflement would seem to be another fictional exploration of the disappointments suffered by the rationalist radicals of Godwin's circle, a reworking of the frustrations embodied in the predicament of Caleb Williams: 'Why', St. Leon asks himself, 'was every power of the social constitution, every caprice of the multitude, every insidious project of the noble, thus instantly in arms against so liberal and grand an undertaking?'[15] St. Leon abandons his experiments, having learned that his obsession with them has destroyed his familial loyalties, and he turns instead to cultivate the 'dearest ties of human existence'—a conversion which even Godwin's sworn enemy the *Anti-Jacobin Review* had to applaud as a welcome sign.[16] The same novel even contains a hideous giant named Bethlem Gabor, whose sufferings have made him a misanthrope. 'I hate mankind', declares Gabor; 'I was not born to hate them. . . . But they have forced me

---

[14] William Godwin, *St. Leon, A Tale of the Sixteenth Century* (London, 1831), 362–3.
[15] Ibid., 424.
[16] *Anti-Jacobin Review and Magazine*, v (1800), 152.

to hate them.'[17] There is more than a hint of Frankenstein's monster here, as there is of its creator in the disastrous scientific career of St. Leon.

From her mother's writings Mary Shelley undoubtedly derived an interest in the theory of education, and a tendency (prominent in many digressive passages of her novel) to stress the influence of a character's upbringing and early impressions. Mary Wollstonecraft, herself a governess and schoolteacher, repeatedly explored these issues in her work, especially in the celebrated *Vindication of the Rights of Woman* (1792), which is in part an extension—and critique—of Rousseau's educational doctrines, redirected against the artificiality with which young women were 'formed' by their upbringing. In the pages of the *Vindication* at least two incidental reflections can be found which seem to anticipate the themes of *Frankenstein*. In one, Mary Wollstonecraft defends herself against her contemporaries' horror of rational innovation and experiment:

Everything new appears to them wrong; and not able to distinguish the possible from the monstrous, they fear where no fear should find a place, running from the light of reason, as if it were a firebrand; yet the limits of the possible have never been defined to stop the sturdy innovator's hand.[18]

In the reactionary climate of the 1790s rationalist innovation and reform had been successfully identified with the 'monstrous',[19] and Mary Wollstonecraft herself came to be displayed as a monstrous figure: when Godwin's posthumous memoir of her revealed that she had once attempted suicide when abandoned by a lover, the fact was deemed to illustrate the dire consequences of straying from virtue's path and woman's lot, just as Percy Shelley's drowning was later interpreted as a fitting judgement upon his atheism. Mary Godwin's strong identification with her mother's memory taught her to question the category of the 'monstrous' and to sympathize with moral outcasts; as an unmarried mother herself (she became Mary Shelley only in December 1816), she needed little reminding.

---

[17] Godwin, *St. Leon*, 415.

[18] Mary Wollstonecraft, *Vindication of the Rights of Woman*, ed. Miriam Brody Kramnick (Harmondsworth, 1975), 265.

[19] The *Anti-Jacobin Review* (v. 427) called Godwin's followers 'spawn of the same monster'; and Thomas De Quincey recalled in 1837 that 'most people felt of Mr Godwin with the same alienation and horror as of a ghoul, or a bloodless vampyre, or the monster created by Frankenstein'. *The Collected Writings of Thomas De Quincey*, ed. David Masson (Edinburgh, 1890), iii. 25.

A second Frankensteinian theme adumbrated in the *Vindication* is the questioning of heroic exertion. While agreeing with Bacon that the greatest human achievements are made by those who are unmarried, Wollstonecraft insists that she shall not therefore recommend all women to abandon marriage and domestic life, since 'the welfare of society is not built on extraordinary exertions; and were it more reasonably organized, there would be still less need of great abilities, or heroic virtues'.[20] She is no more impressed by masculine heroism than she is by other ingredients of aristocratic ideology; rational and democratic reform could bring it down to its true size. Like Godwin in his treatment of Falkland's inflated honour, Wollstonecraft recognizes the danger and the redundancy of the heroic ideal, particularly in its artificial divorce from the domestic. *Frankenstein* too investigates the same problem, from its opening contrast between the ardent but isolated adventurer Robert Walton and his sister's settled sanity, to Victor's closing speech against the alleged cowardice of Walton's crew.

To these parental influences we may add some of the more important sources in Mary Shelley's early reading. One story of her girlhood has her hiding behind a sofa while Coleridge himself read to Godwin his 'Rime of the Ancient Mariner'. Coleridge's hypnotic tale of guilt and isolation is clearly a significant source for the ice-bound voyage of *Frankenstein*'s frame-narrative, and possibly for its doomed and transgressing hero too. Mary Shelley was careful to emphasize the connection herself, by having Frankenstein quote (anachronistically) the 'Rime' to express his fear of the monster (*F*, 54/59). In her revisions of 1831 she reinforced the allusions to the poem by both Victor and Walton, making the latter attribute his enthusiasm for polar exploration to Coleridge's inspiration (*F*, (231)/21). It seems that in the confessional mode of the 'Rime', especially in its contrast between the Mariner and the Wedding-Guest, Mary Shelley found some hints towards a narrative structure which could frame and partly domesticate the trials of the Romantic outcast.

There is some evidence, as Burton R. Pollin has suggested,[21] that the myth of Pygmalion and his animated statue Galatea helped to stimulate the Frankenstein story, particularly in the form given to

[20] Wollstonecraft, *Vindication*, 155.
[21] Burton R. Pollin, 'Philosophical and Literary Sources of *Frankenstein*', *Comparative Literature*, xvii (1965), 100–1.

it by Mme de Genlis in a dramatic sketch, 'Pygmalion et Galatée', from her *Nouveaux contes moraux* (1802–3), which Mary Shelley read in the summer of 1816. 'Pygmalion et Galatée' uses the device of the naïve creature's initiation into human customs as a vehicle of social criticism, showing its heroine's horror upon learning of slavery, tyranny, poverty, and human guile, just as Mary Shelley has the monster respond to Safie's history lessons in the De Lacey cottage.

By far the most important literary source for *Frankenstein*, though, is Milton's *Paradise Lost*, as repeated allusions in the novel remind us, beginning with the title-page itself and culminating in the monster's own avid reading of the epic poem, which he takes to be true history. As the monster reflects upon his reading, he first compares his condition with Adam's, but then feels a frustration akin to Satan's, if not worse (*F*, 125–7/129–31). Victor, who ought to correspond to God in this new creation, comes also to feel like Satan; he too bears a hell within him. The monster's earliest memories resemble those of Adam in *Paradise Lost* Book VIII, while his first sight of his own reflection in water is a travesty of Eve's similar revelation in Book IV. Likewise, the monster's vengeful declaration of war against human kind arises from a bitter feeling of exclusion from human joys, a hopeless envy described in terms similar to Satan's (*Paradise Lost*, iv. 505 ff.; ix. 114 ff.).

*Frankenstein*'s relationship to Milton's epic is, however, more than a matter of incidental borrowings. Unlike the story of Pygmalion, the subject-matter of *Paradise Lost* happens to be the most powerfully authorized creation myth in Western culture. Moreover, it elaborates upon the connections between *two* kinds of myth: a myth of creation and a myth of transgression. *Frankenstein* does this too, but its sinister travesty collapses the two kinds of myth together so that now creation and transgression appear to be the same thing, as they are also in William Blake's *Book of Urizen*. The accusations of impiety which greeted the publication of *Frankenstein* may surprise us today, but it seemed to some of Mary Shelley's first readers that the novel was calling into question the most sacred of stories, equating the Supreme Being with a blundering chemistry student. The particular impiety of Mary Shelley's Miltonic travesty forms part of that common Romantic reinterpretation of *Paradise Lost* which follows the Gnostic heresy in elevating Satan to the role of sublimely heroic rebel.[22] Blake's remark in *The Marriage of Heaven and Hell*, that Milton was unwittingly of the Devil's party, and Percy Shelley's qualified admiration for Satan in his Preface to *Prometheus Unbound* are well-known instances, but William Godwin too conducted a defence of Satan's principled opposition to tyranny in his *Political Justice* (*EPJ*, 309), while Mary Shelley herself, in one of her unpublished corrections to the 'Thomas' copy of *Frankenstein*, refers to Satan's 'sublime defiance' (*F*, 125/ — ). The widespread cult of Prometheus in Romantic literature is often only a slightly Hellenized variant of the same heretical tendency.

As many commentators have pointed out, Milton had, by submitting God's providence to rational debate, inadvertently exposed the foundations of his religion to subversion. Nowhere is this clearer than in the very speech which Mary Shelley uses as her epigraph to *Frankenstein*, in which Adam bewails the injustice of his position:

> Did I request thee, Maker, from my clay
> To mould me man? Did I solicit thee
> From darkness to promote me?
>
> (*Paradise Lost*, x. 743–5)

As Adam complains a few lines later, God's justice seems 'inexplicable'. In the full context of Milton's poem, Adam's complaint can be discredited on several theological grounds, and the Christian readings are in the literal sense the authorized ones; but the Romantic revision of Milton is precisely a decontextualizing movement which, in plundering *Paradise Lost* for meanings, tears elements of the poem free from their doctrinal framework. *Frankenstein* takes part in this desecration by dramatizing Romanticism's sympathy for the Devil.

Actual devils, however, do not appear in *Frankenstein*. Victor calls his creature a devil and a demon, but he knows better than anyone in the tale that the monster is not literally a paid-up and fork-carrying member of that order. This absence of any demonic tempter behind Victor's transgression is the main reason why we have to eliminate the Faust myth from our list of sources (Mary Shelley appears not to have known Goethe's recent version, at least until after *Frankenstein*'s composition); it is also the factor that most clearly marks the story's distance from Milton. It is tempting to jump from

[22] See Paul A. Cantor, *Creature and Creator: Myth-Making and English Romanticism* (Cambridge, 1984).

the continuing significance of the Faust myth in Western culture[23] to the hasty conclusion that all modern stories of transgression are derivatives of it, but to do this with *Frankenstein* would be to obscure a vital feature of the novel's modernity. While Faust's damnation and the Fall of Adam and Eve are brought about by the machinations of Mephistopheles and Satan, Victor Frankenstein has no serious tempter other than himself, his chemistry professor remaining a minor, innocent figure. If Frankenstein is any kind of Faust, he is a Faust without a Mephisto, that is, hardly a Faust at all; and if he is a Prometheus, as the novel's subtitle suggests, then he is a Prometheus without a Jove.

The novelty of *Frankenstein* which sets it apart from the phantasmagoria of Faust and of the Gothic novel is, as George Levine rightly insists, its starkly secular nature.[24] Eschewing the *geistig* world of Germanic mythology, it belongs in many ways with the more earthbound materiality of that other English myth, *Robinson Crusoe*. The gross physical insistence of *Frankenstein*'s central figure cruelly mocks the emptiness of spiritual aspiration, in what can be read as an ironic commentary upon Romantic idealism's 'angelic' transcendence of the flesh.[25] At the same time, the narrative logic of the novel observes (perhaps even invents) the rules of what we now call science fiction, tracing a chain of probable consequences from a single implausible premiss without resort to magical interventions. The impiety which early readers found in *Frankenstein* lies partly in the fact that its story is, as Levine says, 'acted out in the absence of God',[26] that it follows the logic of a godless world; its tensions interest us because they thrive upon that disorientation which follows the subtraction of God and Mephistopheles from the known creation. Mary Shelley's impiety goes a step further than many of Romanticism's Satanic heresies, revising *Paradise Lost* in so decontextualized a manner that the great context Himself is removed, turning the novel into 'a *Paradise Lost* without angels, or devils, or God'.[27] God is mentioned in the novel only as a minor character in Milton's epic,

---

[23] On the modernity of Faust see Marshall Berman, *All That Is Solid Melts Into Air: The Experience of Modernity* (New York, 1982).

[24] Levine and Knoepflmacher (eds.), *Endurance of 'Frankenstein'*, 6–7.

[25] On *Frankenstein*'s critique of 'angelism' see Gerhard Joseph, 'Frankenstein's Dream: The Child as Father of the Monster', *Hartford Studies in Literature*, vii (1975), 97–115.

[26] Levine and Knoepflmacher (eds.), *Endurance of 'Frankenstein'*, 7.

[27] Ibid., 7.

or in blasphemous exclamations, and the only character to invoke His name piously ends up on the gallows, hanged for a crime she never committed, having made a false confession at the prompting of her priest.

Among the simpler interpretations of *Frankenstein* as a moral fable of presumption, it is often asserted that Victor Frankenstein is trying to 'play God' or usurp divine powers. Although Mary Shelley's 1831 Introduction hints at such a view, the novel offers very limited grounds for it: Victor aims at first not to rival God but to be useful to humanity by eliminating disease, and all he creates is a single living creature. If this is a blasphemous crime, then all parents stand condemned for it too. From the monster's point of view, though, Victor is a 'god' of sorts, and it is through this perspective that the novel's impieties emerge, the most mischievous of them being the incident in which the monster swears to Victor a solemn oath 'by you that made me' (*F*, 143/147). The monster's 'god' comes to be seen as an ineptly negligent creator whose conduct towards his creation is callously unjust. If Adam's complaint in the epigraph is borne in mind as well, the novel begins to look like a nightmarish parody of patriarchal religion, in which the Son is made, not begotten, the Flesh is made Word,[28] and women cede the power of Conception to men while being legally framed as criminals (like Eve) or torn to pieces. It is not too hard to imagine the pious readers of 1818 feeling that their God and His creation were being grimly mocked.

Lowry Nelson Jr. has suggested that *Frankenstein* inaugurates a line of 'unchristian' or diabolical novels of a distinctive Romantic or mythic cast, which includes *Wuthering Heights* and *Moby Dick* (and, we could add, *Heart of Darkness* among others), and which is remarkable for its common use of complex narrative frames surrounding a central transgressing anti-hero.[29] In *Frankenstein* as in these other works the diabolical nature of the narrative form inheres in what we could call its 'dialogical' openness. Since there is no Mephisto or recognizably evil tempter, and no Jove for the modern Prometheus to offend, the moral framework of the novel is dissolved into an open contest or debate between Victor and the

[28] See Milton A. Mays, '*Frankenstein*, Mary Shelley's Black Theodicy', *Southern Humanities Review*, iii (1969), 146–59; and Judith Wilt, '*Frankenstein* as Mystery Play', in Levine and Knoepflmacher (eds.), *Endurance of 'Frankenstein'*, 31–48.
[29] Nelson, 'Night Thoughts', 251 ff.

monster, in which the reassuring categories of Good, Evil, Guilt, and Justice can never be allotted a settled place. Other Gothic or Godwinian writers of this period, like Charles Brockden Brown in *Wieland* (1798) and James Hogg in *Confessions of a Justified Sinner* (1824), found double or multiple narration to be an ideal device for undermining the certainties of religious delusion; Mary Shelley achieves a similar effect in the narrative design of *Frankenstein*. As most readers of the novel attest, its most challenging effect comes from the reversal of sympathies demanded by the monster's narrative. This jolt is reinforced by the 'doubling' in the relationship between the monster and Victor (and in Victor's resemblance to Walton too), so that all identities in the novel are unstable and shifting, the roles of master and slave, pursuer and pursued alternating or merging. As in the Revolution debates, the accuser of monstrous offspring is himself accused of being a monstrously negligent parent. When Victor and his monster refer themselves back to *Paradise Lost*— a guiding text with apparently fixed moral roles—they can no longer be sure whether they correspond to Adam, to God, or to Satan, or to some or all of these figures. Like the iceberg on which Frankenstein makes his first appearance in the novel, their bearings are all adrift. Interpretation of the novel encounters much the same problem.

### (iii) *It speaks*

Among the interpretative possibilities offered by *Frankenstein*, two need to be dismissed from the start, not as 'wrong' but as premature, since they come to have their place in the myth as it grows up around the novel. These are the readings which see *Frankenstein* as a technological prophecy or as a moral fable of blasphemous human presumption, and sometimes as both. The technological reading adopted by Martin Tropp and by Brian Aldiss in his novel *Frankenstein Unbound* (when he is not too busy contriving for his narrator a time-warped route into Mary Godwin's bed) tends to jump ahead from the text of *Frankenstein* to issues embraced by the myth at a later stage, distorting the status of the monster as he appeared in 1818. In Mary Shelley's novel Victor Frankenstein constructs his monster with no technological ends even remotely in view; not as a machine, a robot, a helot, or any other labour-saving convenience, but as the Adam of a new race which will love and venerate its creator (*F*, 49/54). More importantly, the monster has no mechanical characteristics, and is a fully human creature. Indeed, in his range of sympathies and his need for companionship he is perhaps more human than his creator, as Harold Bloom has observed.[30] The monster's most convincingly human characteristic is of course his power of speech. Since much of the myth's subsequent history revolves around this point, it is worth dwelling upon. The decision to give the monster an articulate voice is Mary Shelley's most important subversion of the category of monstrosity. As we have seen, the traditional idea of the monstrous was strongly associated with visual display, and monsters were understood primarily as exhibitions of moral vices: they were to be seen and not heard. For the readers of *Frankenstein*, though, as for the blind De Lacey, the visibility of the monster means nothing and his eloquence means everything for his identity. Moreover, his namelessness helps to dislodge him from that traditional notion of the monstrous which fixes its objects with a moral label or caption. He has himself acquired command over the 'godlike science' of language (*F*, 107/112), slipping free from its defining functions while mobilizing its persuasive power. The full effect of these reversals depends upon the emphasis which the novel gives to his very human needs and feelings, and to their painful frustration. Although the monster is the result of what is formally a 'mechanical' assembly, once animated he is as unexpectedly human as he is unexpectedly ugly. To read him even allegorically as a machine at this stage would be more than just premature; it would mean missing the monster's most disturbing immediate significance.

Rather than tie *Frankenstein* too soon to the issue of technology as such, it would be safer to say that the novel dramatizes certain doubts about the rewards of knowledge, in a broader sense. Knowledge is shown to be double-edged, its benefits and hazards depending upon the circumstances, and the spirit, in which it is pursued. It is not just Victor's experience which shows this; in many ways the monster learns the lesson more clearly. Mary Shelley's description of his first experiences is designed as an accelerated exposition both of infant development and of the early history of the human species. This empiricist version of Adam's story is perhaps partly inspired by Volney's *Ruins*, a book from which the monster learns of human

[30] Harold Bloom, '*Frankenstein*, or the New Prometheus', *Partisan Review*, xxxii (1965), 618.

history, and in which the chapter on the 'Original State of Men' presents the earliest man as 'an orphan, deserted by the unknown power that had produced him',[31] learning purely by his senses. A crucial stage in the monster's education comes with his discovery of fire:

One day, when I was oppressed by cold, I found a fire which had been left by some wandering beggars, and was overcome with delight at the warmth I experienced from it. In my joy I thrust my hand into the live embers, but quickly drew it out again with a cry of pain. How strange, I thought, that the same cause should produce such opposite effects! (*F*, 99/104)

In discovering pain and pleasure arising from the same source, the monster has felt the contradictory nature of experience. He will feel its confusing force again in the 'mixture of pain and pleasure' inspired in him by the De Laceys' affections (*F*, 103–4/108) and in the record of human history which displays us as both vicious and virtuous (*F*, 115/119). His empiricist translation of the Eden and Prometheus myths here obviously preserves their sense of the ambivalence of knowledge, and in this episode at least it is the monster rather than Victor who is the modern Prometheus. Unlike Victor but like Prometheus, he uses his knowledge helpfully, collecting firewood for the de Laceys; but it is with fire too that he destroys their cottage and later himself.

The monster's further reflections on his discoveries also condense the novel's issues. As he compares his own position (and his appearance) with that of the De Laceys, he finds that 'sorrow only increase[s] with knowledge' (*F*, 116/120). 'Increase of knowledge', he adds later, 'only discovered to me more clearly what a wretched outcast I was.' (*F*, 127/131.) This is another lesson which Victor too—like Godwin's heroes—has to learn more slowly and painfully: the condition of solitude cannot be cured, only sharpened, by knowledge. All three of the narrators in the novel are self-educated, and fall victim to this problem; seeking knowledge *in* solitude, they are condemned to find only a more distressing knowledge *of* solitude. Bearing in mind this implied critique of solitude—to which we shall need to return later—we can concede that the novel is indeed about the perils of discovery.

A straightforward cautionary tale, however, it is not. Although Mary Shelley's revisions and Introduction of 1831 did, as we shall

---

[31] C. F. C. Volney, *The Ruins, or a Survey of the Revolutions of Empires* (London, 1878), 17.

see, nudge the story in the direction of a parable of presumption, the grounds for this sort of reading are shifting and uncertain in the text as a whole, particularly in the first edition of 1818. The novel's inconclusiveness breaks out at the very moment when Victor Frankenstein seems to be drawing most tidily the moral of the tale:

Farewell, Walton! Seek happiness in tranquillity, and avoid ambition, even if it be only the apparently innocent one of distinguishing yourself in science and discoveries. Yet why do I say this? I have myself been blasted in these hopes, yet another may succeed. (*F*, 215/217-8)

This last escape clause could be read as evidence of Victor's incorrigible blindness, but it seems more likely to be an equivocation of Mary Shelley's own, perhaps reflecting her mixed feelings about her literary ambitions, and apparently aligning her with her mother's refusal to endorse the superstitions of Pandora's box and similar anti-scientific fables. In this sense *Frankenstein* shares in that duplicity with which many Gothic novels ( *Vathek*, *The Monk*, and *Zastrozzi* among them) appear to reprove their villains while covertly driving them on to further blasphemous outrages. At the eleventh hour the text defers judgement, allowing true progress and discovery still to be made by 'another'—by those who find a way out of the trap in which Frankenstein has been caught.

It is the nature of this trap that has to be defined by those more careful interpretations which look beyond *Frankenstein*'s ostensible moral. The exegetical possibilities here range from psychological analyses of Victor's deficiencies to more or less allegorical readings of the novel as social criticism. In their simplest versions the psychological analyses see the monster as a projection of Frankenstein's unconscious urges; as an Id splitting away to enact those repressed desires which its controlling Ego (i.e. Victor) cannot openly acknowledge.[32] So the murders of Elizabeth, William, and Justine can be accounted for as outbursts of sibling rivalry, Elizabeth in particular being unconsciously held responsible for Mme Frankenstein's death. There is, again, a danger in this 'divided

[32] See e.g. Tropp, *Mary Shelley's Monster*, 19-33; Nelson, 'Night Thoughts', 247-8; Masao Miyoshi, *The Divided Self: A Perspective on the Literature of the Victorians* (New York, 1969), 84. Mary Poovey, in her haste to present Victor's creature as a straightforward phallocratic weapon, argues implausibly that 'The monster is simply the agent that carries out Frankenstein's desire.' 'My Hideous Progeny: Mary Shelley and the Feminization of Romanticism', *PMLA* xcv (1980), 336.

self' approach of reading later developments of the myth—the Jekyll and Hyde story especially—into the novel prematurely, but the text certainly offers a credible basis for psychoanalytic interpretations. The powerful episode of the dream which immediately follows upon the success of Victor's experiment is only the most obvious point of departure:

I slept indeed, but I was disturbed by the wildest dreams. I thought I saw Elizabeth, in the bloom of health, walking in the streets of Ingolstadt. Delighted and surprised, I embraced her; but as I imprinted the first kiss on her lips, they became livid with the hue of death; her features appeared to change, and I thought that I held the corpse of my dead mother in my arms; a shroud enveloped her form, and I saw the grave-worms crawling in the folds of the flannel. I started from my sleep with horror; a cold dew covered my forehead, my teeth chattered, and every limb became convulsed; when, by the dim and yellow light of the moon, as it forced its way through the window-shutters, I beheld the wretch—the miserable monster whom I had created. He held up the curtain of the bed; and his eyes, if eyes they may be called, were fixed on me. His jaws opened, and he muttered some inarticulate sounds, while a grin wrinkled his cheeks. He might have spoken, but I did not hear; one hand was stretched out, seemingly to detain me, but I escaped, and rushed down stairs. (*F*, 53/58)

This extraordinary passage firmly associates the first appearance of the monster with the simultaneous emergence of macabre incestuous disturbances in Victor's mind. In taking flight from the monster (whose outstretched hand is a greeting rather than a threat), Victor can be seen to be shunning the recognition of his own desire; his failure to acknowledge either as his own will make him their slave.

A strict equation of Frankenstein and his monster with Ego and Id runs the risk of becoming schematic, since Victor is in many ways more impulsive than his very rational creature, whose constant reminders of his creator's obligations towards him make him more of a Superego than an Id. There is still much to be said, though, for seeing their relationship as a drama of repression, an enactment of that Freudian formula so useful for the understanding of Gothic fiction, 'the return of the repressed'. The climax of this development in *Frankenstein* arrives with the fulfilment of the monster's promise, '*I shall be with you on your wedding night*'—a threat whose meaning Victor has repressed, assuming that he alone is the intended victim.

I had been calm during the day; but so soon as night obscured the shapes of objects, a thousand fears arose in my mind. I was anxious and watchful,

while my right hand grasped a pistol which was hidden in my bosom; every
sound terrified me; but I resolved that I would sell my life dearly, and not
relax the impending conflict until my own life, or that of my adversary,
were extinguished.

Elizabeth observed my agitation for some time in timid and fearful silence;
at length she said, 'What is it that agitates you, my dear Victor? What is
it you fear?'

'Oh! peace, peace, my love,' replied I, 'this night, and all will be safe:
but this night is dreadful, very dreadful.'

I passed an hour in this state of mind, when suddenly I reflected how
dreadful the combat which I momentarily expected would be to my wife,
and I earnestly entreated her to retire, resolving not to join her until I had
obtained some knowledge of my enemy. (*F*, 192/194–5)

As with Adam in *Paradise Lost*, it is just this moment of separation
from his wife which allows the fatal attack on her to be made. The
fact that Victor leaves Elizabeth in the mistaken hope of obtaining
knowledge makes the passage an unusually condensed résumé of the
action of the novel as a whole.

Perhaps more disturbingly, as Robert Kiely has pointed out,[33] the
ambiguity of this passage, in which the identity of the 'adversary'
is left unspecified, allows us to read Victor's agitation as a sign that
he fears the 'dreadful . . . combat' of sexual initiation itself, the more
traditional 'impending conflict' of the wedding night. The coincidence
of terms seems to imply that Victor's fear of sexuality and Elizabeth's
murder are parts of a single 'complex'; and if we remember that the
creation of the monster is an attempt to create life without encountering
female sexuality, we begin to see how this connection might work.
Nuptial forebodings are of course an established preoccupation of
the Gothic from Bluebeard to Hammer Films, but few fictional
wedding nights can have been as loaded with guilt as Frankenstein's.
Just as Victor has called himself the true murderer of William,
Justine, and Henry (*F*, 174/177), so he knows that he is his wife's
assassin too, having condemned her indirectly but certainly to death
by tearing up the unfinished female monster. In the relentless logic
of this 'return of the repressed', what returns is not so much the
monster as the content of Victor's earlier dream: the transformation
of Elizabeth into a corpse, which in dream-logic is itself an 'exchange'
for the transformation of a corpse into a living being.

[33] Robert Kiely, *The Romantic Novel in England* (Cambridge, Mass., 1972),
165–6.

Observing Victor's anxious demeanour after his return home from Ingolstadt, his father and Elizabeth herself both guess that he wishes to break off his engagement to his childhood sweetheart, having formed another attachment while at university. Although in the plainest sense he proves them wrong by marrying Elizabeth, they are still right in a deeper sense. The monster is indeed a sort of matrimonial rival to Elizabeth, a dependant whose ties to Victor are, he claims, indissoluble until death (*F*, 94/99). Frankenstein delays his marriage because he remembers his solemn promise, his 'engagement' (*F*, 149/152) to the monster. In so far as the monster is Victor's own persecuting *Doppelgänger*, he is in Freudian terms a symptom of a profound narcissism, displayed in his solitary and guilty attempt to achieve reproduction without a sexual partner. Viewed from a further stage of Freudian interpretation, Frankenstein's enterprise is a model of sublimation. As we saw in the wedding-night passage quoted above, he resolves not to join his bride in the marriage bed until after he has 'obtained some knowledge' of his enemy. This fatal moment of postponed consummation recapitulates the pattern of his researches at Ingolstadt, which delay his return to the affections of his family. Accounting for his inability to tear himself away from his loathsome experiments, Victor tells us: 'I wished, as it were, to procrastinate all that related to my feelings of affection until the great object, which swallowed every habit of my nature, should be completed.' (*F*, 50/55.) Victor's case of deferred gratification in his abstinent withdrawal from Elizabeth into his researches reflects clearly that general exchange of sexual for artistic or scientific fulfilments which Freud saw as the necessary price of cultural achievement. *Frankenstein* seems to formulate a law of psychic economy (essentially that of the return of the repressed) according to which the cost of sublimation has to be paid in an equal and opposite brutalization. It is of this cost, perhaps, that the monster's outrages are designed to remind us.

The discovery of narcissism and sublimation at work in Frankenstein's project offers a preliminary clue to the nature of the problem against which the tale warns, and a point of entry to the dimension of social criticism in the novel. Since, as we have observed, there is no God for Frankenstein to disobey, his transgression has to be defined in purely secular terms. There may be no divine prohibition that Victor can be said to flout, but there is still a society against which he can offend, members of it he can harm, and a creature for him to neglect. M. A. Goldberg is surely right to argue, in these terms, that Victor's offence is a sin against society and against the monster;[34] just as the feminist readings of the novel point out that he usurps not the privilege of God but the reproductive power of women. The terms of Mary Shelley's implicit criticism of Frankenstein appear now to be those of social obligation and irresponsible solitude. Victor's transgression is not a punctual disobedience—an eating of the apple or a signing away of his soul—but rather a continuous career which includes his early researches and his later neglect of the monster. What matters about his act of creation is not any heavenly law that has forbidden it but the nature of the entire transgressive process in which it is approached and carried through. In this light the monster's otherwise inexplicable ugliness can be accounted for more confidently as the visible symbol of the circumstances, the unhealthy conditions of production in which he is assembled.

Frankenstein's creation of his monster is a very private enterprise, conducted in the shadow of guilt and concealment, undertaken in narcissistic abstraction from social ties. The result of his 'secret toil' (*F*, 49/54) can be taken as embodying the socially irresponsible logic of private production itself. The monster is the spirit of private production brought to life, his asocial origin emphasized by his namelessness; through him Mary Shelley can show how a merely asocial course of private action harbours within it and realizes a fully anti-social potential. Frankenstein's sublimated 'abstinence'—a form of renunciation to which the nineteenth-century bourgeoisie often referred as an explanation for its ascendancy—produces a creature who is obliged to abstain from social intercourse. Victor's victory, the triumph of his ascetic masculine heroism, is a conquest over his own social and sexual being, fulfilled in a creature to whom social and sexual ties are denied. In this kind of 'social' reading of the novel the monster can be seen as a projection, not of some hidden part of Frankenstein's psyche but of his asocial conduct. Victor hides away from his friend, from his family, and from his fiancée to turn corpses into a living being. The monster, precisely *because* Victor's own solitary condition is forced (branded, as it were) upon him, turns

---

[34] M. A. Goldberg, 'Moral and Myth in Mrs Shelley's *Frankenstein*', *Keats–Shelley Journal*, viii (1959), 27–38.

Victor's friend, family, and bride from living beings into corpses. Victor, miserable because he is asocial, makes the monster in his own image, thereby making him miserable and so antisocially malevolent. No recourse to the uncanny or the spiritual is really needed to account for the monster's appearance as Victor's 'double', and for the many correspondences which pair them. The trick is not done with mirrors but with a strict and old-fashioned causal logic, within which one of the connecting links involves a further issue of social criticism in *Frankenstein*: that of injustice, which Milton Mays and David Punter have read as the major theme of the novel.[35]

While the monster's condition may be an exact mirror image of Victor's divorce from social bonds, there is one crucial difference between them, namely that Victor's solitude is voluntary and the monster's is enforced. The fundamental injustice here is the same as that of which Adam accuses God: the creature has no say in its creation, yet it has to suffer the consequences more painfully than the creator. For the monster, his very existence is a miscarriage of justice, and his career of crime is really a prolonged protest against this anomaly. Although he explains with perfect Godwinian logic that he is malicious because he is miserable (*F*, 141/145), he is really driven by a conscious sense of equity rather than by mere frustration or vengeful rage; which is not to say that his actions are just. On the contrary, the victims of his attacks are all *innocents*, which is exactly his grim but satirical point. His outrages against the Frankenstein clan may be accepted as impetuous revenge, but in his framing of Justine as William's murderer, the monster's evident malice aforethought is likely to shock the fair-minded reader. It is criminal madness, but there is certainly a method in it, since what the monster is doing is providing an illustration of the arbitrary injustice of the human society which condemns him on sight.

The novel is peopled with characters who have been punished for crimes which they did not commit: the monster, Safie's father, Justine Moritz, the De Lacey family, and even Victor Frankenstein himself; the injustices against Justine and Victor being the work of the monster. Victor is arrested in Ireland after the murder of Henry Clerval, and the monster's message is brought home to him: as he

[35] Mays, 'Black Theodicy', 147–53; David Punter, *The Literature of Terror: A History of Gothic Fictions from 1765 to the present day* (London, 1980), 127.

admits in prison (but fortunately not in his gaoler's language), he *is* Henry's murderer. The injustice is much more flagrant in the case of the tellingly-named Justine. Considering murder as a fine art, as we are at liberty to do only in fiction, we have to appreciate the setting up of this innocent servant as the monster's *chef d'œuvre*, a perfectly executed representation of his own inequitable position, which implicates Victor, the good burghers of Geneva, and the Church in the worst of judicial crimes. If the monster is denied the solace of a female companion, he can at least fabricate a female partner-in-crime, with the help of the law's blindness. The Genevese court, indeed, is tricked into doing what Victor finally refuses to do for his creature: it makes a female 'monster' of Justine, and the priest even comes close to convincing Justine herself of her monstrous nature (*F*, 82/87), forcing her to confess falsely to the murder. Only by staging parodies of the injustice he suffers can the monster reproduce his outcast kind; so long as there are victims, he is not altogether alone.

'If there be any sight more humiliating than all others,' wrote William Godwin, 'it is that of a miserable victim acknowledging the justice of a sentence against which every enlightened spectator exclaims with horror.' (*EPJ*, 654.) Justine's confession and conviction are contrived to illustrate this Godwinian point, elaborated by Elizabeth, the single 'enlightened witness' to question the verdict. She draws the appropriate conclusion from the trial as she throws the accusation of monstrosity back upon society: 'When I reflect . . . on the miserable death of Justine Moritz, I no longer see the world and its works as they before appeared to me . . . now misery has come home, and men appear to me as monsters thirsting for each other's blood.' (*F*, 88/92.) Elizabeth has learned to look upon human institutions in much the same way as the monster does in his more extended reflections on social injustices.

The monster's initial *naïveté* is a useful device by which Mary Shelley can lift the veil of familiarity from our view of social institutions, exposing their inequalities afresh:

Every conversation of the cottagers now opened new wonders to me. While I listened to the instructions which Felix bestowed upon the Arabian, the strange system of human society was explained to me. I heard of the division of property, of immense wealth and squalid poverty; of rank, descent, and noble blood.

The words induced me to turn towards myself. I learned that the possessions most esteemed by your fellow-creatures were, high and unsullied descent united with riches. A man might be respected with only one of these acquisitions; but without either he was considered, except in very rare instances, as a vagabond and a slave, doomed to waste his powers for the profit of the chosen few. And what was I? Of my creation and creator I was absolutely ignorant; but I knew that I possessed no money, no friends, no kind of property. (*F*, 115/119–20)

The tortuous contrivance by which the monster is brought to reflect on these issues should not lead us to assume that this passage is some kind of extraneous supplement to the novel's main concerns. We are not dealing here with an 'organically' integrated work (if such a thing can exist), so the implausible lengths to which the author is prepared to go in order to include this social criticism appear rather to stress its importance than to betray its superfluity. The monster's application of these lessons from Volney to his own predicament, and his identification with the propertyless, invite us to regard him as a representative of the oppressed classes, while Victor appears to represent the callous neglect with which the ruling orders treat them.

Although *Frankenstein* is not exactly 'a straightforward allegory of the class struggle', as Paul O'Flinn has called it,[36] the social and political metaphors of monstrosity which we reviewed in the last chapter would undoubtedly have been present in the minds of Mary Shelley and her readers, particularly in passages like that quoted above. Telling the story of a monster out of the control of its philosophical creator, *Frankenstein* reanimates recognizably the terms of the debate over the French Revolution. As Lee Sterrenburg has argued,[37] the monster is derived from the lurid imagery of Burke's counter-revolutionary polemics, but manages at the same time to voice the opposing views of Mary Wollstonecraft and others, indicting the prevailing system from the standpoint of the oppressed and outcast. The mythically productive equivocation of *Frankenstein* appears to emerge ultimately from this double—indeed contradictory—derivation from contending political positions. Read from the Burkean position, as it usually is, the novel seems to warn against the recklessness of the radical *philosophe* who tries to construct a

[36] Paul O'Flinn, 'Production and Reproduction: The Case of *Frankenstein*', *Literature and History*, ix (1983), 199. O'Flinn sees the political origin of *Frankenstein* as the pattern of revenge and reprisal in the Luddite risings in England, rather than as the prior, and more lastingly traumatic, shock of the French Revolution.

[37] Sterrenburg, 'Mary Shelley's Monster', in Levine and Knoepflmacher (eds.), *Endurance of 'Frankenstein'*, 143–71.

new body politic. But read from the position of Paine, Wollstonecraft, or Godwin, it seems to suggest that the violence of the oppressed springs from frustration with the neglect and injustice of their social 'parent'. Mary Shelley's own response is an uneasy combination of fearful revulsion and cautious sympathy for the monster; in short, an anxious liberalism, as O'Flinn remarks. The subsequent mythic career of the tale will also turn out to be a tug-of-war between the two contending political attitudes held in *Frankenstein*'s unstable balance.

A more specific reading of the monster's social identity has been offered by Franco Moretti, who suggests that the piecing together of Frankenstein's creature is an image of the assembly in the late eighteenth century of the industrial proletariat, a new social 'body' thrown together from the *disjecta membra* of declining classes and later welded by the factory system into a dangerously powerful aggregation.[38] This perceptive analogy is another of those readings which rely slightly prematurely upon important developments in the later myth. Paul O'Flinn, though, reminds us that wage-labour does rear its collective head elsewhere in *Frankenstein*, in the form of the crew which Walton has recruited from whaling ships. This crew threatens a mutiny unless Walton turns back from the increasing dangers of his polar expedition, much to the disgust of Frankenstein, who calls them cowards who prefer their firesides to glorious heroism. At this final stage of the novel, Walton's choice—whether to follow Victor's example of solitary endeavour or to return to his sister's domestic sphere—is settled for him by the employees whose lives he has risked, and he is saved from his folly by collective strike action.

Modern criticism has been able to read *Frankenstein* in a number of ways which go well beyond the formerly accepted interpretation of the novel as a simple cautionary tale; in so many ways, indeed, that the variety becomes bewildering. The possibilities surveyed in the last few pages cover only the main lines of recent enquiry. Paul Sherwin has listed several more, as they apply to the monster alone:

---

[38] Franco Moretti, *Signs Taken for Wonders: Essays in the Sociology of Literary Forms*, trans. S. Fischer, D. Forgacs, and D. Miller (London, 1983), 83–108. Much of this work is concerned to refute Formalist misconceptions of literature's necessary radicalism, and for this reason—acceptable enough in itself—Moretti's account of *Frankenstein*, the first Marxist study attempted, accepts too readily the second-hand readings of the novel as a conservative fable.

If, for the orthodox Freudian, he is a type of the unconscious, for the Jungian he is the shadow, for the Lacanian an *objet a*, for one Romanticist a Blakean 'spectre', for another a Blakean 'emanation'; he also has been or can be read as Rousseau's natural man, a Wordsworthian child of nature, the isolated Romantic rebel, the misunderstood revolutionary impulse, Mary Shelley's abandoned baby self, her abandoned babe, an aberrant signifier, *différance*, or as a hypostasis of godless presumption, the monstrosity of a godless nature, analytical reasoning, or alienating labor.[39]

The source of this dizzying profusion of meanings appears to lie in Mary Shelley's overloading of the novel with approximately parallel 'codes' of signification—psychological, pedagogic, sexual, Miltonic, political—which overlap and interfere with one another at so many points that no single line of interpretation can convincingly fend off all the others. The first critical responses to *Frankenstein*'s publication (perhaps one should say, its release) tried immediately to contain its chaotic abundance, and to resolve its equivocations.

### (iv) *It escapes*

The reception of literary works is no straightforward matter of 'the reader' either consuming or producing the text's meanings, but a struggle which takes place among and between *different* readers who are already disposed in various camps, constituencies, and cultural factions, as *Frankenstein*'s early reception shows quite clearly. The novel did not appear under Mary Shelley's own name until the second edition of 1823, so the only clue which readers had in 1818 about the anonymous author lay in the dedication to William Godwin. This was quite enough for the Tory *Quarterly Review* to damn it, while others were put on their guard against *Frankenstein*'s possibly subversive and atheistic content. William Beckford, a pioneer of the Gothic novel in England, recoiled in disgust from this latest of his offspring, writing in the flyleaf of his copy: 'This is, perhaps, the foulest Toadstool that has yet sprung up from the reeking dunghill of the present times.'[40] The *Quarterly Review*, along with the *Edinburgh Magazine*, drew attention to the novel's affinities with Godwin, and denounced it as 'a tissue of horrible and disgusting absurdity'. The objection continued:

[39] Paul Sherwin, '*Frankenstein*: Creation as Catastrophe', *PMLA* xcvi (1981), 890.
[40] Cited by Howard B. Gotlieb, *William Beckford of Fonthill* (New Haven, 1960), 61.

Our taste and our judgement alike revolt at this kind of writing, and the greater the ability with which it is executed the worse it is—it inculcates no lesson of conduct, manners, or morality; it cannot mend, and will not even amuse its readers, unless their taste have been deplorably vitiated . . .[41]

This reader at least, although seething with moral indignation, discerned no cautionary fable in the book; on the contrary, the basis of his objection is just this absence of a guiding 'moral'.

The *Edinburgh Magazine* likewise found the views expressed in *Frankenstein* to be 'bordering too closely on impiety', even more dangerously than Godwin's novels.[42] More astutely, this reviewer recognizes that *Frankenstein* 'has an air of reality attached to it, by being connected with the favourite projects and passions of the times'; it calls contemporary events 'wondrous and gigantic', presumably referring to the French Revolution and the Napoleonic wars. This review also carries the first attempt at the now established 'moral' reading: 'It might, indeed, be the author's view to shew that the powers of man have been wisely limited, and that misery would follow their extension.' It is worth noting that this remark is offered tentatively as a guess at the author's intention, to offset the more powerful feeling of *Frankenstein*'s disturbing impiety ('some of our highest and most reverential feelings receive a shock from the conception on which it turns', particularly the idea of a mere man as creator). Sir Walter Scott in *Blackwood's* was kinder, admitting that *Frankenstein* showed 'uncommon powers of poetic imagination', although it 'shook a little even our firm nerves'.[43]

The conservative reviewers were not alone in emphasizing the Godwinian heresies of *Frankenstein*. Percy Shelley also wrote an appreciation which (although unpublished until 1832) was obviously intended to appear as an anonymous review, since it pretends ignorance of the author's identity and sex. In it he draws attention to the novel's similarities to Godwin in style and subject, admiring the way the monster's crimes are explained by definite causes rather than by any unaccountably evil propensity. For Percy Shelley the moral of *Frankenstein* is clear: 'Treat a person ill, and he will become wicked.'[44] Another heretic, whose taste the *Quarterly Review*

---

[41] *The Quarterly Review*, xviii (1818), 385.

[42] *The Edinburgh Magazine and Literary Miscellany*, ii (1818), 249–53.

[43] *Blackwood's Edinburgh Magazine*, ii (1817–18), 619.

[44] *The Prose Works of Percy Bysshe Shelley*, ed. R. H. Shepherd, 2 vols. (London, 1888), i. 418.

would have regarded as vitiated, was the reviewer of *Frankenstein*'s second edition in *Knight's Quarterly Magazine*, who enthused about the book's 'extreme power', and continued:

For my own part, I confess that *my* interest in the book is entirely on the side of the monster. His eloquence and persuasion, of which Frankenstein complains, are so because they are truth. The justice is indisputably on his side, and his sufferings are, to me, touching to the last degree.[45]

So far there is little sign, from either the horrified or the enthusiastic, of *Frankenstein* being received as a conservative parable of presumption. The novel appeared to these early readers to inculcate, in the *Quarterly Review*'s words, 'no lesson', unless it were the radical Godwinian critique of injustice.

The moral outrage provoked among *Frankenstein*'s more pious readers did, however, help to resolve this problem of interpretation by influencing the story's adaptation for the stage. The first dramatic version of *Frankenstein* appeared in 1823 with the staging of Richard Brinsley Peake's *Presumption: or the Fate of Frankenstein* at the English Opera House, T. P. Cooke playing the part of the monster. Mary Shelley herself went to see a performance, and although she was amused by it and impressed by Cooke's acting, she decided that 'The story is not well managed.'[46] This is a remarkable understatement. The tendency of Peake's management of the tale can be guessed at from the title alone, which so baldly advertises the morally improving nature of the adaptation. What is more interesting is that, according to Elizabeth Nitchie's 'Stage History of *Frankenstein*', the production had to face what the playbills described as 'abortive attempts . . . to prejudice the Publick' in the form of placards apparently displayed by certain 'friends of humanity' who appealed to fathers of families to boycott the play. Under the pressure of this moral campaign, the theatre management went out of its way to announce that 'The striking moral exhibited in this story, is the fatal consequence of that presumption which attempts to penetrate, beyond prescribed depths, into the mysteries of nature.'[47] One may

---

[45] *Knight's Quarterly Magazine*, iii (1824), 198.

[46] *The Letters of Mary Wollstonecraft Shelley*, ed. Betty T. Bennett, 2 vols. (Baltimore, 1980–3), i. 378 (to Leigh Hunt, 9 Sept. 1823).

[47] Cited by Elizabeth Nitchie, *Mary Shelley, Author of 'Frankenstein'* (Westport, Conn., 1953), 221. This section of Nitchie's book is reprinted from her article 'The Stage History of *Frankenstein*', *South Atlantic Quarterly*, xli (1942), 384–98.

well understand that Peake's play had to pander to the conscience of the churchgoing paterfamilias. The same seems to apply to H. M. Milner's version, *The Daemon of Switzerland*, which was produced in the same year and was advertised as the illustration of an 'Instructive Lesson'.

A glance at Peake's adaptation (later retitled *Frankenstein, A Romantic Drama*) will show how the moralizing of the tale works. After creating the monster off-stage, Victor appears before the audience and describes his creature's ugliness in terms which are lifted verbatim from the novel, but then he suddenly departs from his literary source by announcing that 'a flash breaks in upon my darkened soul, and tells me my attempt was impious'.[48] He goes on to cry, 'Oh that I could recall my impious labour, or suddenly extinguish the spark which I have so presumptuously bestowed.' (*FRD*, 7.) Earlier in the play Peake has introduced the comic character of Fritz, the country bumpkin who acts as Victor's assistant and who prepares the audience to interpret the tale according to received Christian notions of sin and damnation by telling them that 'like Dr Faustus, my master is raising the Devil' (*FRD*, 3). Peake makes several minor alterations in the story (Elizabeth becomes Victor's sister and is engaged to Clerval, while Victor is enamoured of Agatha De Lacey, who becomes the monster's victim), but the important changes are the dropping of Walton's frame-narrative and above all the silencing of the monster, who in this version has, as Frankenstein tells us, 'the mind of an infant' (*FRD*, 7). The monster is still responsive to music, he discovers the mixed blessings of fire, and he chops wood for the De Laceys, but he is never allowed to develop beyond blind power and rage, still less to learn of human language and customs before he is buried with his creator in an avalanche. From a sensitive critic of social institutions, the monster has been transformed into a rampaging embodiment of Victor's unleashed 'impiety', who is never given a hearing. In short, he is assimilated firmly into the traditional role of the monster as a visible image of presumptuous vice.

Peake's adaptation of the tale, and the fame of Cooke's rendering of the inarticulate monster (or '————' as he was called in the

---

[48] Richard Brinsley Peake, *Frankenstein, A Romantic Drama in Three Acts* (London, 1884), 7. Subsequent page references in the text are to this edition, abbreviated as *FRD*.

theatre programme), set the pattern for nearly all subsequent stage versions, and eventually for the 1931 screen version too, which even preserves Fritz along with the virtually silenced monster. As Nitchie's stage history records, the formula was successful and recognizable enough to spawn several burlesques—tributes to its possibilities as an established myth:

The laboratory at the top of a staircase leading from the back of the stage, with a door for the monster to break down and a window for the frightened servant to peer through, was part of the setting for each play. There was almost invariably a cottage to be burnt. The monster always leaped the railing of the staircase; he always seized and snapped Frankenstein's sword; he always experienced wonder at sounds and was charmed by music. He was always nameless. He was always painted blue.[49]

While the monster was being recuperated into the traditional form of visible monstrosity in this congealing of a dramatic cliché, he was also beginning his career as an object of rhetorical allusion. In the year after the first stage productions of the story, the Foreign Secretary George Canning spoke in the House of Commons in a debate on West Indian slave emancipation, remarking of the slave that 'To turn him loose in the manhood of his physical strength, in the maturity of his physical passion, but in the infancy of his uninstructed reason, would be to raise up a creature resembling the splendid fiction of a recent romance.'[50] Mary Shelley felt flattered by the attention shown to her tale in such quarters, but seems not to have noticed how *Frankenstein* was being used by nervous liberal statesmen to delay reform, nor how the monster (and worse, the slave) was being transformed by such rhetoric into a mindless brute. Canning, a former contributor to the *Anti-Jacobin Review* and a founder of the *Quarterly Review*, was clearly reclaiming the monster as a Burkean bogy figure to illustrate the danger of reform turning into rebellion. The same tradition of colourful rhetoric was maintained by the radical Tories of *Fraser's Magazine*, for whom Thomas Carlyle wrote in his early days. *Fraser's* seems to have invented the problem of the monster's 'soul' before even Mary Shelley herself did:

A state without religion is like a human body without a soul, or rather like an unnatural body of the species of the Frankenstein monster, without a

[49] Nitchie, *Mary Shelley*, 225.
[50] *Hansard's Parliamentary Debates*, 2nd ser., x (London, 1824), col. 1103. See Mary Shelley's *Letters*, i. 417, 564.

pure and vivifying principle; for the limbs are of different natures, and form a horrible heterogeneous compound, full of corruption and exciting our disgust.[51]

The allusion here not only absorbs the monster into the old image of the body politic, but provides retrospectively a pious explanation for Victor Frankenstein's disastrous failure.

When Mary Shelley came to revise her novel for the third edition of 1831, on which virtually all modern editions have been based, she incorporated several of the more conservative readings implied in the dramatic and rhetorical uses to which the story had been put since 1818. Now distancing herself from her radical past, the author strengthened the cautionary element of the novel to the point where it could be read as an 'improving' work. Despite her misgivings about Peake's handling of the story, she even introduced his title into the book: the word 'presumption' appears for the first time in a new speech given to Victor, who now describes the monster as 'the living monument of presumption and rash ignorance which I had let loose upon the world' (F, (245)/80). Victor is twice made to describe his action in creating the monster as 'unhallowed' (F, (247)/89; (256)/185), and is given a chance to mention, for the first time, the problem of 'the mockery of a soul' with which he has endued his creature (F, (255)/183). Galvanism, unmentioned in 1818, also creeps into the text along with occasional phrases which stress the unhallowed nature of Victor's transgression, like the reference to his 'fervent longing to penetrate the secrets of nature' (F, (238)/39). Elizabeth's radical speech against retributive justice, in the dialogues before Justine's execution, is excised and replaced, absurdly, with some saintly advice from Justine, who now tells Elizabeth: 'Learn from me, dear lady, to submit in patience to the will of Heaven!' (F, (246)/88.)

The figure of Walton is adapted to this process of conservative revision, turned into a far more deluded explorer than he was in 1818 so as to correspond to the new 'presumptuous' Frankenstein. 'I would sacrifice my fortune, my existence, my every hope,' declares this revised Walton, 'to the furtherance of my enterprise. One man's life or death were but a small price to pay for the acquirement of the knowledge which I sought.' (F, (231-2)/28.) In reply Victor

---

[51] *Fraser's Magazine* (Nov. 1830), 481. Cited by Sterrenburg, 'Mary Shelley's Monster', 166.

hints strongly at the similarity of their presumptuous endeavours: 'Unhappy man! do you share my madness? Have you drank also of the intoxicating draught? Hear me—let me reveal my tale, and you will dash the cup from your lips!' (*F*, (232)/28.) By the end of the novel Walton accordingly comes to regret his own 'mad schemes' (*F*, (258)/212). This revision of *Frankenstein*'s narrative frame effects a decisive adjustment of the sense in which the central episodes are to be understood. In the 1818 text Victor tells Walton his story because he thinks his rescuer might find it interesting and useful. In the 1831 version, though, the similarities between the respective enterprises of the two men are drummed home in order to give Frankenstein's narrative a fully cautionary status: 'when I reflect', Victor tells Walton, 'that you are pursuing the same course, exposing yourself to the same dangers which have rendered me what I am, I imagine that you may deduce an apt moral from my tale.' (*F*, (232–3)/30.)

Provided thus with a moral, *Frankenstein* at last became an acceptable text, its meanings brought into line with the improving lessons of its dramatic versions. But while the developing tradition of stage, cartoon, and—eventually—screen *Frankenstein*s managed more successfully to rein in the excesses of the story's multiple significance by exhibiting the monster as an awful warning, there remained a sphere in which the monster could live on in the less prejudicial condition of eloquent invisibility: the literary tradition. In this chapter I have sought to fend off the intrusion of later mythic developments into the reading of the 1818 novel, isolating the text from its offspring all the better to highlight the subsequent process of transformation from text to myth. In the following chapters this quarantine will be lifted, and the myth will be traced as it appears in nineteenth-century literature, often contaminated, distorted, masked, or disfigured, but unmistakably at large.

# 4

## Tales of Transgression, Fables of Industry: Hoffmann, Hawthorne, Melville, and Gaskell

> What a range of meanings and perpetual pertinence
> has the story of Prometheus!
>
> Ralph Waldo Emerson, 'History'

Mary Shelley was not alone in fictionalizing the various preoccupations which we find at work in *Frankenstein*; stories of doomed experimenters and obsessive chemists were favourites with early nineteenth-century readers. In France Balzac himself tried his hand at this kind of tale in his *La Recherche de l'Absolu* (1834), in which the protagonist Balthazar Claes, who has studied chemistry under Lavoisier, encounters a Polish chemist who inspires him to search for 'the Absolute'—the single element to which all matter can be reduced. The quest is of course fatal in its consequences, especially for Claes's domestic peace, as his wife foresees. She accuses Claes of regarding people merely as mechanisms animated by electrical fluid, and warns him against the Pole: 'Did you look at him closely? Only the tempter could have those yellow eyes, blazing with the fire of Prometheus.' Claes's science is, she warns, encroaching on God's power just as Satan had done in his reckless pride.[1]

The more familiar home of such Frankensteinian themes, though, lay in the European and American short-story tradition, where the emergent sub-genres of horror story, science fiction, and detective tale mingled productively in the early part of the century. Many of the most impressive short stories of this period are tales of transgression which show a particular interest in production—whether artistic, craft, or scientific—as an obsessive and self-destructive activity. The model for most of these Romantic fables is of course

---

[1] Honoré de Balzac, *The Quest of the Absolute*, trans. Ellen Marriage (London, 1908), 80–2.

63

the Faust myth, but in these versions the Faustian figure is radically modernized, his former acquisition of merely abstract knowledge now rewritten as the perfecting of productive technique.[2] These stories are often also explorations of the Romantic crisis of artistic identity, self-reflexive fictions of creative aspiration and its uncertainties. In many of the best tales of E. T. A. Hoffmann and Nathaniel Hawthorne, artists of various kinds discover the destructive and damning qualities of their own creations, which typically develop autonomous powers and overwhelm their creators. As we are not yet dealing with a conscious or clearly defined 'science fiction' (the word 'scientist' itself does not appear before 1834), the kind of creator-figure we find in these stories is a peculiar mixture of artist, philosopher, craftsman, and chemical experimenter. Through these versatile and obsessive creators, Romantic story-tellers offered their own artistic dilemmas as metaphors for the production and reproduction of life in every domain from the sexual to the industrial.

Given the then incipient division of art from technology, Romantic authors could better subsume the full range of human activity under their sense of the 'creative' by using a conventional figure of creativity drawn from economically retarded societies in which a cherished integration of imagination and manual skill was still embodied in a single person. This would seem to explain partly the strong Germanic influence on the short-story tradition in the nineteenth century, and why the protagonists in Hoffmann, Hawthorne, and their imitators are so often skilled craftsmen; theirs are tales of mystery in the archaic sense of 'mystery' as a skilled and secretive trade. So we find in these stories a gallery or arcade of watchmakers, jewellers, violin-makers, goldsmiths, architects, opticians, and assorted experimenting doctors or professors, all of them obsessively independent producers who create marvels from their private researches, usually without Mephistophelean assistance. These figures are, in short, classical petty-bourgeois producers whose special knowledge and skill have allowed them to become their own masters, answerable to nobody and often feared by their fellow burghers.

What is repeatedly shown in these tales of transgression is how the secret skill which makes the protagonist independent and severs his social ties becomes an obsessional end in itself and masters the

---

[2] Goethe's *Faust* itself, in its second part, follows the same path to modern industry, as Berman emphasizes in *All That Is Solid*, 37–86.

master. In particular, the pursuit of craft skills to the point of artistic perfectionism is often shown—especially by Hoffmann—to stand in direct competition with sexual love. Hoffmann's young protagonists typically find themselves distracted from their fiancées by some delusion associated with their work or that of their masters, in the same pattern by which Victor Frankenstein neglects Elizabeth for his workshop. This element of sublimating distraction is one of the few original features of the tale most carefully preserved in stage and film versions of *Frankenstein*; Victor as a kind of secretive Bluebeard thus stands as one of the more popular components from which the cliché of the Mad Scientist will be constructed. The products of similarly obsessed creators in Hoffmann and Hawthorne are often poisonous or otherwise blighted, mocking the ideals of artistic perfectionism and metaphorically revealing the blighting of the creator as he seals himself off from the sources of life in other people.

Nathaniel's fiancée Clara in Hoffmann's 'The Sandman' takes the experimenter's syndrome for granted when she writes to her intended of his recent experiences:

The uncanny night-time activities with your father were no doubt nothing more than secret alchemical experiments . . . and your mother can hardly have been pleased about it, since a lot of money was undoubtedly wasted and, moreover, as is always supposed to be the case with such laboratory experimenters, your father, altogether absorbed in the deceptive desire for higher truth, would have become estranged from his family.[3]

True to the same pattern, Nathaniel is seduced away from the devoted Clara by the sinister optician Coppola and by the charms of Professor Spalanzini's perfect clockwork doll Olympia, with whom he falls in love. Finally driven insane by a series of delusions, Nathaniel almost kills Clara before leaping to his death from a tower. Similarly the artist Berthold in 'The Jesuit College at Glogau', who speaks of his art in terms of Promethean struggle, finds his life divided sharply between his obsessive work and his love, and is suspected of killing his wife and child to remove all distractions from his painting. Councillor Krespel, who dismantles violins to discover their secrets, throws his pregnant wife out of a window when she interrupts his

[3] *Tales of Hoffmann*, trans. R. J. Hollingdale, Stella and Vernon Humphries, and Sally Hayward (Harmondsworth, 1982), 95–6. Subsequent page references in the text are to this edition, abbreviated as *TH*.

music, and metonymically 'kills' his daughter by dismantling a violin especially associated with her.

The pattern of fatal oppositions between love and work is repeated in a particularly fascinating story by Hoffmann, 'The Mines at Falun' (1819), upon which Wagner once planned to base an opera. The tale is a kind of *Moby Dick* in reverse: a melancholic and introspective sailor, Elis Fröbom, meets an old miner and is ensnared by the attractions of subterranean life. As in Melville's novel, the industry is endowed with a metaphysical value beyond its financial rewards, and it is this lure of higher aspirations which draws the protagonist on to his eventual destruction.

Elis Fröbom was almost terrified by the old man's words. 'What are you advising me to do?' he cried. 'Am I to leave the beautiful earth and the sunlit sky and go down into the dreadful depths and burrow like a mole, grubbing for ores and minerals, for the sake of vile profit?'

'People despise what they want to know nothing about!' the old man cried angrily. 'Vile profit! As if the horrors perpetrated on the face of the earth by trade and commerce were nobler than the work of the miner, whose indefatigable industry opens up nature's most secret treasure-houses. You speak of vile profit, Elis Fröbom! — well, something higher than that might be involved. If the blind mole burrows by blind instinct, it may be that the eyes of man acquire more penetrating sight in the deepest depths of the earth, until they can recognize in the wonderful stones they find a reflection of that which is hidden above the clouds. You know nothing about mining, Elis; let me tell you about it.' (*TH*, 316)

As the old man describes the world of mining, Elis begins to feel the charm of a world whose magic has been known to him from earliest boyhood in strange and secret presentiments. They are perhaps not so strange if we remember that he is being invited to penetrate Mother Nature; and indeed that night Elis is conquered in a dream by the huge and terrifying subterranean 'Queen' at the same time that he hears the voice of his dead mother.

Repelled at first by the chasm of the open-cast mine and its resemblance to Dante's Inferno, Elis bashfully falls in love with Ulla, the daughter of a mine overseer, and becomes a miner himself. But the mysterious old miner reappears to warn him that the Prince of Metals jealously demands an exclusive devotion with which Elis's love for Ulla conflicts. Other miners tell him that the old man is the ghost of the bachelor Torbern, whose understanding of 'the hidden powers which rule in the womb of the earth' (*TH*, 329) had transcended mere material greed, but who had been killed in a collapse; his ghost recruits miners in times of labour shortage and guides them to the best veins of ore. When it appears that Ulla is accepting the advances of a rich merchant, Elis rushes to the mine to devote himself to it instead; in a vision, he discovers the richest veins, and is clasped to the breast of the Queen. Ulla's apparent betrayal turns out to have been staged by her father to force a proposal from Elis, so their engagement can now go ahead. In the midst of their bliss, though, Elis feels haunted by his commitment to the Queen, while Ulla senses something pulling him away from her as he raves about 'the paradise which shone in the womb of the earth' ( *TH*, 334). As the wedding day nears, Elis's state improves, but on the nuptial morning he sets off again to the mine to find, as a bridal gift, a blood-red carbuncle which he has seen in a dream and which reflects 'the heart of the Queen at the mid-point of the earth' (where Lucifer is placed in Dante's Inferno) ( *TH*, 335). Elis is then killed in a landslide.

In this tale Hoffmann outlines, almost at the same time as Mary Shelley, a series of Frankensteinian problems, most obviously a complex involving the fusion of productive labour and sexual obsession. As in *Frankenstein*, the hero is clearly gripped by fantasies of his dead mother, and the tale is almost too overtly a 'mine' for depth psychology. Yet, like other tales of Hoffmann, it pursues the conflict between normal bonds of affection and a professional 'mystery' which exacts a single-minded devotion from its followers. It gives us not just a Freudian nuptial trauma but an image of the world of work as a rival to the sexual claims of the fiancée. Only when Elis hears that there is more to mining than the mundane value of 'vile profit' does he become embroiled in its fantasized appeal. Thus it is suggested (as it is in *Moby Dick*, as we shall see) that Elis's self-destruction follows from his aspiring beyond the bourgeois safety of the balance-sheet, in ardent pursuit of Nature's secrets. Hoffmann hints at a mysterious force of attraction which entices young men into frantic labours apparently unjustified by the simple market value of the ores extracted. The brilliant gems and metals seen in Elis's visions seem to reflect all his desires both sexual and spiritual, and it is worth noting that although he starts by scorning vile profit, his obsession is put in motion by the prospect of marrying his overseer's daughter. Elis's industry is rewarded in just this way by Ulla's father, so his frantic accumulation can be seen as a means towards a respectable end. At the close of the tale, though, what seems to Ulla and her father to be a means has become an end in itself. In this kind of concern with the obsessional appeal of production, 'The Mines at Falun' stands alongside *Frankenstein* as another remarkable modern parable of the industrial condition.

Nathaniel Hawthorne, in his many fictional studies of self-destructive artists, craftsmen, alchemists, and other alienated producers, is clearly an imitator of Hoffmann, although the American's tales show a more measured and artistically finished quality. Often, as in 'The Artist of the Beautiful', it is apparent that Hawthorne's central concern is with the dilemmas of the Romantic artist, yet in this and in many closely related tales he also brings into focus wider questions of society, science, and solitude which are posed in ways which are strikingly familiar to the reader of *Frankenstein*. Hawthorne's stock figure in these allegorical sketches is an isolated man whose mentality and special pursuits tear him from the warmth of (usually female) society until he hardens into a frozen or petrified monster. Indeed, the protagonist of 'The Man of Adamant' literally turns to stone after rejecting the sympathies of woman; conversely, the 'monstrous egotism'[4] of Roderick Elliston in 'Egotism, or the Bosom Serpent' is finally cured by woman's love. Hawthorne repeatedly plays upon a contrast between the human warmth of domesticity and the self-defeating coldness and abstraction of egotistical endeavour, as in 'The Ambitious Guest' or 'The Christmas Banquet'. Similar patterns of characterization are at work in the longer romances too: in the prying heartlessness of Chillingworth in *The Scarlet Letter*, and in Hollingsworth's pseudo-philanthropic egoism in *The Blithedale Romance*.

Hollingsworth had a closer friend than ever you could be. And this friend was the cold, spectral monster which he had himself conjured up, and on which he was wasting all the warmth of his heart, and of which, at last — as these men of mighty purpose so invariably do — he had grown to be the bond-slave. It was his philanthropic theory![5]

Before this Frankensteinian narcissism destroys the warm-blooded

---

[4] Nathaniel Hawthorne, *Selected Tales and Sketches*, ed. Hyatt H. Waggoner (New York, 1964), 193. Subsequent page references in the text are to this edition, abbreviated as *STS*.

[5] Nathaniel Hawthorne, *The Blithedale Romance* (Harmondsworth, 1983), 55 (ch. 7).

Zenobia, she accuses Hollingsworth of being a monster and a 'cold, heartless, self-beginning and self-ending piece of mechanism'.[6] Hawthorne's interests extend beyond the spectres conjured up by egotism, to take in similarly alienated figures who are not just heartless individualists but also producers in a more practical sense: alchemists, artists, or both. 'The Artist of the Beautiful' is unusual in the sympathy which Hawthorne extends to its hero, the poetical watchmaker Owen Warlock; the tale is less a critique of egotism than an indulgent self-examination of the artist's predicament, but it is still worth noting how Hawthorne makes Owen lose the girl Annie, as a result of his creative obsession, to a more earthly blacksmith and suffer 'a sensation of moral cold that makes the spirit shiver as if it had reached the frozen solitudes around the pole' (*STS*, 253). Trying to improve upon nature by manufacturing a butterfly-like automaton, Owen cuts himself off from the blessings of truly humanized nature. Appropriately it is Annie's child who finally crushes Owen's painstakingly constructed model butterfly.

Owen's malign counterpart in Hawthorne is the physician Rappaccini, whose exile from human sympathies fits more closely the developing stereotype of the Mad Scientist: the hero Giovanni is told by Professor Baglioni that Rappaccini 'cares infinitely more for science than for mankind. His patients are interesting to him only as subjects for some new experiment.' (*STS*, 274.) In Hawthorne's works clinical detachment of this kind is always a symptom of moral disease. Rappaccini is not just a sinister experimenter, though, but a creator whose works are fabricated on recognizably Frankensteinian principles. The plants in his poisonous artificial garden

would have shocked a delicate instinct by an appearance of artificialness indicating that there had been such commixture, and, as it were, adultery, of various vegetable species, that the production was no longer of God's making, but the monstrous offspring of man's depraved fancy, glowing with only an evil mockery of beauty. They were probably the result of experiment, which in one or two cases had succeeded in mingling plants individually lovely into a compound possessing the questionable and ominous character that distinguished the whole growth of the garden. (*STS*, 283)

Taking individually beautiful components, as Victor Frankenstein had done, Rappaccini has combined them to produce not an abortive

[6] Ibid., 218 (ch. 25).

Adam but a poisonous Garden of Eden, which similarly exhibits the nature of the temperament behind its creation. And for Rappaccini's crime it is his creature who suffers: his daughter (and finest 'flower') Beatrice, who is condemned to solitude by her poisonous constitution and who regards herself as a monster when she infects Giovanni.

Perhaps a more interesting figure among Hawthorne's deluded creators is Aylmer in 'The Birthmark'. Like Owen Warlock and like Frankenstein, Aylmer is a modern disciple of Albertus Magnus and a latter-day rival to Pygmalion. Seeking to improve upon nature, he attempts to correct the only blemish in his wife's otherwise perfect beauty — a hand-shaped birthmark which comes to symbolize earthly imperfection in general. In this story too we see 'the love of science . . . rival the love of woman in its depth and absorbing energy' (*STS*, 203). So strong is the rivalry, in fact, that Aylmer's attempt to eradicate the birthmark succeeds in killing his wife along with her supposed blemish.

Several of these characteristics of heartless isolation and abortive production are united in the most Frankensteinian figure in Hawthorne's fiction, that of Ethan Brand. In his story we can detect a significant shift from a Faustian to a Promethean model of transgression. The legend which surrounds Brand in the tale attributes to him the conjuring of a devil from the furnace of his lime-kiln, but the activity which he and the devil are alleged then to pursue is described as if it were a process of production, 'the man and the fiend each laboring to frame the image of some mode of guilt which could neither be atoned for nor forgiven' (*STS*, 305). A lime-burner by trade, Ethan is a maker, and a suitably Promethean one at that, as his fiery surname hints. Although he is for a while led off on a fruitless quest for the Unpardonable Sin, he finds it at last only by making it. Hawthorne shows in Brand's project a familiar process of dehumanization which is revealed at last to be a process of transgressive production.

So much for the intellect! But where was the heart? That, indeed, had withered, — had contracted, — had hardened, — had perished! It had ceased to partake of the universal throb. He had lost his hold of the magnetic chain of humanity. He was no longer a brother-man, opening the chambers or the dungeons of our common nature by the key of holy sympathy, which gave him a right to share in all its secrets; he was now a cold observer, looking on mankind as the subject of his experiment, and, at length, converting man and woman to be his puppets, and pulling the wires that moved them to such degrees of crime as were demanded for his study.

Thus Ethan Brand became a fiend. He began to be so from the moment that his moral nature had ceased to keep the pace of improvement with his intellect. And now, as his highest effort and inevitable development,—as the bright and gorgeous flower, and rich, delicious fruit of his life's labor,—he had produced the Unpardonable Sin! (*STS*, 314)

By 'producing' the Unpardonable Sin, Brand has produced himself too, remaking himself as a man whose heart, after his final self-immolation, is so hard as to withstand the furnace. His long search for the Unpardonable Sin has been a wasted effort, more pointless even than the spinnings of the dog in the story who chases his own tail, since Brand's goal too is in himself. Ethan Brand's activity combines all those disorders which Hawthorne habitually analyses: individualism, isolation from human sympathies, intellectual irresponsibility, and an instrumental attitude to others. Brand comes to define the Unpardonable Sin as the one he has himself practised: 'The sin of an intellect that triumphed over the sense of brotherhood with man and reverence for God, and sacrificed everything to its own mighty claims!' (*STS*, 306.)

As if to emphasize the fact that Brand's sin is a misdirected labour, Hawthorne takes care to contrast with him the figure of Lawyer Giles. Whereas Brand has risen from manual to intellectual labour, Giles has gone the other way.

This poor fellow had been an attorney . . . but flip, and sling, and toddy, and cocktails, imbibed at all hours, morning, noon, and night, had caused him to slide from intellectual to various kinds and degrees of bodily labor, till at last, to adopt his own phrase, he slid into a soap-vat. In other words, Giles was now a soap-boiler, in a small way. He had come to be but the fragment of a human being, a part of one foot having been chopped off by an axe, and an entire hand torn away by the devilish grip of a steam engine. (*STS*, 307)

If Ethan Brand's intellectual labour condemns him to burn in his own kiln, Giles's manual labour dismembers him in the grip of a mechanical devil; his soap-boiling and Brand's lime-burning both hint at the infernal. As Leo Marx has pointed out, this macabre vision of manual labour as dismemberment seems to arise from Hawthorne's visit in 1838 to the new factories in the Berkshires.[7] Hawthorne addresses in 'Ethan Brand' the problem of Schiller's fragmented humanity,

---

[7] Leo Marx, *The Machine in the Garden: Technology and the Pastoral Ideal in America* (New York, 1967), 267–9.

allegorizing that division of labour which the Transcendentalists of
Brook Farm had tried to overcome in their Utopian schemes, under
the sceptical eye of Nathaniel Hawthorne himself.
Thanks to R. W. Emerson and his associates, the problem
of modern fragmentation as formulated in German Idealist and
Carlylean terms was to become a central preoccupation of mid-
century American writing, the novelty of the American adventure
having called forth fundamental questions about life, labour, and
human ambition in an individualist and scientific age. Emerson's own
anxiety, expressed in 'The American Scholar', was that the advanced
division of labour in modern industrial society was fragmenting any
sense of human integrity:

The state of society is one in which the members have suffered amputation
from the trunk, and strut about so many walking monsters, — a good finger,
a neck, a stomach, an elbow, but never a man.
   Man is thus metamorphosed into a thing, into many things. . . . The priest
becomes a form; the attorney a statute-book; the mechanic a machine; the
sailor a rope of the ship.[8]

This kind of Transcendentalist social criticism emphasizes both
the dismemberment of the body politic and the subordination of
men and women to their own creations, under the new reign of
the commodity. As Emerson lamented in his 'Ode Inscribed to
W. E. Channing',

> 'Tis the day of the chattel,
> Web to weave, and corn to grind;
> Things are in the saddle,
> And ride mankind.
>
> There are two laws discrete,
> Not reconciled, —
> Law for man and law for thing;
> The last builds town and fleet,
> But it runs wild,
> And doth the man unking.[9]

This running wild of the huge productive energies of the nineteenth
century, particularly in the unprecedented conquests of nature going

   [8] Ralph Waldo Emerson, *Selected Essays*, ed. Larzer Ziff (Harmondsworth,
1982), 84–5.
   [9] Ralph Waldo Emerson, *Poems* (Boston, 1904), 78.

forward in Britain and America, is a recurrent nightmare for the mid-century writer. The feeling that 'things are in the saddle' reappears in the paradoxical formulations of H. D. Thoreau, whose hut at Walden adjoined a new railroad track. 'We do not ride on the railroad', Thoreau wrote, 'it rides upon us.' Reflecting on his neighbours' enslaved existence, he believes that 'men are not so much the keepers of herds as herds are the keepers of men', and again that 'when the farmer has got his house, he may not be the richer but the poorer for it, and it be the house that has got him'. Thoreau summarizes the incompatibility of liberty and property by agreeing with Emerson that 'men have become the tools of their tools'.[10]

The prospect which so troubled these Transcendentalist writers was that the 'Adam' of Tom Paine's new world would turn out to be a miscreant, and that the created wealth of the New World would turn (or had already turned) against 'Man', its supposed master. Instead of conquering nature, Americans would find themselves becoming the slaves of their own products, whose power would run wild. Frankensteinian forebodings of this kind were prompted not just by railroads or machinery but also by larger problems of nationhood in the United States. Another of Emerson's Transcendentalist associates, the feminist Margaret Fuller, applied the Frankenstein myth to the prospects of American literature itself. Arguing against premature attempts to synthesize a peculiarly national literature, Fuller contended that such an achievement would have to await the further fusion of races on the American continent and the advent of greater leisure alongside material progress; 'national ideas shall take birth' only then, she maintains. 'Without such ideas', Fuller warns, 'all attempts to construct a national literature must end in abortions like the monster of Frankenstein, things with forms, and the instincts of forms, but soulless, and therefore revolting.'[11] Fuller's analogy is not quite clear, but it appears to warn against assembling a literature from the existing cultural *disjecta membra* available in the United States before a unified American 'soul' has emerged. The almost unavoidable corollary is that the United States themselves form already a Frankenstein monster, the federal attempt to make one from many (*e pluribus unum*) having proved either

[10] Henry David Thoreau, *Walden, and Civil Disobedience* (Harmondsworth, 1983), 136, 99, 76, 80.

[11] *The Writings of Margaret Fuller*, ed. Mason Wade (New York, 1941), 359–60.

abortive or, at best, embryonic. America itself might become a colossal, powerful, but alarmingly uncontrolled creation running wild.

It is partly out of this ferment of ideas in mid-century America that the major writings of Herman Melville emerge, and partly too from the example of his literary hero and sometime neighbour Nathaniel Hawthorne. Melville's focus of interest, like Hawthorne's, is usually on the outcast or *isolato*, often a fatherless figure doomed to wander the world. And like Emerson and Thoreau, Melville is particularly alert to the contradictory promise of America's new empire of productive forces: 'Seeking to conquer a larger liberty,' he wrote, 'man but extends the empire of necessity.' This striking aphorism appears as one of the epigraphs to a short story, 'The Bell-Tower', in which Melville most concisely reproduces the themes of *Frankenstein*. The tale is often regarded as a reworking of Hawthorne's 'Ethan Brand', but it is likely to have been based also on *Frankenstein*, a copy of which was sent to Melville by his publisher in 1849. The meaning of 'The Bell-Tower' is summarized, rather too emphatically and proverbially, in its final paragraph: 'So the blind slave obeyed its blinder lord; but, in obedience, slew him. So the creator was killed by the creature. So the bell was too heavy for the tower. So the bell's main weakness was where man's blood had flawed it. And so pride went before the fall.'[12] The pride of the protagonist Bannadonna takes, as so often in Melville, a phallic form: he erects a tower to house his perfect bell, but this bell is in fact blemished by a fragment of flesh from a foundry worker killed in anger by Bannadonna during its casting. To chime the hours, Bannadonna secretly constructs an automaton whose hammering action kills him. The bell later crashes down and is finally destroyed along with the tower by an earthquake.

Bannadonna's dream, described by Melville as Promethean and compared with those of Albertus Magnus and Cornelius Agrippa, has been to construct a superior creature as a helot. 'All excellences of all God-made creatures, which served man, were here to receive advancement, and then to be combined in one.' (*BBS*, 209.) The difference from Frankenstein or Faust is, as Melville is at pains to stress, that Bannadonna does not believe in a mysterious secret of

[12] Herman Melville, *Billy Budd, Sailor and Other Stories*, ed. Harold Beaver (Harmondsworth, 1967), 213. Subsequent page references in the text are to this edition, abbreviated as *BBS*.

life; he is 'a practical materialist' (*BBS*, 210) aiming to achieve Frankensteinian ends by means of applied mechanics:

> In short, to solve nature, to steal into her, to intrigue beyond her, to procure some one else to bind her to his hand;—these, one and all, had not been his objects; but, asking no favors from any element or any being, of himself, to rival her, outstrip her, and rule her. He stooped to conquer. With him, common sense was theurgy; machinery, miracle; Prometheus, the heroic name for machinist; man, the true God. (*BBS*, 210)

It is as if Melville were criticizing *Frankenstein* for being too Faustian, too alchemical to be a fully modern version of the Prometheus myth. Despite the tale's setting in Renaissance Italy, Bannadonna's 'utilitarian ambition' (*BBS*, 210) more accurately represents the nineteenth-century Prometheanism of industry. It attempts no romantic seduction or inveigling of Nature but an individualistic effort of competition against her, carried on in what Melville implies is a 'stooping' mechanical efficiency rather than in transcendental aspiration.

Melville's response to *Frankenstein* is not to convert it again into a moral fable—although he does his worst in the last lines of 'The Bell-Tower'—but to outstrip it himself, to make it both more secular and yet more potently mythical too. The achievement of the earlier and far greater *Moby Dick* follows this paradoxical pattern, representing the Prometheanism of modern industry in almost pedantic realist reportage while at the same time inflating it mythically into the grandest of Titanic enterprises. Through such a paradoxical design can be shown the larger contradictions behind the self-destructiveness of Melville's age—both the mechanical inventiveness of the nineteenth century and the restless ambition which drives it.

Like *Frankenstein* but more ostentatiously, Melville's *Moby Dick* is an assemblage and pastiche of older myths. Most obviously, the novel recalls the myths of Job and Jonah along with other biblical tales, and employs—like earlier Gothic novels—a clearly Shakespearian tragic pattern in its plotting. *Moby Dick* is an allusive omnivore, digesting myths as remote as those of Osiris or Narcissus and as recent as *Paradise Lost* or *Robinson Crusoe*, but among the more prominent of the myths which the novel absorbs and reworks is that of Prometheus. Like Victor Frankenstein, Captain Ahab embodies both the transgressive and the creative aspects of Prometheus, in such a contradictory manner that Captain Peleg has to describe him as 'a grand, ungodly, god-like man' (ch. 16).[13] Ahab's Promethean traits extend beyond his rebellion against divine power to include a tormented capacity for remaking himself, most strikingly apparent in this account of his obsession:

. . . it must have been that, in Ahab's case, yielding up all his thoughts and fancies to his one supreme purpose; that purpose, by its own sheer inveteracy of will, forced itself against gods and devils into a kind of self-assumed, independent being of its own. Nay, could grimly live and burn, while the common vitality to which it was conjoined, fled horror-stricken from the unbidden and unfathered birth. Therefore, the tormented spirit that glared out of bodily eyes, when what seemed Ahab rushed from his room, was for the time but a vacated thing, a formless somnambulistic being, a ray of living light, to be sure, but without an object to color, and therefore a blankness in itself. God help thee, old man, thy thoughts have created a creature in thee; and he whose intense thinking thus makes him a Prometheus; a vulture feeds upon that heart for ever; that vulture the very creature he creates. (ch. 44)

Ahab's obsessive purpose is seen here to be an independent creature of his own fashioning, which now feeds upon the remaining human elements within him. He is caught here in the process of becoming his own self-created monster.

Ahab is of course already partly an artificial man, recognizable by the ivory leg which is both a reminder of and a defiant challenge to the divine malevolence he detects behind the White Whale. In a sequence of more or less comic scenes involving the replacement of this leg, Ahab elaborates upon the myth of Prometheus in his dialogues with the ship's carpenter and blacksmith, whom he nicknames 'manmaker' and 'Prometheus' respectively (ch. 108). 'I do deem it now a most meaning thing,' he says, 'that that old Greek, Prometheus, who made men, they say, should have been a blacksmith, and animated them with fire; for what's made in fire must properly belong to fire; and so hell's probable.' (ch. 108.) Warming to his hellish theme, Ahab himself tries on the role of Prometheus by imagining the creation of an artificial man:

Hold; while Prometheus is about it, I'll order a complete man after a desirable pattern. Imprimis, fifty feet high in his socks; then, chest modelled after the Thames Tunnel; then, legs with roots to 'em, to stay in one place; then,

[13] References to *Moby Dick* are by chapter rather than by page. My text is Harold Beaver's Penguin edition (Harmondsworth, 1972).

arms three feet through the wrist; no heart at all, brass forehead, and about a quarter of fine brains; and let me see—shall I order eyes to see outwards? No, but put a sky-light on top of his head to illuminate inwards. (ch. 108)

Behind the foolery here is a grandiose self-portraiture, an enlarged projection of Ahab's own ambition, complete with its heartlessness and its solipsism. Like the ship's surgeon and anatomist Dr Cuticle in *White-Jacket*, 'a curious patch-work of life and death, with a wig, one glass eye, and a set of false teeth',[14] Ahab's willed resistance to common human sympathies has refashioned him as an artificial being, the creature and plaything of his own monomania. He is both sides of the Promethean creation at once, both obsessed creator and outcast creature.

To emphasize his Promethean role Ahab becomes a blacksmith himself and forges his own harpoon, which we foresee will bring about his death ('have I been but forging my own branding-iron, then?'), baptizing it in the name of the Devil (ch. 113). He has already described himself as an iron artefact, indeed as the all-conquering and world-embracing railroad engine. 'The path to my fixed purpose is laid with iron rails, whereon my soul is grooved to run. Over unsounded gorges, through the rifled hearts of mountains, under torrents' beds, unerringly I rush! Naught's an obstacle, naught's an angle to the iron way!' (ch. 37.) Beneath this expansionist brag lies an ironic admission that Ahab has re-created himself in the image of a mechanical beast of burden, enslaving himself to what he imagines is a conquest of nature. Ahab's Promethean self-making is both heroic and pathetic, for in seeking a larger liberty he has but extended the realm of necessity.

Victor Frankenstein's first disciple is a navigator, Robert Walton, who attempts with Frankenstein's help to inspire his crew to complete a dangerous voyage. He is saved from the consequences of his ambition by the threat of mutiny by his sailors, who have been recruited, as it happens, from whaling ships. *Moby Dick* can be read as a study of what happens when the crew fails to mutiny against Frankensteinian leadership. The crew of the *Pequod* allows itself to be welded into another instrument of Ahab's mania. The old captain regards the mentality of his sailors as that of the 'manufactured man' (ch. 46), while in the preparations for the final chase the men around

---

[14] Herman Melville, *White-Jacket*, ed. Hennig Cohen (New York, 1967), 246 (ch. 61).

him appear to Ishmael as if their human feelings had been 'ground to finest dust, and powdered, for the time, in the clamped mortar of Ahab's iron soul. Like machines, they dumbly moved about the deck, ever conscious that the old man's despot eye was on them.' (ch. 130.) Melville had explained in *White-Jacket* that a ship's captain regards his subordinates as 'disintegrated parts of himself, detached from the main body';[15] Ahab has remade from such parts a disciplined organic instrument subordinate to his will. As he exclaims at the climax of the chase, 'Ye are not other men, but my arms and legs; and so obey me.' (ch. 134.)

Animated by Ahab's controlling will, the arms and legs of the crew, and their separate racial and personal identities, are brought together to compose a floating body politic.

They were one man, not thirty. For as the one ship that held them all; though it was put together of all contrasting things—oak, and maple, and pine wood; iron, and pitch, and hemp—yet all these ran into each other in the one concrete hull, which shot on its way, both balanced and directed by the long central keel; even so, all the individualities of the crew, this man's valor, that man's fear; guilt and guiltiness, all varieties were welded into oneness, and were all directed to that fatal goal which Ahab their one lord and keel did point to. (ch. 134)

It is the crew as a whole which is the 'manufactured man' shaped by Ahab in his role as the Prometheus of nineteenth-century industry. The crew is deliberately and allegorically presented to us as a medley of different races and temperaments, all of its members being islanders, individualists, and *isolatoes*. 'Yet now, federated along one keel, what a set these Isolatoes were!' (ch. 27.) They stand, in short, for the federated American republic, afloat upon Melville's allegorical waters. But they do not form a federation of equals; the red man, the brown man, and the black boy are all mere instruments subordinate to the white captain and his white obsession. The nineteenth-century American whaling ship, as H. Bruce Franklin reminds us,[16] combined many of the worst features of Northern wage-slavery with those of Southern chattel-slavery, driving its victims—Melville included—to desertion or mutiny.

That reactionary relapse into concealed feudal tyrannies imagined in Gothic novels is also the concern of *Moby Dick*, which envisages

---

[15] Ibid., 215 (ch. 52).
[16] H. Bruce Franklin, *The Victim as Criminal and Artist: Literature from the American Prison* (New York, 1978), 31-2.

the possibility of America's federated parts being reassembled in the service of a guiding principle—a 'keel'—both oppressive and self-destructive. The danger is the same as that announced in *White-Jacket*: a 'monstrous grafting of tyranny upon freedom'.[17] The individuals or *isolatoes* of the *Pequod*'s crew succumb to a Shakespearian rhetoric and to a resurgent European mode of hierarchy in which Ahab galvanizes them through 'the Leyden jar of his own magnetic life' (ch. 36). Rather than squeeze hands in that democratic brotherhood dreamed of by Ishmael, they surrender their destinies to a 'head' who turns them into mere arms and legs. Since Ahab is waging war against Nature in the shape of the White Whale, he requires a prior conquest over his men; called into life as a collective instrument, their task is to suffer for their captain's transgression. While Ahab attempts to subdue Nature, pursuing her to her hiding-places like Frankenstein (*F*, 49/54), the crew is expected to suffer the consequences. The fate of the *Pequod* asks us to question the logic of industrial development stirring into life in America and across 'the all-grasping western world' (ch. 87).

Read in a Frankensteinian perspective, *Moby Dick* can be seen to harbour three monsters: the dehumanized Ahab, the 'manufactured man' which is the crew, and finally the White Whale itself. Moby Dick is frequently referred to as a monster, often simply because of his huge size and destructive capacity, but he has other claims to the title. In the episode of 'The Spirit-Spout', Ishmael and the rest of the crew sense a malevolence in the whale's appearance, 'as if it were treacherously beckoning us on and on, in order that the monster might turn round upon us, and rend us at last in the remotest and most savage seas' (ch. 51). This ambiguous point at which the quarry becomes a trapper and the hunter becomes the hunted is precisely that of *Frankenstein*'s closing episodes, in which the monster appears to flee Victor but leaves him food and directions in order to lure him to the Arctic. In both novels the effect of the confusion between pursuer and pursued is to cast the antagonists as twin 'moments' within a single self-destructive complex, in which revenge can be revealed as suicide and heroism as folly pursuing its own tail. As in *Caleb Williams* and *Frankenstein*, the quest turns in upon itself statically, and the antagonists of *Moby Dick* confront one another as mirror images. That the White Whale acts, or at least appears

---

[17] Melville, *White-Jacket*, 296 (ch. 71).

to the Puritan paranoiac, as Ahab's 'double' has often been remarked by readers of *Moby Dick*; the two share the same wrinkled brow and the same solitary and maimed grandeur. Yet their equivalence is ultimately a figment of Ahab's obsessed mind: as a white whale, Ahab's quarry is simply a whale, a dumb brute, but as Moby Dick—humanly named and adorned with legend—he becomes a 'monster', apparently wilfil in provoking and mocking Ahab's urge to subdue Nature.

If the monstrous quality of the White Whale is a projection of Ahab's persecution mania, then it should come as no surprise to find Ahab blending into this mirror image, and becoming a vengeful monster himself. On the other hand the whale, with the help of Ishmael's bragging cetology, appears in heroic guise, and even as an inscrutable divinity towards whom Ahab is acting as a presumptuous blasphemer. By the end of the story Moby Dick has become a fully American hero by resisting and eluding the Europeanized tyranny of Ahab's monomania. His human counterpart and panegyrist Ishmael also slips away from the despotic nightmare and offers through his narrative a fraternal and pastoral alternative to Ahab's lust for conquest. The whale is a mute 'monster', but he is given a displaced voice through his advocate Ishmael, a virtuoso of rhetorical energy and style. Between them, these two survivors offer the dialogical rebuttal of Ahab's obsession, as the monster does to Victor's. Goaded into self-defence, the whale remains innocent because dumb; forced to become, in human eyes, a 'monster', he is never truly part of the human world. His articulate equivalent is Ishmael, a fellow-victim and outcast orphan, while the true monster is the Frankensteinian figure of Ahab himself, dismembered, unnaturally vengeful, self-enslaved, and self-exiled from land and from women.

Even more than *Frankenstein*, *Moby Dick* is a novel which excludes women from its action, yet it manages similarly, if less pointedly, to problematize the masculine heroism which its setting isolates. Melville's men appear to be redeemed to the extent that they are feminized: Ishmael and Queequeg are seen to be bound together in what is almost a parody of the marriage-bed and its harmony, and they are later 'wedded' by the monkey-rope, while Queequeg acts as a 'midwife' to Tashtego. By contrast, Ahab's regime aboard the *Pequod* bristles with phallic menace. Only in the chapter entitled 'The Symphony' does his rigour unbend as he observes the sexualized heavings of sea and sky. Here he admits to Starbuck that his forty years at sea have been a 'desolation of solitude'. For the first time, Ahab mentions

that young girl-wife I wedded past fifty, and sailed for Cape Horn the next day, leaving but one dent in my marriage pillow—wife? wife?—rather a widow with her husband alive! Aye, I widowed that poor girl when I married her, Starbuck . . . (ch. 132)

The image of his wife and child which he sees in Starbuck's eye is the last lifeline by which Ahab could pull himself back to his 'humanities'. In rejecting it, he joins Victor Frankenstein, Elis Fröbom, and Hawthorne's transgressors as another victim of industrial sublimation.

The earliest and most outspoken champions of the modern Melville revival rightly stressed the connections between *Moby Dick* and the dynamic energies of territorial and industrial expansion in mid-century America. Both D. H. Lawrence in *Studies in Classic American Literature* and Charles Olson in *Call Me Ishmael* read the *Pequod* as an image of American industry, and Ahab as the white American urge to subdue Nature by mechanical efficiency. Many critics have seen Ahab as a latter-day Faust, but Olson recognizes that after the industrial revolution Faust could never be the same again.[18] Faust has become Prometheanized; and in the nineteenth-century world of industrial development, transgression and damnation have become identified less with devilry than with production. The world of *Moby Dick* is no alchemical laboratory but an authentic and exhaustively catalogued American whaling ship setting out to convert real spermaceti and blubber into dollars for its owners. The problem of defining Ahab's transgression, however, is that his project is not simply an over-reaching extension of capitalist enterprise as such; on the contrary, it appears to be a hijacking or usurpation of the *Pequod* for private purposes at odds with those of mundane profit-making. As in 'The Mines at Falun', it is the conversion of the industrial into a route to 'higher' goals which proves fatal.

Starbuck, the pious and (as his name suggests) dollar-orientated first mate, voices the horror of the respectable New England bourgeois at Ahab's motives.

I am game for his crooked jaw, and for the jaws of Death too, Captain Ahab, if it fairly comes in the way of the business we follow; but I came here to

---

[18] Charles Olson, *Call Me Ishmael* (New York, 1947), 59.

hunt whales, not my commander's vengeance. How many barrels will thy vengeance yield thee even if thou gettest it, Captain Ahab? it will not fetch thee much in our Nantucket market. (ch. 36)

Ahab scorns this as an accountant's view of the world, and it is only then that Starbuck resorts to moral objections, condemning Ahab's pursuit as blasphemous. From the point of view of the *Pequod*'s owners, Ahab is a profitable instrument who has now rebelled in pursuit of his own higher goal, diverting the lucrative resources of the crew and the ship towards the symbolic conquest of Nature's malevolence in the shape of the White Whale. Yet Starbuck, the loyal representative of the company's interests, is forced nevertheless to obey the man to whom the supreme powers of captain and industrial manager have been delegated. Ahab's maritime *coup d'état* may be illegal, but to the impotent Starbuck it is also irresistible, because all he can offer the crew, in competition with Ahab's inspiring heroic purpose, is a frugal and drily legalistic accountancy. Melville is, in effect, enquiring into the possibility that simple capitalist enterprise can harbour within it—in its acquisitive mentality, in its forms of labour-discipline and delegated power—tendencies towards untrammelled despotism and destructive energy which its sober guardians are powerless to resist once they are unleashed.

The good Quakers of Nantucket are obliged by the law of the market to employ heathen harpooners and a satanic captain, because their labour is more productive. Once out of their sight, though, the Quakers' ship becomes a weapon to strike at their own God in open rebellion. Starbuck seems quite unprepared for this transformation, having failed to discern beneath the *Pequod*'s innocent commercial status a power susceptible to irrational development. What Ahab's usurpation represents is the subordination of simple commercial transactions to an underlying thirst for capital *accumulation*, an uncontrolled expansionist drive which uses each transaction or productive act merely as a step to the next. This process was still very much a mystery even to those who were most eagerly practising it, and so it can only be represented symbolically, in the somewhat lurid and melodramatic terms of biblical or Shakespearian vengeance, in pseudo-Masonic rituals and other codes incompatible with Starbuck's mercantile common sense. Even Ahab cannot understand the nature of the force which drives him; like Queequeg, who cannot decipher the hieroglyphs tattooed upon his own skin, the captain is inscrutable to himself.

What is it, what nameless, inscrutable, unearthly thing is it; what cozzening, hidden lord and master, and cruel, remorseless emperor commands me; that against all natural lovings and longings, I so keep pushing, and crowding, and jamming myself on all the time; recklessly making me ready to do what in my own proper, natural heart, I durst not so much as dare? is Ahab, Ahab? (ch. 132)

Never stably identical with himself, Ahab is indeed not Ahab but the instrument of an accumulative frenzy which grips nineteenth-century industry, possessing the possessor and commanding the commander. Ahab's combination of technical efficiency with general loss of control and purpose, of localized tyranny with generalized anarchy, encapsulates perfectly the very logic of capitalist accumulation and expansion: 'all my means are sane,' he realizes, 'my motive and my object mad.' (ch. 41.)[19]

The singular achievement of *Moby Dick* is now generally acknowledged as an unprecedented combination of high tragic dignity and mythological resonance with the meticulous, even pedantic realism of reportage, in which Melville plays off Ahab the mythic quester and tragedian against Ishmael the encyclopaedic cetologist and practical mariner. The novel's divergent registers somehow balance one another, the central chapters on the parts and dimensions of the whale and on the bloody details of its exploitation serving as a 'ballast'—as many critics have expressed it—to the symbolic and metaphysical soaring which is the book's counter-movement. This cetological material holds what would otherwise be transcendental freewheeling down to the observable facts of the nineteenth-century world, while on the other hand the anatomizing of the whale and the inventory of the ship are lifted and propelled beyond the merely documentary by the impetus of the book's mythic, symbolic, and romance elements. Yoked together in *Moby Dick* are two contrary impulses—of documentary realism and of symbolic romance—which tend to pull in opposite directions throughout the history of the novel form, and whose magnetic repulsion was especially powerful in the nineteenth century as an ugly, urbanized, industrial world proved increasingly indigestible to the traditions of literary romance.

---

[19] Melville was of course not a Marxist but a radical democrat of a sceptical disposition. However, the common objection to Marxist readings of *Moby Dick*— that Melville also celebrates capitalist industry's heroic achievements as well as condemning its recklessness—is quite misplaced, since the same is true of Marx and Engels themselves in their *Communist Manifesto*.

Melville's ability thus to digest fictionally the hard facts of nineteenth-century industry relies to a great extent on his use of transgression myths—those of Frankenstein and Faust, with the stories of Ethan Brand and others—as the foundation for *Moby Dick*'s design and narrative movement. It is the mobilization of such myths which gives the novel a means (perhaps the only means) of grasping imaginatively the new complexities of the modern world and especially the motive forces of industrial expansion; forces whose impersonal and invisible movements concealed themselves behind the phenomena they produced and which were therefore not readily accessible to realist representation. Melville's resort to myth in *Moby Dick* is not an atavistic invocation of primeval archetypes but a remarkably modern effort to dramatize the dynamics of nineteenth-century industrial expansion.

In many respects the achievement of *Moby Dick* invites comparison with that of a contemporary work which also attempts to assimilate romance and industrial life: Elizabeth Gaskell's *Mary Barton*. According to Gaskell's preface, this novel was born from the realization of 'how deep might be the romance in the lives of some of those who elbowed me daily in the busy streets of the town in which I resided'.[20] The strength of its earlier chapters lies in a realist commitment to reproducing the speech, manners, domestic environment, and personal histories of the Manchester factory-workers and their families. Yet along with this element in *Mary Barton* goes an element of romance, of the kind which rapidly curdles into melodrama. These two sides of the novel sit so uneasily together that it is almost possible to divide *Mary Barton* into a first half of powerful and sympathetic reportage and a second half of melodramatic degeneration. The crucial dividing line falls, very significantly, across the discussion in Chapter 15 of John Barton's support for Chartism.

Gaskell had originally intended John Barton to be the hero of the novel and the central object of our sympathies but, partly under her publishers' pressure and partly because of her own problems with the character, she discarded this plan as the book took shape. The first part of *Mary Barton* tries to lead readers to understand the disaffection and protests of workers like John Barton, but it reaches

---

[20] Elizabeth Gaskell, *Mary Barton: A Tale of Manchester Life*, ed. Stephen Gill (Harmondsworth, 1970), 37. Subsequent page references in the text are to this edition, abbreviated as *MB*.

a conclusion and a crisis of a kind which obliges Gaskell to dislodge this character from the centre of sympathy and to substitute for him his daughter Mary, who takes over as the beautiful romance heroine. The discarding of John Barton is a rapid and even spectacular operation: he becomes an opium addict, a Chartist, and a trade-unionist in quick (and, we are left to infer, logical) succession. Gaskell's commentary reveals several of her motives for the sudden change of direction:

2. The Working Class as Monster: in Tenniel's 'The Brummagem Franken-stein' (*Punch*, 1866), an enormous proletarian waits for the vote to be given to him by the Birmingham Liberal MP John Bright, a leader of the Reform agitation in the 1860s.

John Barton's overpowering thought, which was to work out his fate on earth, was rich and poor; why are they so separate, so distinct, when God has made them all? It is not His will, that their interests are so far apart. Whose doing is it?

And so on into the problems and mysteries of life, until, bewildered and lost, unhappy and suffering, the only feeling that remained clear and undisturbed in the tumult of his heart, was hatred to the one class and keen sympathy with the other.

But what availed his sympathy? No education had given him wisdom; and without wisdom, even love, with all its effects, too often works but harm. He acted to the best of his judgement, but it was a widely-erring judgement.

The actions of the uneducated seem to me typified in those of Frankenstein, that monster of many human qualities, ungifted with a soul, a knowledge of the difference between good and evil.

The people rise up to life; they irritate us, they terrify us, and we become their enemies. Then, in the sorrowful moment of our triumphant power, their eyes gaze on us with a mute reproach. Why have we made them what they are; a powerful monster, yet without the inner means for peace and happiness? (*MB*, 219)

In a novel which offers a considered response to the sufferings of the Manchester workers, and an effort to sympathize with them, such a passage has considerable significance. It is the point at which a class at first represented as suffering passively now 'rises up into life' in protest, and has therefore to be distanced and reinterpreted as a monster, strong but childishly misguided. The working class now becomes 'the uneducated'; at the moment when it tries to overcome its subordination it has to be told that its actions are based upon a fundamental ignorance of Manchester Political Economy and its eternal truths: 'Distrust each other as they may, the employers and employed must rise or fall together. There may be some difference as to chronology, none as to fact.' (*MB*, 221.)[21]

In Gaskell's allusion to *Frankenstein* we have a prominent example of a creative misreading which wrenches the myth into new patterns

---

[21] Despite such confident expositions of economic fact against the childish imaginings of the workers, Gaskell claims in her Preface that she knows 'nothing of Political Economy, or the theories of trade' (*MB*, 38), soon after remarking upon the 'unhappy state of things between those so bound to each other by common interests, as the employers and the employed must ever be' (*MB*, 37). The illusion of disinterestedness here in taking for granted the common interest of contending classes is a perfect instance of ideological blindness.

while applying it directly to the central tensions of an industrializing social order. The misreading here is more than just a matter of calling the monster by the name of his maker; it brings in too the stage versions' redefinition of the monster as a soulless being and as an inarticulate child. This allows Gaskell to represent the working class as an unfortunate but morally irresponsible creature which lashes out blindly and mutely at its begetter in the deluded belief that the employers are in some way to blame for its misery. It is no more human than Mary Wollstonecraft's blind elephant, although Gaskell does allow it the charitable condescension due to a child. If the employers are to blame, it is, according to Gaskell, only for failing to provide their workers with 'soul' in the form of religious example, and with an education which could explain that their miseries are the necessary consequences of immutable market forces, their prosperity tied forever to that of their masters. The repeated refrain which Gaskell raises against working-class violence in *Mary Barton* is 'They know not what they do' ( *MB*, 223, 439). What begins as an account of the sufferings of the working class ends by equating the passion of the crucified Christ with that of the Manchester bourgeoisie.[22]

In this extraordinary series of mythological displacements Gaskell herself manages to double up as both Victor Frankenstein and Pontius Pilate. While her intended message in *Mary Barton* is one of sympathy and brotherhood, ironically she comes to wash her hands of her proletarian hero and to recoil from him as a monster when he appears to be asserting his independence from his employers and from his literary creator. Gaskell enacts, in other words, the same repudiation of the monster and his claims of which Victor Frankenstein had been guilty. She accompanies this gesture with a litany of disclaimers on behalf of the employers' class, shifting responsibility to the eternal laws of supply and demand, which her ideology identifies in turn with the injunctions of Christian charity: when it is weak and incapable, the working class deserves pious sympathy, but when it is in a position to assert itself, it is to be reviled as a monstrous beast. The result is that just when John Barton is about to transform himself from passive victim to articulate champion of his class, Gaskell has to drug him and turn him into

---

[22] Cf. the inverted *pietà* which Gaskell contrives at the end of the riot scene in Chapter 22 of her *North and South*.

a mute and vengeful monster. His form of class resistance is narrowed into a personal grudge and dramatized as the reflex savagery of an inarticulate assassin. *Mary Barton* falls asunder into reportage on the one side and lurid melodrama on the other, split apart by Gaskell's recoiling from and silencing of the working-class monster.

That Melville is able to overcome the danger of such a split in *Moby Dick*, that he can mythicize the everyday reality of the whaling industry while preserving its authenticity, can be attributed ultimately to his radical-democratic reinterpretation of the grand style and of tragic propriety.

If, then, to meanest mariners, and renegades and castaways, I shall hereafter ascribe high qualities, though dark; weave round them tragic graces; if even the most mournful, perchance the most abased, among them all, shall at times lift himself to the exalted mounts; if I shall touch that workman's arm with some ethereal light; if I shall spread a rainbow over his disastrous set of sun; then against all mortal critics bear me out in it, thou just Spirit of Equality, which has spread one royal mantle of humanity over all my kind! (ch. 26.)

Melville is able to elevate his mariners in this way because he believes in their 'democratic dignity', and because he himself has been formed by their experiences, viewing the world of his novels from the forecastle rather than from the bridge. It is not just that, as a matter of their personal experience, Melville was able to describe actual labour whereas Gaskell—along with other misnamed 'industrial' novelists in Britain—could give us only the domestic sickbed or the riot at the factory gates. It is also a matter of instinctive identifications: unlike Gaskell, Melville has no occasion to recoil from his 'monsters', the crew and the whale. His impatience with the anti-democratic rhetoric of popular monstrosity is highlighted in the repartee of his idealized mariner Jack Chase in *White-Jacket*. The ship's poetaster Lemsford bewails the philistinism of a public which ignores him:

'Blast them, Jack, what they call the public is a monster, like the idol we saw in Owhyhee, with the head of a jackass, the body of a baboon, and the tail of a scorpion!'

'I don't like that,' said Jack; 'when I'm ashore, I myself am part of the public.'[23]

The difference is resolved by an evasive distinction between public and people, but Melville's democratic reservation still stands, signalling

---

[23] Melville, *White-Jacket*, 191–2 (ch. 45).

his suspicion of the traditionally reactionary uses to which the 'monstrous' has been put, and reminding us of his own place within the monstrous body of democracy. Himself a renegade, castaway, and deserter, Melville can give the outcasts and victims of industrial Prometheanism a human voice, while Gaskell silences them or relegates them to a faltering infancy.

The point at which Elizabeth Gaskell transforms her workers from reasonable beings into Gothic banditti in *Mary Barton* has a certain ironic significance. During the negotiations between the employers and a trade union delegation, Mary's prospective seducer Harry Carson vigorously opposes the workers' right to organize, and scribbles a caricature of the lean and hungry delegates for the amusement of his fellow-capitalists. This cartoon is later picked up by one of the workmen, and it inflames them to the point of drawing lots for Carson's assassination. Although we are meant to take Carson's caricature as another sign of his callous insensitivity, a portrayal of the workers of just the kind that Gaskell wants to supersede in her own work, it comes instead to set the tone of Gaskell's subsequent treatment of her workers: in her portrayal of working-class organization as a murderous conspiracy Gaskell herself degenerates into literary 'caricature'. Such contradictions in her treatment of the working class revolve around the ambivalence of her central and repeated insistence upon the mutual dependence between masters and men. As it appears in her other 'industrial' novel, *North and South*, Gaskell's argument formulates a Christian paternalist qualification to the *laissez-faire* doctrines of Manchester: Margaret Hale tells the employer Thornton that 'the most isolated of your Darkshire Egos has dependants clinging to him on all sides; he cannot shake them off . . .'[24] Through her heroine Gaskell espouses here what could be called the official morality of the Victorian novel, chiding liberal individualism in the name of social responsibility. But the reminder of Christian brotherhood has its more sinister underside, which Gaskell's appeal to the Frankenstein myth in *Mary Barton* brings into focus. For if the capitalists truly cannot shake off the terrifying power which they have brought into being (and since they live off its labour, they cannot) then they are saddled, like Victor Frankenstein, with a threatening monster who will never leave them in peace. Gaskell's

---

[24] Elizabeth Gaskell, *North and South*, ed. Dorothy Collin (Harmondsworth, 1970), 169.

3. Parnell as Frankenstein: a fortnight after the Phoenix Park murders (May 1882), Tenniel's 'The Irish Frankenstein' in *Punch* pins the blame on the Irish Nationalist leader Charles Stewart Parnell. The caption gives an '*Extract from the Works of* C.S.P–RN–LL, M.P.': '"The baneful and blood-stained Monster * * * yet was it not my Master to the very extent that it was my Creature? * * * Had I not breathed into it my own spirit? * * *"'

use of the Frankenstein myth announces the awful recognition by the Victorian bourgeoisie that its prosperity is inescapably haunted.

It is this indelible historical fear that Harry Carson's professional counterparts—the cartoonists of the Victorian press—play upon in their adaptations of Frankenstein's monster. True to the older traditions of the monstrous as a visible vice, they depict in their political allegories a creature who embodies pure brutal menace. The most vicious of their caricatures were reserved for the Irish nationalists, always regarded in Britain as mindless and primitive brutes; but the Frankenstein myth also appears in cartoons which depict the sometimes linked threat of the British working class, as in Tenniel's 'The Brummagem Frankenstein'. Tenniel preserved in his two Frankenstein cartoons the Burkean prophecy which warns that middle-class radicals (here, the Irish nationalist Charles Stewart Parnell and the Liberal orator John Bright) will surely be overwhelmed by the uncontrollable masses they incite. Frankenstein had come to stand as the reflected image of the Victorian bourgeois order as it faced nervously the Irish and the working class stirring into independent political life.

# 5

# The Galvanic World:
# Carlyle and the Dickens Monster

> Their system of education is factitious. The universities
> galvanize dead languages into a semblance of life. Their
> church is artificial. The manners and customs of society
> are artificial;—made-up men with made-up manners;—
> and thus the whole is Birminghamized, and thus we have
> a nation whose whole existence is a work of art . . . Man
> is made as a Birmingham button.
>
> Ralph Waldo Emerson, *English Traits*

IN the the chain of connections traced in the last chapter from the
monsters of German Idealism to those of the American literary
renaissance and of the British industrial novel, one vital link was
omitted: the work of Thomas Carlyle. Carlyle was, among other
things, the translator and biographer of Schiller and a translator of
Hoffmann too in his selection of *German Romance*, where he cites
'the gory profundities of *Frankenstein*'[1] as symptoms of the Germanic
spirit in modern fiction. As a mediator between the Germans'
awareness of modern fragmentation and the anglophone fiction of
industry, Carlyle is inescapable: Gaskell quoted him on the title-page
of *Mary Barton*, Dickens dedicated *Hard Times* to him, and his
extravagant, mythologically allusive rhetoric was a pervasive influence
on Melville's *Moby Dick*. Not only did Carlyle provide these writers
with a definitive diagnosis of the Machine Age; he put forward too
the major Romantic reinterpretation of the French Revolution in
Britain, thereby encouraging readers in the 1840s to view the
movement of history in their own century providentially and
indeed mythically.

The historical significance of the Frankenstein myth derived, as
we have seen, from images of political monstrosity brought vividly
before the attention of the British public by the early debates over
the French Revolution. In his exhilarating historical narrative,

---

[1] *The Works of Thomas Carlyle*, Centenary Edition, 30 vols. (London, 1896–9),
xxi. 2. Subsequent page references in the text are to this edition, abbreviated as *W*.

*The French Revolution* (1837), Carlyle revives the Frankensteinian reading of modern history chiefly by resuscitating Burkean themes while drastically revising Burke's view of France. To some extent Carlyle endorses the Burkean narrative, in which a parricidal gang of atheist experimenters desecrates its inheritance and creates a constitutional monster which devours it. From his earliest significant writings Carlyle feels acutely the desiccating curse of Enlightenment materialism, and his revulsion from it usually appears in lurid anatomical images. In 'Signs of the Times' Carlyle ridicules a 'dissecting' view of life which is so mechanical as to produce absurdities like that of the inventor Vaucanson, the creator of a mechanical duck ( *W*, xxvii. 65). Extending his attack to the whole complexion of modern thinking, Carlyle complains that 'we see nothing by direct vision; but only by reflection, and in anatomical dismemberment' ( *W*, xxvii. 76). In *Sartor Resartus* he has Teufelsdröckh cry out that 'The Universe is not dead and demoniacal, a charnel-house with spectres', as the doctrines of 'the monster UTILITARIA' would have us believe ( *W*, i. 150, 188). Carlyle insistently associates Enlightenment philosophy with corpses and absurd mechanical contrivances; in his summary of France's intellectual climate before the Revolution, he elaborates the macabre consequences of its corrosively analytic tradition:

Honour to victorious Analysis; nevertheless, out of the Workshop and Laboratory, what thing was victorious Analysis yet known to make? Detection of incoherences, mainly; destruction of the incoherent. From of old, Doubt was but half a magician; she evokes the spectres which she cannot quell. ( *W*, ii. 53)

Out of the laboratory of the experimenting Enlightenment, Carlyle implies, comes the spectre of the Revolution itself. This Burkean reading, which casts the dissecting, anatomizing *philosophes* in the fabulous role of sorcerer's apprentice, brings into play Carlyle's repeated motif of ungovernable spectres and inadvertent self-destroyers — of whom we will find several more in his work. Carlyle here and throughout *The French Revolution* presents the dynamics of historical events as a cycle of poetic justice and fitting retribution, even more relentlessly than Burke had.

Keeping one eye on the lessons to be drawn by Britain in the 1830s, Carlyle differs from Burke in extending the fabulous narrative of poetic justice to include not only the sorcerer-*philosophes* but also the French monarchy. In the grand providential vision of *The French Revolution* royalists and revolutionaries alike can be seen as inevitably doomed, both parties being but twin facets of a great Sham which is necessarily burst apart by the reassertion of Reality. Carlyle's rather risky strategy is no less than to redeem the Revolution's admonitory stature while maintaining the utmost Burkean scorn for its atheist experimenters. This he manages by reducing most of the revolutionary leadership to a fragile epiphenomenon driven by the demiurge of unconscious spiritual forces in the populace, of which Robespierre and company are only the false prophets. In direct contrast with Burke, then, Carlyle argues that the *ancien régime* deserved its downfall; indeed, produced it and was directly responsible for it. In the tones of biblical prophecy Carlyle addresses the French nobility prior to the Revolution: 'Dance on, ye foolish ones; ye sought not wisdom, neither have ye found it. Ye and your fathers have sown the wind, ye shall reap the whirlwind. Was it not, from of old, written: *The wages of sin is death*?' ( *W*, ii. 48.) The same biblical figure and tone is invoked when Carlyle warms to the theme of the Terror in Book V, but now the logic of sowing and reaping is emphasized as the revelation of Truth itself.

The harvest of long centuries was ripening and whitening so rapidly of late; and now it is grown *white*, and is reaped rapidly, as it were, in one day. Reaped, in this Reign of Terror; and carried home, to Hades and the Pit! — Unhappy Sons of Adam: it is ever so; and never do they know it, nor will they know it. With cheerfully smoothed countenances, day after day, and generation after generation, they, calling cheerfully to one another, Well-speed ye, are at work, *sowing the wind*. And yet, as God lives, they *shall reap the whirlwind*; no other thing, we say, is possible, — since God is a Truth and His World is a Truth. ( *W*, iv. 203)

Carlyle presents the inevitability of the Revolution both as a punishment for the monarchy's negligence and as a refutation of the *philosophes'* atheism. This allows him to rejoice in its cleansing destruction, interpreting it as a divine scourge.

Carlyle's almost pathological clinging to the pattern of poetic justice makes retribution the only reliable Truth to be discerned in a world which he otherwise depicts as a swirling vortex of shams and rubbish. It should not surprise us, then, to find the same structure recurring under different guises throughout *The French Revolution*, the sowing–reaping metaphor being only the most authoritative image of poetic justice. There are others more striking; for example,

4. A Militarist Frankenstein: *Punch*'s 'The Russian Frankenstein and His Monster' (1854) celebrates the sending of an Allied force to the Crimea to punish the presumptuous Tsar Nicholas I, whose militarism would surely backfire on him. He who lives by the cannon shall die by the cannon, this rather poor cartoon implies.

Carlyle's use of the prophetic words of Vergniaud: 'The Revolution, like Saturn, is devouring its own children.' ( *W*, iv. 201.) And there is Carlyle's favourite, which he appears to have picked up from Schiller,[2] and which he deploys widely in his other works: the Bull of Phalaris. With this image Carlyle is able much more graphically to represent the deserved downfall of the French monarchy as the product of an independently active power which turns against those who first put it in motion. Carlyle brings the image out for his grand apostrophe on the special occasion of the King's execution.

To this conclusion, then, hast thou come, O hapless Louis! The Son of Sixty Kings is to die on the Scaffold by form of Law. Under Sixty Kings this same form of Law, form of Society, has been fashioning itself together, these thousand years; and has become, one way and another, a most strange Machine. Surely, if needful, it is also frightful, this Machine; dead, blind; not what it should be; which, with swift stroke, or by cold slow torture, has wasted the lives and souls of innumerable men. And behold now a King himself, or say rather Kinghood in his person, is to expire here in cruel tortures; — like a Phalaris shut in the belly of his own red-heated Brazen Bull! It is ever so; and thou shouldst know it, O haughty tyrannous man: injustice breeds injustice; curses and falsehoods do verily return 'always *home*', wide as they may wander. ( *W*, iv. 106–7)

Here Carlyle has extended the fabulous framework of Burke's attack on the Revolution, in order to incriminate the monarchy itself; he has subsumed the King's repressive machinery of injustice under a higher justice which it had vainly ignored.

The reassuring certitude of the poetic justice invoked in such passages acts as a centripetal counterweight to the equally fabulous portrayal of revolutionary atrocities and excesses, allowing Carlyle to revel in anarchy without ever finally succumbing to it. He can afford to expand the events of the French Revolution to alarming mythic proportions because myths can offer the reassurance of justice alongside their fearful distortions and metamorphoses. The great protagonists of the Revolution can thus be presented mythically as Titanic figures: the storming of the Bastille 'was the Titans warring with Olympus', and Danton is 'the great Titan' ( *W*, ii. 197; iv. 251); likewise Mirabeau ('the first of the modern Titans' ( *W*, xii. 5–6)) does battle with half the monsters of classical mythology:

---

[2] In his early *Life of Friedrich Schiller* Carlyle quotes from *The Robbers* an allusion to the brazen bull ( *W*, xxv. 17).

There is one Herculean Man; in internecine duel with him, there is Monster after Monster. Emigrant Noblesse return, sword on thigh, vaunting of their Loyalty never sullied; descending from the air, like Harpy-swarms with ferocity, with obscene greed. Earthward there is the Typhon of Anarchy, Political, Religious: sprawling hundred-headed, say with Twenty-five million heads; wide as the area of France; fierce as Frenzy; strong in very Hunger. With these shall the Serpent-queller do battle continually, and expect no rest. ( *W*, iii. 137)

Along with the extravagant titanizing of Carlyle's heroes—Mirabeau, Danton, Napoleon—goes, as here, a conversion of their adversaries (and sometimes of the whole French nation) into a menagerie of monsters and macabre phantoms. The tumbril is described, perhaps predictably, as 'a black spectre', and the deputies voting on the King's execution appear 'Like Phantoms in the hour of midnight; most spectral, pandemonial!' ( *W*, iv. 192, 102). The events of the Revolution are 'monsters and prodigies' bred in the gloomy womb of Orcus, and the creature which arises from them—'The Revolution Prodigy'—can be seen 'shaping itself rapidly . . . into terrific stature and articulation, limb after limb' ( *W*, iv. 25, 140). And just as Burke had dwelt upon the unnatural manufacture of saltpetre from the ruins of noble mansions, so Carlyle, not to be outdone in ghoulish suggestions, lingers over the raiding of coffins to make cannon-balls, the sale of blond perukes from victims of the guillotine, and the tanning of the victims' skins for wash-leather and breeches. The deliberate effect of Carlyle's figurative energy and frantic mythologizing inflation in the rhetoric of *The French Revolution* is to persuade us of the portentous, heroic significance of 'the crowning Phenomenon of our Modern Time' ( *W*, ii. 212); to remind us that the wonders of ancient myth, far from having been buried by the upstart sceptics of the Enlightenment, have risen again to mock them, and to bury them. Carlyle even exclaims (in pointed contrast to Burke's cry that the Age of Chivalry was gone) that 'The age of Miracles has come back!' ( *W*, ii. 213). Carlyle welcomes the Revolution as a miraculous revelation of Truth which puts to shame the periods of Falsehood which precede and follow it, as the naked Truth of Sansculottism, however terrifying, discredits the superficial 'culottism' of clothed Shams. The Revolution reaffirms the Truth of what eighteenth-century scepticism would have dismissed as barbarous Fancy: that the fabulous, the Titanic, and the monstrous are now the great facts of 'our Modern Time'.

Carlyle's fabulous presentation of modernity depends often upon an image of small-minded men conjuring up creatures of greater stature, and greater Truth, than themselves, and then being unable to control or even to recognize the forces they are playing with. From as early as his *Life of Schiller*, the figure of the conjurer unable to control the spectres he has invoked recurs in Carlyle's work in varying forms. Discussing the growth of mechanism in his 'Signs of the Times', Carlyle warns that 'the shadow we have wantonly evoked stands terrible before us and will not depart at our bidding' ( *W*, xxvii. 66). 'Things,' he writes in *Past and Present*, 'if it be not mere cotton and iron things, are growing disobedient to man.' ( *W*, x. 5.) More vivid as an image of this disobedience is Carlyle's repeated use of Phalaris' Bull. In 'The Hero as Man of Letters' he indicates the form of poetic justice awaiting the man who sees nothing in the universe but mechanism.

The man, I say, is become spiritually a paralytic man; this godlike Universe a dead mechanical steamengine, all working by motives, checks, balances, and I know not what; wherein, as in the detestable belly of some Phalaris'-Bull of his own contriving, he the poor Phalaris sits miserably dying! ( *W*, v. 173)

This can be recognized as a fitting retribution, of course: atheism, as Carlyle says, punishing itself in its own prison. The more telling uses of Phalaris' Bull, though, are those in which the victim is not the Bull's creator but another innocent creature. Here, the sacrifice appears as the most shocking injustice: in *Past and Present*, Carlyle explains that the unbearable provocation which drives the working class to Chartism and revolution is not death or hunger in itself but

to live miserable we know not why; to work sore and yet gain nothing; to be heart-worn, weary, yet isolated, unrelated, girt-in with a cold universal Laissez-faire: it is to die slowly all our life long, imprisoned in a deaf, dead, Infinite Injustice, as in the accursed iron belly of a Phalaris' Bull! ( *W*, x. 210–11)

The importance of the mythical Bull is that it is a man-made, factitious prison crushing the God-given life out of its impoverished victims. Carlyle argues in *Chartism* that if the workers' sufferings were providentially ordained they would represent some justice and leave room for hope, but the atheistic modern world of mechanism excludes any hope, thereby fuelling the explosive forces of Despair: 'If men had lost belief in a God, their only resource against a blind No-God, of Necessity and Mechanism, that held them like a hideous

World-Steamengine, like a hideous Phalaris' Bull, imprisoned in its own iron belly, would be, with or without hope,—*revolt*.' ( *W*, xxix. 146.) The modern world of the steam-engine thus appears as a man-made contrivance for human sacrifice, mechanically embodying a kind of injustice which must always finally recoil upon its creators, as it had upon the French monarchy.

Given Carlyle's belief that the age of Miracles has come back, it is only to be expected that the fabulous Titanism he attributes to the French Revolution should be extended also to the Machine Age which it ushered in, and that his extravagant mythological rhetoric should be applied to the two most awesome new powers of that age: machine power (or steam) and democracy (or the urban crowd). The machine was of course already ripe for mythic hyperbole. In *Chartism* Carlyle foresees the day when 'Arkwright shall have become mythic like Arachne', and presents England as a Prospero sending forth 'Fire-demons panting across all oceans' ( *W*, xxix. 184, 181). Machine power is both horrifying and exhilarating for Carlyle. 'The huge demon of Mechanism smokes and thunders, panting at his great task, in all sections of English land; changing his *shape* like a very Proteus;' yet, for all its Heroic stature, it is this same 'immeasurable Proteus steam-demon' which throws up unemployment, discontent, and starvation in its huge convulsions ( *W*, xxix. 141–2, 143).

More interesting in the context of those adaptations of the Frankenstein story that we find in Gaskell and the Victorian cartoonists, is Carlyle's demonizing of the lower classes, particularly the urban crowd. In his frenzied passages on the Sansculottes in *The French Revolution*, Carlyle allows himself plenty of scope to imagine the huge destructive energies of the Parisian mob, and indeed of the twenty million French men and women 'whom, however, we lump together into a kind of dim compendious unity, monstrous but dim, far off, as the *canaille*' ( *W*, ii. 33). Taken together, 'this monstrous twenty-million class' looms through the pages of Carlyle's history as 'the fire-breathing Spectre of DEMOCRACY' ( *W*, ii. 115, 21). To the traditional figure of the many-headed monster of the multitude Carlyle has added a transcendental justification, elevating the mob to the status of a historical Truth: as for early Christian interpreters, so for Carlyle the monster appears as a revelation of providence, a retributive scourge. If this is the mission of the French Sansculotte, so it is also for what Carlyle calls the Irish 'Sans-Potato':

5. Irish Nationalism as Monster, again: Thomas Carlyle's image of the
'Irish giant, named of Despair' turns vicious through the eyes of British
racism in Meadows's 'The Irish Frankenstein'(*Punch*, 1843), a response to
Daniel O'Connell's Repeal Movement.

. . . but the Irish Giant, named of Despair, is advancing upon London itself,
laying waste all English cities, towns and villages . . . I notice him in Piccadilly,
blue-visaged, thatched in rags, a blue child on each arm; hunger-driven, wide-
mouthed, seeking whom he may devour: he, missioned by the just Heavens,
too truly and too sadly their 'divine missionary' come at last in *this*
authoritative manner, will throw us all into Doubting Castle, I perceive! . . .
Prophecy of him there has long been; but now by the rot of the potato (blessed

be the just gods, who send us either swift death or some beginning of cure
at last!), he is here in person, and there is no denying him, or disregarding
him any more . . . ( *W*, xx. 94)

Carlyle's monstrous images of the oppressed are not, as Burke's were,
mere objects of horror and panic, but providential portents. 'Huge
Democracy, walking the streets everywhere in its Sack Coat' ( *W*,
x. 250–1) is presented as a fright to the reader, but to Carlyle this
allegorical figure is a strangely satisfying sign of justice working itself
out in history.

Although the monstrous mass tends to be converted into a sign
in Carlyle's writings, it is at the same time, and paradoxically, a *dumb*
sign, requiring an articulate hero or prophet to read it. Carlyle's
repeated insistence upon the inarticulacy of the masses makes this
a basic pivot of his whole theory of history and politics. 'The
frightfullest Births of Time', Carlyle wrote in *The French Revolution*,
'are never the loud-speaking ones, for these soon die; they are the
silent ones, which can live from century to century!' ( *W*, iv. 313.)
It is the virtuous silence of the poor, as contrasted with the chatter
of demagogues and deputies, which most impresses—and most
suits—Carlyle. 'The voice of the poor, through long years, ascends
inarticulate, in *Jacqueries*, meal-mobs; low-whimpering of infinite
moan.' ( *W*, ii. 53.) History, as Carlyle argues in the *Latter-Day
Pamphlets*, is an inarticulate Bible, the sense of which can be read
from the unspoken feelings of the common people, but only if you
avoid listening to what they actually say (or worse, vote), which is
a mere surface froth of vanity. The popular voice which is heard
in *The French Revolution* is thus given as the cry of 'a dumb tortured
animal' ( *W*, ii. 13).

According to Carlyle's scheme, explained in *Heroes, Hero-
Worship, and the Heroic in History*, inarticulacy is as much a
characteristic of the hero as it is of the mass. 'The Great Man . . . is
a Force of Nature: whatsoever is truly great in him springs-up from
the *in*articulate deeps.' ( *W*, v. 112.) Accordingly, Carlyle lays great
stress on the essential dumbness of Mahomet and Cromwell in his
accounts of these inspired leaders. What wells up in the inarticulate
hero and the dumb mass alike is the transcendent Truth of history;
both are signs or, in the traditional and semi-allegorical sense,
monsters. The silence or silencing of the monster is, as I have argued
above, the guarantee of its fitness for representation within a

univocal discourse. Carlyle's monsters have to express providential truths yet remain dumb; like oracles, they must not presume to understand what it is that is spoken through them, relinquishing this task of translation to the hierophant Carlyle himself.

The political consequences of Carlyle's strict division of meaning and utterance can, on the one hand, come close to justifying popular riots as the appropriate self-expression of the dumb: 'The speaking classes speak and debate each for itself; the great dumb, deep-buried class lies like an Enceladus, who in his pain, if he will complain of it, has to produce earthquakes!' ( W, xxix. 185.) On the other hand, in his search for 'a clear interpretation of the thought which at heart torments these wild inarticulate souls' ( W, xxix. 122), the dumbness which Carlyle has foisted on the working class is exploited as an opening for quite unwarrantable authoritarian ventriloquism—a strategy which governs the argument of *Chartism*:

> What is the meaning of the 'five points,' if we will understand them? What are all popular commotions and maddest bellowings from Peterloo to the Place-de-Grève itself? Bellowings, *in*articulate cries as of a dumb creature in rage and pain; to the ear of wisdom they are inarticulate prayers: 'Guide me, govern me! I am mad and miserable, and cannot guide myself!' ( W, xxix. 157)

The ease with which Carlyle manages completely to reverse the sense of the Chartists' Five Points is breathtaking, but quite explicable too, once the essential inarticulacy of the masses is granted. In a characteristically Romantic gesture,[3] the voice to be heard is intercepted by the educated hierophant who relays it in his own dialect and for his own ends. Certainly, the masses' supposed dumbness is the greatest possible convenience to Carlyle, allowing him to put the most implausibly anti-democratic slogans into their mouths. It is true that Carlyle favoured compulsory elementary education to overcome popular inarticulacy, but even in advocating this measure he maintained a connection between the illiterate and the monstrous. The people should be provided with schoolteachers, he argued, 'so that, in ten years hence, an Englishman who could not read might

---

[3] Interceptions of this kind are central to Wordsworth's 'The Solitary Reaper' and 'Resolution and Independence', and may be detected in the odes of Keats and Shelley; the perfect formulation of the device appears in the *Suspiria De Profundis*, where De Quincey says of his Ladies of Sorrows, '*Theirs* were the symbols, *mine* are the words.' *Collected Writings* xiii, 365.

be acknowledged as the monster, which he really is!' ( *W*, xxix. 198).
It is partly from such hints in Carlyle that there is formed the
identification of Frankenstein's monster with 'the uneducated' which
we have in Gaskell's *Mary Barton*.

While Carlyle's use of the fabulous and the monstrous provides,
as I have argued, a stable centre of Truth in a world otherwise
depicted as a swirling mass of debris and dust, it serves also the
opposite, centrifugal, direction of his vision. In this direction the most
consistently unnerving manifestations of the monstrous in Carlyle's
writings are his images of modern humanity as a disconnected and
fragmented automaton. His satire of the rationalist Machine Age
replaces human functions with mechanical contrivances, as for
instance in his ironic proposal to construct mechanical men, after
the example of Albertus Magnus, for the teaching of religion or
languages ( *W*, xxix. 195–6; i. 84–5). Behind such jokes lies a
deep and unsettling conviction that human identity is not given
but constructed, and in modern conditions is more likely to be
constructed abortively or randomly. 'For ours is a most fictile
world;' Carlyle explains, 'and man is the most fingent plastic
of creatures.' ( *W*, ii. 6.) Carlyle's desperate search for a stable
authority has its source in this very acute sense of the infinite
malleability and factitiousness of human identity. Thus, Marat
is described in *The French Revolution* as having been abortively
kneaded together by Nature out of leavings and waste clay, while
in *Sartor Resartus* especially, the men and women of the nineteenth
century are seen to have been fabricated, like scarecrows, merely
from clothes.

In the exuberant satire of *Sartor Resartus* Carlyle gives us, through
the voice of Teufelsdröckh, an ironic reworking of the idea of
modern Prometheanism.

. . . the Tailor is not only a Man, but something of a Creator or Divinity.
Of Franklin it was said, that 'he snatched the Thunder from Heaven and
the Sceptre from Kings:' but which is greater, I would ask, he that lends,
or he that snatches? For, looking away from individual cases, and how a
Man is by the Tailor new-created into a Nobleman, and clothed not only
with Wool but with Dignity and a Mystic Dominion, — is not the fair fabric
of Society itself, with all its royal mantles and pontifical stoles, whereby,
from nakedness and dismemberment, we are organised into Polities, into
nations, and a whole coöperating Mankind, the creation, as has here been
often irrefragably evinced, of the Tailor alone? ( *W*, i. 231)

Unable to face naked realities, this clothes-society is stitched together from its component rags by a degraded mockery of a Prometheus: what we have here is not even a body politic but an empty shirt politic which, Carlyle implies, could function just as well with nothing human inside it. In a more serious and impassioned protest against the rule of garments over naked humanity, Carlyle makes Teufelsdröckh identify clothes with the covering of life by dead matter. The passage is distinctly, and perhaps deliberately, Frankensteinian:

While I — good Heaven! — have thatched myself over with the dead fleeces of sheep, and bark of vegetables, the entrails of worms, the hides of oxen or seals, the felt of furred beasts; and walk abroad a moving Rag-screen, overheaped with shreds and tatters raked from the Charnel-house of Nature, where they would have rotted, to rot on me more slowly! Day after day, I must thatch myself anew; day after day, this despicable thatch must lose some film of its thickness; some film of it, frayed away by tear and wear, must be brushed-off into the Ashpit, into the Lay-stall; till by degrees the whole has been brushed thither, and I, the dust-making, patent Rag-grinder, get new material to grind down. O subter-brutish! vile! most vile! For have not I too a compact all-enclosing Skin, whiter or dingier? Am I a botched mass of tailors' and cobblers' shreds, then; or a tightly-articulated, homogeneous little Figure, automatic, nay alive? ( W, i. 44)

There is an almost suffocating impression here of life smothered by rotting remains; but more unsettling still is the final question, which will not allow clothes to stand safely outside of the human, any more than the machine is conceived as a purely external menace for Carlyle. Clothes and machines alike, with all they stand for, infect and even define the 'inner' sphere of human identity, finally substituting themselves for it, in Carlyle's anticipation of the Hollow Men.

The question, 'Am I a botched mass of tailors' and cobblers' shreds . . . ?', with all its feeling of lost authenticity and of factitious, abortive identity, resounds far into the work of Charles Dickens, as we shall see. Its macabre suggestion of a modern life composed of the decomposing, cannibalized parts which exist in a mockery of organic coherence continues in Carlyle's repeated ghoulish images of generalized galvanism. These are pervasive in his writings, beginning with the complaint in 'Signs of the Times' that the scientist of Newton's stature has been superseded by one who 'behind whole batteries of retorts, digesters and galvanic piles imperatively "interrogates Nature"' ( W, xxvii. 62), and extending to the several references to the merely galvanic life of European politics and religion in the *Latter-Day Pamphlets*. In this gloomy and rabid volume Carlyle defines the situation of 'the Free Man' thus: 'To him in the waste Saharas, through the grim solitudes peopled by galvanized corpses and doleful creatures, there is a loadstar' ( *W*, xx. 251–2). For Carlyle the nineteenth century was to be defined not just as the Machine Age — as if technology were the end of the problem — but more fully as a Galvanic World in which the inward sanctuary of organic human authenticity has been abandoned to the rule of the corpse.

The galvanic world is ushered in by the greatest ever convulsion of the body politic — the French Revolution, in which Sansculottism leads a disturbed 'galvanic-life', while in the movements of the counter-revolution, the dead Church 'is not allowed to lie dead; no, it is *galvanized* into the detestablest death-life' ( *W*, iv. 143; iii. 151). In *The French Revolution* Carlyle expands these images into a larger metaphor for France in its agonized convulsions:

France is as a monstrous Galvanic Mass, wherein all sorts of far stranger than chemical galvanic or electric forces and substances are at work; electrifying one another, positive and negative; filling with electricity your Leyden-jars, — Twenty-five millions in number! As the jars get full, there will, from time to time, be, on slight hint, an explosion. ( *W*, iii. 113)

In *Sartor Resartus* Carlyle returns to the galvanic metaphor to conduct a more sustained and consistent examination of the loss of religious principles in modern society. His argument runs like a post-mortem on a once integral body politic:

For if Government is, so to speak, the outward SKIN of the Body Politic, holding the whole together and protecting it; and all your Craft-Guilds, and Associations for Industry, of hand or of head, are the Fleshly Clothes, the muscular and osseous Tissues (lying *under* such SKIN), whereby Society stands and works; — then is Religion the inmost Pericardial and Nervous Tissue, which ministers Life and warm Circulation to the whole. Without which Pericardial Tissue the Bones and Muscles (of Industry) were inert, or animated only by a Galvanic vitality; the SKIN would become a shrivelled pelt, or fast-rotting raw-hide; and Society itself a dead carcass, — deserving to be buried. ( *W*, i. 172)

Thus does Carlyle anatomize the decomposition of organic, spiritually vital social existence into the artificial, gregarious mass of a society governed by scientific rationality and the cash-nexus alone. Such a society may present the signs of busy and energetic movement, but 'these spasmodic, galvanic sprawlings' ( W, i. 185), Carlyle insists, are not life at all.

Carlyle's galvanic metaphor is employed consistently to contrast the faithless society with the organic order inspired by transcendental truths. So in *Heroes* we find Carlyle asking 'what else is alive *but* Protestantism? The life of most else that one meets is a galvanic one merely' ( W, v. 137). But it is in *Past and Present*, where he most systematically juxtaposes religious discipline and sceptical dissolution, that Carlyle's resort to galvanic imagery is most pronounced. Here he looks forward to 'the awakening of the Nation's soul from its asphyxia, and the return of blessed life to us,—Heaven's blessed life, not Mammon's galvanic accursed one' ( W, x. 35). This accursed life of Mammonism is in turn represented as a violation of the natural body politic which replaces its circulation of blood with the circulation of money:

> How human affairs shall now circulate everywhere not healthy life-blood in them, but as it were, a detestable copperas banker's ink; and all is grown acrid, divisive, threatening dissolution; and the huge tumultuous Life of Society is galvanic, devil-ridden, too truly possessed by a devil! ( W, x. 67)

If this is the state of society as a whole, then the galvanic convulsions must work their way down to the individual activities of Mammon's humblest slaves:

> Industrial work, still under bondage to Mammon, the rational soul of it not yet awakened, is a tragic spectacle. Men in the rapidest motion and self-motion; restless, with convulsive energy, as if driven by Galvanism, as if possessed by a Devil: tearing asunder mountains,—to no purpose, for Mammonism is always Midas-eared! ( W, x. 207)

For Carlyle galvanism is the appropriate image for the modern state of possession, in which tremendous energies work themselves out only as undirected physical reflexes. His galvanic world is a world of the living dead, a Limbo for atheists and Mammon-worshippers.

> Ah me, into what waste latitudes, in this Time-Voyage, have we wandered; like adventurous Sinbads;—where the men go about as if by galvanism, with meaningless glaring eyes, and have no soul, but only a beaver-faculty and stomach! ( W, x. 186–7)

Of this galvanic wasteland, Charles Dickens is the Dantean poet. Dickens's debt to Carlyle is well-established: he was reported to have carried *The French Revolution* with him everywhere in 1837, and before dedicating *Hard Times* to Carlyle, he wrote to him to claim that 'No man knows your books better than I'.[4] The influence has important consequences not only for the overt moralizing of Dickens's novels—*A Tale of Two Cities* and *Hard Times* especially—and for the providential pattern of poetic justice at work in their plots, but also for the characteristic texture of what has become known as the 'Dickens World'. Since Dorothy Van Ghent's seminal analysis of this world's features, it is now widely accepted that the apparent weakness of characterization in Dickens's work is often a strength of perception which recognizes what Marx described as 'the personification of things and the reification of people' in modern conditions.[5] In this kind of reversal lies the secret of Dickens's strange effects: buildings, furniture, clocks, machines, and other physical objects are imaginatively animated into an uncanny vitality, while people twitch and stammer in the repetitive gestures of automatism. Those tics and mannerisms which mark so many of his characters are symptoms of Carlyle's galvanic world being absorbed into Dickens's morbid humour, his distinctive melancholy of anatomy.

Dickens will not let his gallows humour rest at the gallows; he takes it one step further to the 'anatomy case'—the fate, that is, of the criminal condemned to posthumous dissection by medical students.[6] As early as *The Pickwick Papers*, grisly humour of this kind flickers around the medics Bob Sawyer and Ben Allen; on their carpet a prostrate figure is discovered by Sam Weller, who exclaims, 'but there's another experiment here, sir. Here's a wenerable old lady a lyin' on the carpet waitin' for dissection, or galwinism, or some other rewivin' and scientific inwention.' (ch. 48.)[7] Even the good Twemlow in *Our Mutual Friend* 'has galvanic starts all over him' in his sleep (Bk. 1, ch. 10), while Uriah Heep, who jerks uncontrollably at the mention of Agnes in *David Copperfield*, is reprimanded by Betsy Trotwood: 'Don't be galvanic, sir!' (ch. 35.) In *Nicholas Nickleby* the

[4] *The Letters of Charles Dickens*, ed. Walter Dexter (London, 1938), ii. 567 (13 July 1854).

[5] Dorothy Van Ghent, 'The Dickens World: A View from Todgers's', *Sewanee Review*, lviii (1950), 417–38; Karl Marx, *Capital, A Critique of Political Economy: Volume One*, trans. Ben Fowkes (Harmondsworth, 1976), 1054.

[6] See Chapter 4 ('Corpses and Effigies') of John Carey, *The Violent Effigy: A Study of Dickens's Imagination* (London, 1973).

[7] References to Dickens's novels are by chapter rather than by page. My texts are the Penguin English Library/Penguin Classics editions (Harmondsworth, 1965–78).

description of the hero's uncle Ralph carries the same suggestions: 'the livid face, the horrible expression of the features to which every nerve and muscle as it twitched with a spasm whose workings no effort could conceal' make this villain appear as ghastly as a revived corpse (ch. 56).

The animation of the apparently inanimate is as important to Dickens's nightmare world as it is to Hoffmann's. The Dickens world is peopled by twitching dummies—like the waxworks and Punch-and-Judy figures of *The Old Curiosity Shop*, like Mrs Wititterly, who is described in *Nicholas Nickleby* as 'a mere animated doll' (ch. 28), and like the spectre recognized by Redlaw the chemical experimenter in *The Haunted Man* as 'the animated image of himself dead' (ch. 1). In his early *Sketches by Boz* Dickens can be seen delighting in such animations of clothes as this from 'Meditations in Monmouth-Street':

We love to walk along these extensive groves of the illustrious dead, and to indulge in the speculations to which they give rise; now fitting a deceased coat, then a pair of trousers, and anon the mortal remains of a gaudy waistcoat, upon some being of our own conjuring up, and endeavouring, from the shape and fashion of the garment itself, to bring its former owner before our mind's eye. We have gone on speculating in this way, until whole rows of coats have started from their pegs, and buttoned up, of their own accord, round the waists of imaginary wearers . . .

This kind of exuberance shows its darker side in the visions of Bill Sykes in *Oliver Twist*; he tells Nancy that she looks 'like a corpse come to life again', and he is indeed later haunted by her image 'like a corpse endowed with the mere machinery of life' (chs. 39, 48).

If the effect of such images is to blur disturbingly the boundary between life and death and to evoke a state of Carlylean galvanic somnambulism, then Dickens's obsession with anatomy carries us even further into unsettling realms of feeling. The most chronic and alarming symptom here is Dickens's regular use of synecdoche in a way which tends to dismember any sense of human wholeness and to offer us a world composed of detachable organs. John Carey has observed that Dickens's imagination is of the kind 'which pulls apart human bodies like dolls and grasps at amputated limbs'.[8] From the punning on the 'hands' in *Hard Times* to the conversion of Mrs Merdle into 'The Bosom' in *Little Dorrit*, this scattering of the human

---

[8] Carey, *Violent Effigy*, 96.

body is a constant feature of Dickens's unnerving humour, reinforced by the appearance of ghoulish dismemberers like Mr Venus the anatomist in *Our Mutual Friend* and Jerry Cruncher the grave-robber (or 'Resurrection-Man') in *A Tale of Two Cities*. Richard Swiveller's encounter with Quilp in *The Old Curiosity Shop* is a fairly representative instance of the dismembering manner in Dickens's descriptions.

Mr Swiveller . . . at last perceived two eyes dimly twinkling through the mist, which he observed after a short time were in the neighbourhood of a nose and mouth. Casting his eyes down towards that quarter in which, with reference to a man's face, his legs are usually to be found, he observed that the face had a body attached; and when he looked more intently he was satisfied that the person was Mr Quilp . . . (ch. 23)

The detachability of bodily parts recurs in *Bleak House*, where Mr Vholes takes off his gloves as if skinning himself, and more light-heartedly in the preparations of the actor Crummles in *Nicholas Nickleby*: 'Mr Crummles put on his other eyebrow, and the calves of his legs, and then put on his legs . . .' (ch. 48). Mr Venus in *Our Mutual Friend* discusses with Silas Wegg the possibility of exhibiting the latter's amputated limb 'as a Monstrosity, if you'll excuse me' (Bk. 1, ch. 7). Behind these cruel jokes lies Dickens's fascination with criminal anatomy. Burke wrote of the French revolutionaries that 'In the groves of their academy, at the end of every visto, you see nothing but the gallows' (*RRF*, 171–2). So at the horizons of the Dickens world loom not just the gallows but the supplementary horrors of the 'anatomy-case' dissection. Squeers threatens Nicholas Nickleby with this fate for stealing clothes and money: 'Do you know that it's a hanging matter—and I an't quite certain whether it an't an anatomy one besides . . . ?' (ch. 38.) Squeers later wishes that Peg were 'dead and buried, and resurrected and dissected, and hung upon wires in an anatomical museum' (ch. 60). Sir John Chester in *Barnaby Rudge* declares that the recently arrested Hugh 'would make a very handsome preparation in Surgeons' Hall, and would benefit science extremely' (ch. 37). Even Mrs Gamp in *Martin Chuzzlewit* is rumoured to have disposed of her late husband's remains to an anatomist. The shadowy figure of Barnaby Rudge senior is associated with this gruesome world on its illegal fringes: 'they who dealt in bodies with the surgeons could swear he slept in churchyards, and that they had beheld him glide away among the tombs on their approach' (ch. 16). There is more to all this ghoulishness than a gratuitous *frisson*; it is of a piece with Dickens's synecdochal, Carlylean representation of character and of the fragmented body; it helps dramatize Dickens's preoccupation with what Carlyle called the plastic and fictile nature of human identity.

The obverse of Dickens's scattering and dismembering of his people is the constant sense in his work of that artificial assemblage which unites their parts into a human patchwork. The Marshalsea debtors' prison in *Little Dorrit* is a perfect example of a world thus modelled on Carlyle's 'Philosophy of Clothes':

The shabbiness of these attendants upon shabbiness, the poverty of these insolvent waiters upon insolvency, was a sight to see. Such threadbare coats and trousers, such fusty gowns and shawls, such squashed hats and bonnets, such boots and shoes, such umbrellas and walking-sticks, never were seen in Rag Fair. All of them wore the cast-off clothes of other men and women, were made up of patches and pieces of other people's individuality, and had no sartorial existence of their own proper. (Bk. 1, ch. 9)

Such fabrication of identity is pervasive among Dickens's characters and has a significance beyond the momentary play of fancy. In *Martin Chuzzlewit*, Pecksniff announces that he is proud 'to have a daughter who is constructed on the best models' (ch. 10), and thus betrays a vanity common in Dickens's negligent parents as they distort and mechanize their offspring. A similar parental delusion occupies the centre of the same novel, and is given a more explicitly Frankensteinian colour and narrative development: Anthony Chuzzlewit trains his son Jonas 'on the strictest principles of the main chance' (ch. 8), a project which Dickens compares with 'those who manufacture idols after the fashion of themselves' (ch. 11). Old Martin describes Jonas, in an apostrophe to the dead Anthony, as 'the creature of your own rearing, training, teaching, hoarding, striving for', and as 'yon monster' (ch. 51). Repeated references to Jonas as a monster carry not just the traditional sense of filial rebellion (Jonas is assumed for some time to be the murderer of his own father), but also the more modern notion of an artificially constructed being. Jonas is not an inexplicably depraved freak but a carefully fabricated distortion of human motive, for which the blame lies largely with his parental creator and intended victim.

The same considerations apply to the production by Thomas Gradgrind of his two 'monsters' in *Hard Times*, the one his son Tom, the other his unnatural protégé Bitzer. Here the artificial assembly of human personality is more sharply presented and more clearly satirized. Referring to the ageing of Tom and Sissy, Dickens mimics Gradgrind's own terms: 'In some stages of his manufacture of the human fabric, the processes of Time are very rapid.' (Bk. 1, ch. 14.) Nor is it just Gradgrind's children and pupils who are seen as manufactured beings; Dickens turns the same implication towards the prosperous beneficiaries of Coketown's wage-labour.

These attributes of Coketown were in the main inseparable from the work by which it was sustained; against them were to be set off, comforts of life which found their way all over the world, and elegancies of life which made, we will not ask how much of the fine lady, who could scarcely bear to hear the place mentioned. (Bk. 1, ch. 5)

Another creation of clothes, the fine lady is 'made' in Coketown, and takes the form, presumably, of Mrs Skewton in *Dombey and Son*, of whom there is nothing but false hair, false teeth, and cosmetics.

Nowhere does Dickens present the factitious nature of human identity more powerfully than in *Great Expectations*, where the narrator's own revelation of his fabricated status is disturbingly vivid. For Pip is the artificial creature of Magwitch, just as Estella is more obviously the mannikin designed by Miss Havisham. Magwitch tells Pip that 'that there hunted dunghill dog wot you kep life in [i.e. Magwitch himself], got his head so high that he could make a gentleman — and, Pip, you're him!' (ch. 39). The estrangement of identity here is reinforced by Magwitch referring to both Pip and himself in the third person, a reminder that their relationship so far has been an entirely abstract and mediated one, established through the cash-nexus alone. Magwitch's fantasy has been that of 'making a gentleman' (ch. 39), but in achieving it he also unmakes a human being. Pip's shock at recognizing at last his own fabrication by others taints his memory of Satis House, where, he now realizes, he was no more than 'a model with a mechanical heart to practise on' (ch. 39). There is, as some critics have noticed, some appropriateness in Pip's being brought up in a forge, because as a gentleman and as Estella's suitor he is a living forgery.

In several of these cases of artificially constructed human beings there are hints of the moral fable, especially in the emphasis Dickens gives to poetic justice in his plotting. Creatures who are produced unnaturally end up recoiling upon their creators or parents in a predictable pattern of nemesis which follows precisely the sowing and reaping cycle Carlyle observed in the French Revolution and in history as a whole. Dickens's Carlylean version of that revolution itself in *A Tale of Two Cities*—complete with harvesting metaphors—is only the most obvious instance.

It was too much the way of Monseigneur under his reverses as a refugee, and it was too much the way of native British orthodoxy, to talk of this terrible Revolution as if it were the one only harvest ever known under the skies that had not been sown—as if nothing had ever been done, or omitted to be done, that had led to it . . . (Bk. 2, ch. 24)

Dickens's argument belongs of course with the 'heterodox' Carlylean claim that the Revolution, indefensible as its horrors were, was provoked by the cruelty and negligence of the nobility. In his closing sermon Dickens's conviction of historical necessity seems even more Carlylean than Carlyle's:

All the devouring and insatiate Monsters imagined since imagination could record itself, are fused in the one realisation, Guillotine. And yet there is not in France, with its rich variety of soil and climate, a blade, a leaf, a root, a sprig, a peppercorn, which will grow to maturity under conditions more certain than those that have produced this horror. Crush humanity out of shape once more, under similar hammers, and it will twist itself into the same tortured forms. Sow the same seed of rapacious licence and oppression over again, and it will surely yield the same fruit according to its kind. (Bk. 3, ch. 15)

Dickens's understanding of Monstrosities, here and elsewhere in his fiction, is that they do not spring fully formed from hell but emerge as the distorted products of human activity, tended, cultivated, or fabricated under crushing social pressures. As the poetic justice of Dickens's plots so often implies, monsters—all the way from Jonas Chuzzlewit to the French Revolution—are our own creatures. This argument informs a central feature of what could be called the moral structure of Dickens's novels. In *David Copperfield*, for example, Uriah Heep, the 'monster of meanness', is, as David comes to realize, the 'harvest' of a 'seed' planted by the hypocritical morality of the charity schools (chs. 54, 39). The same sort of logic appears in Dickens's earlier novels too: a neatly appropriate nemesis is provided in *Barnaby Rudge* for the hangman Dennis, who ends up being hanged with his own rope, and for Sir John Chester, who (like Ralph Nickleby) discovers too late that the young man he has hounded to death is his own son. A significant strengthening of this tendency in his fiction makes itself felt in *Martin Chuzzlewit*, for which Dickens consciously decided to adopt a more coherent structure than he had in his earlier work.

The plotting and the moralizing of *Martin Chuzzlewit* show all the signs of a careful design modelled upon Carlylean nemesis. We have already noted Jonas Chuzzlewit's status as an artificial creature who turns into a parricidal monster; his father Anthony is made to stress the moral of this plot in his final reflections: 'It's a dreadful thing to have my own child thirsting for my death. But I might have known it. I have sown, and I must reap.' (ch. 51.) Anticipating Jonas's doom, Dickens makes sure to remark that 'the fatality was of his own working; the pit was of his own digging' (ch. 46). This kind of proverbial moralizing is so prominent in *Martin Chuzzlewit* because Dickens conceived the novel as an investigation into the genesis of monstrosity—an intention brought clearly to the reader's notice by his 1849 Preface to the 'Cheap Edition'. In this context, Dickens's statement of aims deserves ample quotation:

I conceive that the sordid coarseness and brutality of Jonas would be unnatural, if there had been nothing in his early education, and in the precept and example always before him, to engender and develop the vices that make him odious. But, so born and so bred; admired for that which made him hateful, and justified from his cradle in cunning, treachery, and avarice; I claim him as the legitimate issue of the father upon whom those vices are seen to recoil. And I submit that their recoil upon that old man, in his unhonoured age, is not a mere piece of poetical justice, but is the extreme exposition of a plain truth.

I make this comment on the character, and solicit the reader's attention to it in his or her consideration of this tale, because nothing is more common in real life than a want of profitable reflection on the causes of many vices and crimes that awaken the general horror. What is substantially true of families in this respect, is true of a whole commonwealth. As we sow, we reap. Let the reader go into the children's side of any prison in England, or, I grieve to add, of many workhouses, and judge whether those are monsters who disgrace our streets, people our hulks and penitentiaries, and overcrowd our penal colonies, or are creatures whom we have deliberately suffered to be bred for misery and ruin.

Monsters or creatures?—the interpretative choice is one which brings into focus a whole range of social issues. In the light of Dickens's argument here, what may often appear to be the creaky machinery of the plot in his novels can be seen more clearly to be a fictional demonstration of social conditioning and of social responsibility for the evils perpetrated by individuals.

Accounts of Dickens's political opinions have sometimes asserted too hastily that, as a result of his first trip to America in 1842, he abandoned his early radicalism and along with it his Godwinian views on crime. *Martin Chuzzlewit* and its Preface show him, however, to be reaffirming quite explicitly the essential tenets of this radicalism. From the fact that Dickens never absolves individual miscreants and murderers it does not follow that he has, at this stage, wholly abandoned his view of the criminal's social conditioning, in favour of that theory of innate depravity to which he was later to incline. With Jonas Chuzzlewit, or Uriah Heep, or Bitzer, Dickens is still prepared to explain his more malevolent characters as products of their upbringing. The motiveless malignity of the purely melodramatic villain belongs more to his very early novels, in such creations as Quilp, Fagin, or Ralph Nickleby. In *Martin Chuzzlewit*, though, Dickens uses Jonas's upbringing as an instance of the socially created monster-criminal, in a sense which is clearly enough that of Godwin and the Shelleys. Or it might be more exact to say that he is attempting to revise the meaning of the term 'monster' itself from a prodigious birth to a social construction—an attempt fully in line with Dickens's habitual use of 'manufactured' characters. The monstrous thus becomes an underlying issue for debate within the novel, even in apparently unimportant episodes. As the Preface points out, we do not reflect seriously enough on the nature of monstrosity; and as if to illustrate this, Dickens has the spoilt and shallow Pecksniff daughters abuse the term frequently. Merry Pecksniff is made to touch inadvertently upon Jonas's true nature when, in a perfect moment of dramatic irony, she simpers to old Martin that Jonas is 'such a monster', and again that 'he *is* a monster' (ch. 24). Her complete ignorance of the truth in her own words is underlined when Merry continues to use 'monster' as a frivolous endearment applied to old Martin too.

Dickens's concern with the social genesis of monstrosity continues in his series of Christmas Books, where his allegorical bent is allowed free rein. A crucial but often forgotten episode in *A Christmas Carol* displays Dickens's urge to confront the society represented by Scrooge with its own fruits, forcing it to accept responsibility for its creatures before they become its destroyers.

'Oh Man! look here. Look, look, down here!' exclaimed the Ghost.

They were a boy and a girl. Yellow, meagre, ragged, scowling, wolfish; but prostrate, too, in their humility. Where graceful youth should have filled their features out, and touched them with its freshest tints, a stale and shrivelled hand, like that of age, had pinched, and twisted them, and pulled them into shreds. Where angels might have sat enthroned, devils lurked; and glared out menacing. No change, no degradation, no perversion of humanity, in any grade, through all the mysteries of wonderful creation, has monsters half so horrible and dread. . . .

'Spirit! are they yours?' Scrooge could say no more.

'They are man's,' said the Spirit, looking down upon them. 'And they cling to me, appealing from their fathers. This boy is Ignorance. This girl is Want. Beware them both . . .' (ch. 3)

The combination of menace and pathetic helplessness—a difficult one to manage—recalls Frankenstein's monster, appealing to its creator to acknowledge his responsibility for his work before turning 'wolfish' (an adjective which Dickens uses again in a similar context in *Hard Times*, threatening the 'genteel infidels' of the ruling class that if they suppress the imaginations of the poor, 'Reality will take a wolfish turn, and make an end of you!' (Bk. 2, ch. 6)). These wrinkled, half-threatening, half-pleading creatures are drawn partly, it seems, from the prophecies of Carlyle's *French Revolution*. Towards the end of this work, Carlyle had exhorted his readers to draw timely conclusions from the rise of Sansculottism, the first of which was

That 'if the gods of this lower world will sit on their glittering thrones, indolent as Epicurus' gods, with the living Chaos of Ignorance and Hunger weltering uncared-for at their feet, and smooth Parasites preaching, Peace, peace, when there is no peace', then the dark Chaos, it would seem, will rise . . . ( *W*, iv. 313)

Dickens's purpose in introducing these two starving children into *A Christmas Carol* as the 'monsters' Ignorance and Want is to remind his readers of the same Carlylean lesson, presented again through the fable of sowing and reaping, as a challenge to the irresponsibility of Scrooge's *laissez-faire* principles.

A similar pattern can be seen at work in another of Dickens's Christmas Books, *The Haunted Man*, a tale which carries several Frankensteinian echoes. The protagonist Redlaw is a chemistry teacher with his own private laboratory, who is offered the secret of amnesia to eliminate sorrowful memories. This gift turns out to be both a mixed and an infectious blessing which, as it is transmitted to Redlaw's associates, disrupts their habitual ties and responsibilities to one another; the demon of forgetfulness has finally to be exorcized by the warmth of Milly, a representative of the very spirit of domesticity. In his deluded hope that he will become a benefactor of humanity, Redlaw is urged on by a ghost or double, 'the animated image of himself dead' (ch. 1), and is resisted only by another double, a strange 'baby-monster' (ch. 2) whose significance is explained by the first ghost when questioned by Redlaw. The explanation amounts to an exposition of the principles of Dickensian monstrosity.

'No softening memory of sorrow, wrong, or trouble enters here, because this wretched mortal from his birth has been abandoned to a worse condition than the beasts, and has, within his knowledge, no one contrast, no humanising touch, to make a grain of such a memory spring up in his hardened breast. All within this desolate creature is barren wilderness. All within the man bereft of what you have resigned, is the same barren wilderness. Woe to such a man! Woe, tenfold, to the nation that shall count its monsters such as this, lying here, by hundreds and by thousands!'

Redlaw shrunk, appalled, from what he heard.

'There is not,' said the Phantom, 'one of these—not one—but sows a harvest that mankind MUST reap. From every seed of evil in this boy, a field of ruin is grown that shall be gathered in, and garnered up, and sown again in many places in the world, until regions are overspread with wickedness enough to raise the waters of another Deluge. Open and unpunished murder in a city's streets would be less guilty in its daily toleration, than one such spectacle as this.'

The sermon against Victorian society's negligence continues:

'There is not a father,' said the Phantom, 'by whose side in his daily or his nightly walk, these creatures pass; there is not a mother among all the ranks of loving mothers in this land; there is no one risen from the state of childhood, but shall be responsible in his or her degree for this enormity. There is not a country throughout the earth on which it would not bring a curse. There is no religion upon earth that it would not deny; there is no people upon earth it would not put to shame.' . . .

'Behold, I say,' pursued the Spectre, 'the perfect type of what it was your choice to be. Your influence is powerless here, because from this child's bosom you can banish nothing. His thoughts have been in "terrible companionship" with yours, because you have gone down to his unnatural level. He is the growth of man's indifference; you are the growth of man's presumption. The beneficent design of Heaven is, in each case, overthrown, and from the two poles of the immaterial world you come together.' (ch. 3)

In Dickens's allegorical design, the presumptuous chemist has met his equal or equivalent, a creature cast outside those human ties of remembrance which Redlaw has been tempted to sever. The tale is, again, an allegory of *laissez-faire* and of the wolfish child-monsters Ignorance and Want for whom we are all responsible.

Into the same category of allegorical fable falls the continuation of Dickens's moral crusade in *Hard Times*, where the providential structure of the tale is announced by the titles of its three books: Sowing, Reaping, Garnering. The 'sowing' in question is again the bringing up of children without fostering their human ties; the sower being the deluded Gradgrind, 'a monster in a lecturing castle, . . . taking childhood captive' (Bk. 1, ch. 3), whose dehumanizing contempt for childish Fancy turns him into 'a galvanizing apparatus charged with a grim mechanical substitute for the tender young imaginations that were to be stormed away' (Bk. 1, ch. 2). The 'reaping' and 'garnering' show the perfectly lucid poetic justice according to which Gradgrind's own creatures ruin him. The most obvious instance is that of Bitzer, whose appearance is made to conform to the mechanical spirit of Gradgrindery: he has cold eyes and a skin so unnaturally pale that his very blood must be white. It is this creation of Gradgrind's who explains with perfect consistency that, according to Gradgrind's own principles, he must 'look after number one' even if this means ruining his former teacher and benefactor. In the most traditional sense, Bitzer is a monster of ingratitude; and so is Bounderby, the capitalist who—for the same selfish reasons—repudiates his mother and claims the impossibly unnatural status of 'self-made' man. Closer to Gradgrind's home, Tom too becomes a 'monster' (Bk. 2, ch. 3) in his cynical treatment of his sister Louisa. It is Louisa who takes on the pleading and accusing role of the Frankenstein monster as she comes to curse, to her father's face, the day she was born: 'How could you give me life, and take from me all the inappreciable things that raise it from the state of conscious death?' (Bk. 2, ch. 12.) *Hard Times* translates the fable of Frankenstein into the terms of contemporary Political Economy (with its monstrously dismembering exploitation of 'hands') and Utilitarian education.

Dickens's final Frankensteinian exercise appears in *Great Expectations*, his finest work and the novel most intensely charged with guilt, revulsion, and—as we have noticed—the unease of the fabricated self. Some of the Frankensteinian elements of this work

are fleeting and incidental: Miss Havisham as a corpse-like bride
recalls Victor Frankenstein's prophetic dream and its realization,
while the embedded narrative of Abel Magwitch in Chapter 42
carries odd echoes of the monster's narrative in *Frankenstein*; Pip's
assumption of guilt for his sister's murder also recalls Victor's self-
accusations. Of more central importance, though, as in *Martin
Chuzzlewit* and *Hard Times*, is the fable of an artificially raised
creature turning ungratefully upon its maker. Dickens provides a
comic echo of this major theme in the episode of the servant hired
by Pip in London, who turns out to be an 'avenging phantom':

I had got on so fast of late, that I had even started a boy in boots—top
boots—in bondage and slavery to whom I might have been said to pass
my days. For, after I had made the monster (out of the refuse of my washer-
woman's family) and had clothed him with a blue coat, canary waistcoat,
white cravat, creamy breeches, and the boots already mentioned, I had to
find him a little to do and a great deal to eat; and with both of these horrible
requirements he haunted my existence. (ch. 27)

This is more than just a casual jest about the servant problem, for
it extends the novel's pervasive anxieties about artificiality, echoing
the problem not just of Pip's contrived and burdensome gentility but
also of the rebelliousness built into the story's unnatural creatures.
At a more serious level, Estella's position embodies the same logic.
Accused of being an ingrate by her foster-mother Miss Havisham,
she retorts, 'I am what you made me' (ch. 38). And when Miss
Havisham complains that she is hard and proud, Estella justly
reminds her that this is the inevitable result of her own deliberate
training. Just like Gradgrind, Miss Havisham is guilty of expecting
special treatment inconsistent with the very principles upon which
her creature has been formed. To her, Estella appears as a monster
of ingratitude, but the reader is meant to recognize that the heartless
girl is a monster in the other, more Frankensteinian sense—an
emotional misfit because she is a humanly miscreated anomaly.

What is still more disturbing in *Great Expectations* is the piecemeal
revelation of the narrator's own monstrous status. After his lying
exaggeration of the marvels he has seen at Satis House, Pip's
penitence is presented thus: 'Towards Joe, and Joe only, I considered
myself a young monster' (ch. 9). Indeed, most of Pip's career from
this point until his delirious fever illustrates exactly that he is a
traditional monster of ingratitude towards Joe. This sense of

monstrosity, however, is supplemented and amplified by Dickens's stress on the artificial fabrication of Pip's identity: he is worked upon first by Miss Havisham as a plaything and then reconstructed by Magwitch as a gentleman. The full irony of Pip's relationship with Magwitch is brought out in an intriguing passage which constitutes Dickens's only direct allusion to *Frankenstein*. In the episode of Magwitch's visit to Pip's rooms, the ex-convict, glowing with pride at his creation, asks Pip to display his knowledge of foreign languages by reading aloud.

While I complied, he, not comprehending a single word, would stand before the fire surveying me with the air of an Exhibitor, and I would see him, between the fingers of the hand with which I shaded my face, appealing in dumb show to the furniture to take notice of my proficiency. The imaginary student pursued by the misshapen creature he had impiously made, was not more wretched than I, pursued by the creature who had made me, and recoiling from him with a stronger repulsion, the more he admired me and the fonder he was of me. (ch. 40)

The horrifying recognition of his monstrous status—in the fairground sense, to begin with—is intensified here by Pip's feeling of being exhibited, although the two men are in fact alone; Pip is really being displayed to himself for the first time. This recognition is complicated in fascinating ways by Dickens's apparent reversal of the Frankenstein story and its central relationship. Pip is given both the monster's painful awareness of himself as an anomalous, fabricated being and at the same time Victor Frankenstein's irresponsible revulsion from his creature—a revulsion which further echoes his previous disowning of Joe. (Guilty repudiations abound in this novel: Wemmick's working and domestic identities disavow each other, while Jaggers literally washes his hands of his clients.) Magwitch, for his part, bears the stigmata of the criminal outcast along with the monster's generous and trusting nature, but he combines these with Frankenstein's deluded ambition of becoming a 'creator' of men.

The result of this doubly equivocal inversion of the Frankenstein myth, in which aspects of both creator and creature appear in each of Dickens's two characters, is to put this episode of *Great Expectations* into a relationship with Mary Shelley's novel rather similar to that of *Frankenstein* itself with *Paradise Lost*. Just as Victor and the monster refer themselves back to Milton to define their positions but become uncertain which roles they are playing, so Pip too loses his allusive bearings and is unable honestly to consign Magwitch to the realm of monstrosity when he knows that he belongs there himself. Although Dickens appears to endorse some of the earlier simplifications of the Frankenstein story by referring to Victor's impiety, he succeeds rather in reviving the true complexity of Mary Shelley's own balancing of characters and sympathies in her novel. Here and throughout *Great Expectations* Dickens is pondering the full modern significance of monstrosity, far more seriously than he had felt necessary in his earlier work. In *Barnaby Rudge* it was still possible for him to spin out this kind of melodramatic bombast:

'Villain!' cried Mr Haredale, in a terrible voice—for it was he. 'Dead and buried, as all men supposed through your infernal arts, but reserved by Heaven for this—at last—at last—I have you. You, whose hands are red with my brother's blood, and that of his faithful servant, shed to conceal your own atrocious guilt—You, Rudge, double murderer and monster, I arrest you in the name of God, who has delivered you into my hands.' (ch. 56)

Increasingly, though, Dickens reveals his impatience with such accepted uses of the monstrous, regarding them either as hypocrisy (most of the characters who use the 'monster of ingratitude' cliché in Dickens are monstrous villains themselves) or as dangerously evasive denials of relationship and responsibility. His purpose in later works is repeatedly to implicate his readers in the creation of the monstrous, so that the new Dickens monster of *Great Expectations* appears no longer as an alien to be dismissed, but as a presence beneath our skins.

# 6

## Karl Marx's Vampires
## and Grave-diggers

> I appeared rather like one doomed by slavery to toil in
> the mines, or any other unwholesome trade, than an
> artist occupied by his favourite employment.
>
> Victor, in *Frankenstein*

'A spectre is haunting Europe . . .' So Marx begins *The Communist
Manifesto*, not with the summary of the achievements of contemporary
capitalism, nor with the hopes of the proletariat but, oddly, it seems,
with a Gothic phantom — a relic of precisely that body of medieval
illusions and fantasies which Marx claims has been swept aside or
dispersed by the energy of the new, unashamedly self-interested
bourgeois world. The 'spectre' of Communism, Marx goes on to
explain, is really a nursery tale or bogy, a contrived scare. Yet what
such a figment is doing in the most rational, enlightened, and
calculating culture known to history, and why the bourgeoisie,
having swept away all superstitions, should still be 'haunted' by it
ought to be a puzzle. The problem repeats itself throughout Marx's
writings, in which some of the most gruesomely archaic echoes
of fairy-tale, legend, myth, and folklore crop up in the wholly
unexpected environment of the modern factory system, stock
exchange, and parliamentary chamber: ghosts, vampires, ghouls,
werewolves, alchemists, and reanimated corpses continue to haunt
the bourgeois world, for all its sober and sceptical virtues. I shall
argue that this apparent anomaly in Marx's presentation of bourgeois
society is more than a decorative trick of style, or a boisterous
overspilling of his fondness for imaginative literature and legend.
Rather, it follows from and reinforces certain major elements within
Marx's understanding of capitalism and its place in history; in
particular, of the larger historical ironies of the bourgeoisie's career.

In the bourgeois world, which has abolished all 'ancient and
venerable prejudices and opinions',[1] there should be no place for

---

[1] Karl Marx, *The Revolutions of 1848: Political Writings, Volume 1*, ed. David

fearful ghosts, any more than there is a place for Fancy in Gradgrind's school. This, indeed, is the impression which Marx offers in his 1857 Introduction to the *Grundrisse*:

Is the view of nature and of social relations on which the Greek imagination and hence Greek [mythology] is based possible with self-acting mule spindles and railways and locomotives and electrical telegraphs? What chance has Vulcan against Roberts & Co., Jupiter against the lightning-rod and Hermes against the Crédit Mobilier? All mythology overcomes and dominates and shapes the forces of nature in the imagination and by the imagination; it therefore vanishes with the advent of real mastery over them. What becomes of Fama alongside Printing House Square?[2]

The answer to that final question is that Printing House Square itself becomes mythical, albeit in a qualified modern fashion foreign to the kind of belief and reverence found in Greek religion. 'The Thunderer', though, still steals the thunder of the ancient gods and becomes itself a focus for superstitions appropriate to its age. In this passage Marx is discussing mythology only as the basis for Greek art, attempting to explain why genuine epic poetry cannot survive the age of gunpowder and printing; and he is writing here only of the demystifying capacities of new *forces* of production, not of those social *relations* of production which can engender illusions of their own to fill the gap left by the destruction of older superstitions.

If Marx had intended his statement in the *Grundrisse* to stand as a comprehensive settlement of the issue of mythology and material progress, then it would be seriously one-sided and premature, suggesting that the imagination as such is simply superseded when its projections are realized in actual technologies. It would amount, in fact, to just that kind of naïve bourgeois progressivism which the rest of his work so relentlessly criticizes. For Marx was keenly alert to the ways in which the achievements of bourgeois political reform and capitalist industry could take on the aspect of the mythological and the fabulous. In 1871 we find him taking an approach quite contrary to his *Grundrisse* formulation:

Fernbach (Harmondsworth, 1973), 70. Subsequent page references in the text are to this edition, abbreviated as *RE*.

[2] Karl Marx, *Grundrisse: Foundations of the Critique of Political Economy (Rough Draft)*, trans. Martin Nicolaus (Harmondsworth, 1973), 110. Subsequent page references in the text are to this edition, abbreviated as *G*.

It has hitherto been believed that Christian myth-making was possible only because printing had not yet been invented. Quite on the contrary! The daily Press, and the telegraph that in a moment spreads its inventions over the whole earth, fabricated more myths in a single day (and the bovine bourgeois believes and propagates them) than could have been produced by earlier times in a century.[3]

Far from killing off myths, modern inventions multiply them, even embody them. The productive powers which compete with Vulcan and Hermes are as impressive as the gods which they have replaced. Accordingly, in *Capital* Marx several times within two pages awards some of the larger modern machines the epithet 'Cyclopean', and notes that the latest kind of steam-hammer is 'of such a weight that even Thor himself could not wield it'.[4] Indeed, as Marx tells us in a footnote, the machine is in fact called 'Thor': such was the widespread fashion in the Victorian rhetoric of technological progress.

The more distasteful side of this mythologizing of the machine could be found in the contemporary panegyrics to industry, foremost among them being Andrew Ure's *Philosophy of Manufactures*, a defence of the factory system against restrictive legislation. Ure had this to say of one machine which, by replacing workers, broke the power of unions in the factory to which it was introduced:

Thus the *Iron Man*, as the operatives fitly call it, sprung out of the hands of our modern Prometheus at the bidding of Minerva — a creation destined to restore order among the industrious classes, and to confirm to Great Britain the empire of art. The news of this Herculean prodigy spread dismay through the union, and even long before it left its cradle, so to speak, it strangled the Hydra of misrule.[5]

Ure's gloating had been cited by Engels in his *Condition of the Working Class in England*, thus earning him a place as a target for Marx's repeated scorn in *Capital*, where Ure's 'undisguised cynicism' is characterized as 'the classical expression of the spirit of the factory'

[3] Letter to Ludwig Kugelmann, 27 July 1871, cited by S. S. Prawer, *Karl Marx and World Literature* (Oxford, 1978), 364.

[4] *Capital, A Critique of Political Economy: Volume One*, trans. Ben Fowkes (Harmondsworth, 1976), 506–7. Subsequent page references in the text are to this edition, abbreviated as C.

[5] Andrew Ure, *The Philosophy of Manufactures: Or, An Exposition of the Scientific, Moral, and Commercial Economy of the Factory System of Great Britain* (London, 1835; 3rd edn., 1861), 367.

(*C*, 564). Not the least of Ure's offences in the passage quoted above was to have taken in vain the name of Prometheus, the very Titan whom Marx himself had nominated as 'the foremost saint and martyr in the philosopher's calendar'.[6] One objective of Marx's literary campaign against the likes of Ure is to restore Prometheus's status as the indefatigable rebel, rescuing him from Ure's representation of the 'modern Prometheus' as a common strikebreaker. For Marx the true modern Prometheus is not the machine or even the inventor, but the worker. In an early diatribe against Arnold Ruge, Marx stresses the '*titanic*' and '*gigantic*' stature of the German workers' political culture as compared with the 'dwarf-like' level of bourgeois politics;[7] in the *Grundrisse* he characterizes labour as 'the living, form-giving fire' which converts the instruments and materials of production 'into the body of its soul and thereby resurrects them from the dead' (*G*, 361, 364); and in *Capital*, labour seizes on machines to 'awaken them from the dead' (*C*, 289). As punishment for this creativity, the worker suffers a Promethean torture: 'the law which always holds the relative surplus population or industrial reserve army [i.e. the unemployed] in equilibrium with the extent and energy of accumulation rivets the worker to capital more firmly than the wedges of Hephaestus held Prometheus to the rock.' (*C*, 799.) This is the modern Prometheus—no longer a critical philosopher, as in Marx's earlier formula, but a hero of shaping labour and stubborn resistance.

Marx's casting of the workers in the role of modern Prometheus is only one side, however, of his campaign to subvert the capitalists' Titanic self-image. The other side involves taking them at their word, but employing mythological parallels more appropriate to the grimmer aspects of bourgeois achievement. Accordingly Marx remarks, on the conditions in which phosphorous matches are manufactured, that 'Dante would have found the worst terrors in his Inferno surpassed in this industry' (*C*, 356). Capitalist reality had indeed surpassed the hyperbole of myth, but only by using its vaunted enlightenment and rationality to convert the modern world into the

---

[6] Foreword to Marx's doctoral dissertation, 'The Difference between Democritus' and Epicurus' Philosophy of Nature' (1841), cited by Prawer, *Karl Marx and World Literature*, 23.

[7] Karl Marx, *Early Writings*, trans. Rodney Livingstone and Gregor Benton (Harmondsworth, 1975), 415. Subsequent page references in the text are to this edition, abbreviated as *EW*.

equivalent of a medieval nightmare. As we have noticed in the *Communist Manifesto*, it is this irony whereby the destroyers of medieval superstition come to outdo it in practice that Marx most favours when taunting the bourgeoisie. Hence the delight with which he describes the French National Assembly in its counter-revolutionary role in 1871 as 'that assembly of the ghouls of all defunct regimes . . . eager to feed upon the carcass of the nation'; and with which he portrays the Legitimist party as a corpse which needs to be galvanized back to life.[8] Hence also the capitalist's 'werewolf-like hunger for surplus value' in *Capital* (*C*, 353), and 'the attempts being made to galvanize the corpses of the aristocracy into life' in Marx's article on 'The British Constitution'.[9] In what Marx represents, in *The Eighteenth Brumaire of Louis Bonaparte*, as the theatrical and anachronistic farce of French politics in 1848, 'Men and events appear as Schlemihls in reverse, as shadows which have become detached from their bodies.' (*SE*, 171.) In this shadow-world Marx detects not the real spirit of 1789 but 'only the ghost of the old revolution which walked in the years 1848 to 1851' (*SE*, 148). Marx was so struck by the phantasmagorical nature of French politics in this period that, in *The Class Struggles in France*, he went so far as to describe the National Assembly, in the same breath, as both a vampire and a galvanized corpse (*SE*, 88).

Such ghoulish effects are, again, no mere stylistic flourish but a consistent ironic reversal of the bourgeoisie's own myth, a myth which Marx identifies as his initial obstacle right at the start of the *Grundrisse*: 'The individual and isolated hunter and fisherman, with whom Smith and Ricardo begin, belongs to the unimaginative conceits of the eighteenth-century Robinsonades . . .' (*G*, 83.) The 'Robinsonades'—Utopian fantasies of isolated production— anticipate, as Marx explains, the individualism of the growing capitalist economy, and their illusions reappear when classical political economy explains capital accumulation as the result of 'abstinence' or individual thrift, ignoring the social relations of production. In popularized versions of the Robinson Crusoe story

---

[8] Karl Marx, *The First International and After: Political Writings, Volume 3*, ed. David Fernbach (Harmondsworth, 1974), 220, 196. Subsequent page references in the text are to this edition, abbreviated as *FI*.

[9] Karl Marx, *Surveys from Exile: Political Writings, Volume 2*, ed. David Fernbach (Harmondsworth, 1973), 282. Subsequent page references in the text are to this edition, abbreviated as *SE*.

(as opposed to Defoe's more complex novel) we can see the great myth of the bourgeoisie in its phase of emergent mercantile confidence. As Marx shows, though, it is no longer appropriate to capitalism's maturity, in which the more worrying myth of Frankenstein comes increasingly to correspond to the capitalists' fears in the face of their uncontrollable products.

In the world of the Crusoe fantasy wealth is accounted for as the result of Robinsonian individual effort, thrift, and enterprise realized on the market in the clear light of day by free and fair exchanges between autonomous individuals. Marx's *Capital* seeks to demonstrate that the real sources of capitalist prosperity do not lie in this open-air idyll at all, and that to find them we have to delve into gloomier secret depths, leaving behind the clear light of eighteenth-century rationality—the 'very Eden of the innate rights of man' ( *C*, 280)—for what turns out to be a Dantean Inferno. The end of the second section of *Capital* constitutes a valediction to the Crusoe world, as Marx becomes our Virgil at the gates of the modern factory.

Let us therefore, in company with the owner of money and the owner of labour-power, leave this noisy sphere, where everything takes place on the surface and in full view of everyone, and follow them into the hidden abode of production, on whose threshold hangs the notice 'No admittance except on business'. Here we shall see, not only how capital produces, but how capital is itself produced. The secret of profit-making must at last be laid bare. ( *C*, 279–80)

The truth of capitalist production lies not in the open market but in the enclosed, secret lair or workshop, like all the best family skeletons and Gothic terrors. And it is just because the source of profit is impossible to detect with the naked eye that, as Marx puts it in the third volume of *Capital*, capital 'becomes a very mystical being', a spirit which presides over 'the bewitched, distorted and upside-down world haunted by Monsieur le Capital and Madame la Terre'.[10] This capitalist wonderland is, it seems, possessed by invisible and supernatural forces which operate not in front of our eyes but, in a favourite Marxian phrase, 'behind the backs of' their human agents, who have lost control of their world.

The step which the reader of *Capital* is obliged to take, out of Crusoe's world and into Frankenstein's, is a central imaginative pivot

---

[10] Karl Marx, *Capital, Volume 3*, trans. David Fernbach (Harmondsworth, 1981), 966, 969.

of Marx's presentation of capitalism. It recapitulates the larger ironic contrast we have noticed in the *Communist Manifesto* between the enlightened, disenchanted appearance of the bourgeois world and the shrouded, haunted reality. It will be worth revisiting the *Manifesto* to see how insistently Marx exploits the ironies of fabulous poetic justice in his account of the bourgeoisie's career.

Modern bourgeois society with its relations of production, of exchange and of property, a society that has conjured up such gigantic means of production and of exchange, is like the sorcerer, who is no longer able to control the powers of the nether world whom he has called up by his spells. (*RE*, 72)

The fate of an ostensibly rational economy and technology will merely repeat the nemesis of necromancy. By a strict necessity the forces which the bourgeoisie has summoned up from the nether world will bring its own destruction: 'But not only has the bourgeoisie forged the weapons that bring death to itself; it has also called into existence the men who are to wield those weapons—the modern working class—the proletarians.' (*RE*, 73.) The bourgeoisie has assembled, from the debris of feudal society, a creature whose power as a combination will crush its creator: 'What the bourgeoisie therefore produces, above all, are its own grave-diggers.' (*RE*, 79.) The central fact of modern history, for Marx, is the development of the productive forces (including the proletariat itself) to the point at which they threaten to destroy those social relations of property which have generated them. Surveying the achievements and the fate of the bourgeoisie, Marx emphasizes that 'the forces which it has created have outgrown its control' (*RE*, 295).

Within Marx's historical dialectic, the feverish, Cyclopean industrial development inaugurated in bourgeois society has necessarily to contain the seeds of its own decline and supersession. Trapped within the property-relation, the bourgeoisie's apparently free self-assertion and confident expansion is re-read as the very hastening of its own doom. No longer a rational and autonomous agent in history, the bourgeoisie is revealed as a haunted, *possessed* class, no more in control of its craving for surplus value than it is of the productive forces required to feed it. 'The need of a constantly expanding market for its products chases the bourgeoisie over the whole surface of the globe.' (*RE*, 71.) The world-conquering bourgeoisie is seen in this new light as a thing driven by its addictions, a fugitive—like the Wandering Jew or Victor Frankenstein himself—in the grip of a more powerful demon of his own summoning. That tearing down of old political, social, and natural barriers to its self-expansion which Marx celebrates in his tribute to the bourgeoisie in the *Manifesto*, is now revealed less as a free act than as an ultimately self-destructive compulsion. 'Capital', Marx notes in the *Grundrisse*, 'by its very nature drives beyond every spatial barrier. Thus the creation of the physical conditions of exchange—of the means of communication and transport—the annihilation of space by time—becomes an extraordinary necessity for it.' (*G*, 524.) Necessity—in the form of the iron laws of capital which the bourgeoisie itself invokes—has the bourgeoisie in its tight grip, to the point at which actual capitalists are little more than the 'bearers' of those laws, compelled to execute the demands of capital's self-reproduction, which lead it ultimately to abolish itself: 'The universality to which [capital] irresistibly strives encounters barriers in its own nature, which will, at a certain stage of its development, allow it to be recognized as being itself the greatest barrier to this tendency, and hence will drive towards its own suspension.' (*G*, 410.) The pitiable condition of the capitalist consists in his frantic compulsion to accumulate exchange values which the laws of profit forbid him to squander as use-values in personal enjoyment. The capitalist 'shares with the miser an absolute drive towards self-enrichment. But what appears in the miser as the mania of an individual is in the capitalist the effect of a social mechanism in which he is merely a cog.' (*C*, 739.) Like the worker, the capitalist is reduced to an appendage of his own economic machine, driven by unquenchable and destructive cravings.

The most vivid representation of the bourgeoisie's doomed state of possession by irresistible forces is to be found in Marx's repeated images of capital as a vampire. After Engels had referred to 'the vampire property-holding class' in *The Condition of the Working Class in England*,[11] Marx adopted the image, developing the apparently gratuitous insult into a consistent element of his gothicized portrayal of the bourgeoisie's compulsive condition. In his inaugural address to the International, Marx interprets the resistance to the Ten Hour Bill by Ure, Senior, and other political economists as an admission that 'British industry . . . vampire-like, could but live by sucking blood, and children's blood, too' (*FI*, 79). In *The Civil War*

---

[11] Frederick Engels, *The Condition of the Working Class in England, from Personal Observation and Authentic Sources* (St Albans, 1969), 264.

*in France* the bourgeoisie acts as a vampire towards the peasantry (*FI*, 215), as it does in *The Eighteenth Brumaire*: having at first defended the independence of the peasant smallholding, the bourgeoisie 'has become a vampire that sucks out its blood and brains and throws them into the alchemist's cauldron of capital' (*SE*, 242). But the more important transfusion takes place in the industrial labour process, where the basis of capital's constant thirst becomes clearer. As Marx explains in the *Grundrisse*, 'Capital posits the permanence of value (to a certain degree) by incarnating itself in fleeting commodities and taking on their form, but at the same time changing them just as constantly; . . . But capital obtains this ability only by constantly sucking in living labour as its soul, vampire-like.' (*G*, 646.) This is the necessary movement of 'capital-in-process, creative capital, sucking its living soul out of labour' (*G*, 660). Again, it is the inherent restlessness of the bourgeoisie, as the first great revolutionary class in history, which condemns it to a thirst that can never be quenched. The particular aptness of the vampire image is implied by Marx's term 'living labour', which contrasts with the dead (or 'accumulated') labour embodied in machinery and raw materials—in short, in capital itself, which thus appears as the rule of the dead over the living. As Marx put it most succinctly in *Wage Labour and Capital*, 'It is only the domination of accumulated, past, materialised labour over direct, living labour that turns accumulated labour into capital. Capital does not consist in accumulated labour serving living labour as a means for new production. It consists in living labour serving accumulated labour as a means for maintaining and multiplying the exchange value of the latter.'[12] This is another version, although considerably more analytic, of the familiar complaint that 'things are in the saddle'. It is not just 'things' as objects that Marx is discussing, though, but a *relation* between the life-activity of labour and its own past products, which have come to assume greater power in death, to the point that 'living labour appears as a mere means to realize objectified, dead labour, to penetrate it with an animating soul, while losing its own soul to it' (*G*, 461). If living labour has taken on the role of Promethean creator, it has done so under duress, giving up its breath of life to feed the insatiable thirst of dead labour.

[12] Karl Marx and Frederick Engels, *Selected Works in One Volume* (Moscow, 1968), 81.

It is in *Capital* that these themes are most repeatedly broached. Right from the start, in the Preface to the first edition, monsters and ghouls loom before us: Marx warns the German reader not to dismiss the evils of the factory system as purely English problems—they exist in Germany too, but worsened by the survival of feudal anachronisms in industry. 'We [Germans] suffer not only from the living but from the dead. *Le mort saisit le vif!*' (*C*, 91.) German readers can be complacent about their own industry only because they do not have independent investigators like the English factory inspectorate to open their eyes to the facts. 'Perseus wore a magic cap so that the monster he hunted down might not see him. We draw the magic cap down over our eyes and ears so as to deny that there are any monsters.' (*C*, 91.) *Capital* will set out to show that the monsters are still here, in England as in Germany, and that in different ways '*Le mort saisit le vif*' has become the rule of modern life. 'Capital', Marx writes, 'is dead labour which, vampire-like, lives only by sucking living labour, and lives the more, the more labour it sucks.' (*C*, 342.) To this end the lengthening of the working day is insufficient, and 'only acts as a palliative. It only slightly quenches the vampire thirst for the living blood of labour', which can be satisfied only— appropriately enough—by the introduction of night-shifts (*C*, 367). In the struggle over the length of the working day, the worker discovers that instead of being freely bargained with, he is being bled, and 'that in fact the vampire will not let go "while there remains a single drop of blood to be exploited"'.[13] Capitalism reveals itself 'dripping from head to toe, from every pore, with blood and dirt' (*C*, 926). Lace-making and straw-plaiting 'schools' exploiting the labour of children only four years old are 'blood-sucking institutions' (*C*, 598); the 'capitalized blood of children' is used to finance American capital through English loans (*C*, 920); and in the production process 'the capitalist devours the labour-power of the worker, or appropriates his living labour as the life-blood of capitalism' (*C*, 1007).

In such processes of extracting surplus value, the world of capitalism is revealed as a profound distortion of human life:

Here it is not the worker who makes use of the means of production, but the means of production that make use of the worker. Living labour does not realize itself in objective labour which thereby becomes its objective

---

[13] *C*, 415–6. The quotation is from Engels's article 'The Ten Hours Bill' (1850).

organ, but instead objective labour maintains and fortifies itself by drawing off living labour; it is thus that it becomes *value valorizing itself, capital*, and functions as such. The means of production thus become no more than leeches drawing off as large an amount of living labour as they can. . . . And they now manifest themselves moreover as the rule of past, dead labour over the living. ( *C*, 988 (cf. *C*, 425))

Capital, which appears to be able to perform the miracle of reproducing itself unaided, and of growing spontaneously, is shown to be, beneath the ostensible equity of the wage-bargain, a secret blood-sucker. No longer the self-sufficient fount of wealth, it now appears as a parasite, dead, but by virtue of its parasitism still allowed to linger as undead. The fate of the worker in this topsy-turvy, haunted world is to reproduce and constantly reanimate the 'dead labour' or capital for which she or he exists as nourishment.

Since the process of production is also the process of consumption of labour-power by the capitalist, the worker's product is not only constantly converted into commodities, but also into capital, i.e. into value that sucks up the worker's value-creating power, means of subsistence that actually purchase human beings, and means of production that employ the people who are doing the producing. ( *C*, 716)

This uncanny inversion is the state — or rather, process — of alienation: the surrender of your vital capacities to an 'alien' force which ensures that your own powers are turned against you. The concept (quite distinct from the loose use of the term in the existential sense of exclusion or loss) is central to all of Marx's work from the Economic and Philosophical Manuscripts through to *Capital*, and its place in his writings makes it the most important formulation of that nineteenth-century problem which the continuing use of the Frankenstein myth had come to represent.

In the first place, alienation appears in the immediate production process. As Marx began to see it as early as 1844,

The externalization of the worker in his product means not only that his labour becomes an object, an *external* existence, but that it exists *outside him*, independently of him and alien to him, and begins to confront him as an autonomous power; that the life which he has bestowed on the object confronts him as hostile and alien. ( *EW*, 324)

Similarly, in a letter to the Labour Parliament in 1854, Marx states that the workers have 'allowed the very products of their hands to turn against them and be transformed into as many instruments of their own subjugation' (*SE*, 278). Again the workers are seen as modern Prometheans in the fully Frankensteinian sense—not just infusing the vital spark or life-blood into the body of capital, but enduring its alien and threatening independence as a power over them. During the 1850s Marx developed this theme in his *Grundrisse* notes, showing how the primary separation of labour from the means of production gives machinery a magical appearance of being the true life and force of production. In large-scale industry, the complex combination of labours enhances simple alienation by magnifying the remoteness of the enterprise, as an alien power of combination appears over against the worker:

The combination of this labour appears just as subservient to and led by an alien will and an alien intelligence—having its *animating unity* elsewhere—as its material unity appears subordinate to the *objective unity* of the *machinery* of fixed capital, which, as *animated monster*, objectifies the scientific idea, and is in fact the coordinator, does not in any way relate to the individual worker as his instrument; but rather, he himself exists as an animated individual punctuation mark, as its living isolated accessory. (*G*, 470 (cf. *C*, 1054))

It is hard to believe that Marx did not recall the Frankenstein story when he employed the image of the '*animated monster*'. The phrase will be repeated in the *Grundrisse* and in *Capital*, along with the analysis of machinery as the power of labour turned back upon itself. The means of production confront the worker as 'an alien, commanding personification', in which 'the product of labour, objectified labour, has been endowed by living labour with a soul of its own, and establishes itself opposite living labour as an *alien* power' (*G*, 453–4). Having been given a soul of its own, the machinery entangles the worker in its more powerful limbs, forcing him or her to follow its own rhythms: 'In machinery, objectified labour materially confronts living labour as a ruling power, and as an active subsumption of the latter under itself.' (*G*, 696.) Summarizing this inverted character of productive relations within capitalism, Marx observes that

the objective conditions of labour assume an ever more colossal independence, represented by its very extent, opposite living labour, and that social wealth confronts labour in more powerful portions as an alien and dominant power. The emphasis comes to be placed not on the state of being *objectified*, but on the state of being *alienated*, dispossessed, sold; on the condition that the monstrous objective power which social labour itself erected opposite itself as one of its moments belongs not to the worker but to the personified condition of production, i.e. to capital. (*G*, 831)

In *Capital* this colossal and monstrous alien power appears again as the animated monster of machinery. The omitted seventh part of *Capital*'s first volume, not published until the 1930s, is particularly concerned with this idea: the machines, being autonomous from living labour, appear to possess 'a mind of their own', and Marx adds, quoting Goethe's *Faust*, that by incorporating living labour into the constituents of capital, the machine 'becomes an animated monster, and starts to act "as if consumed by love"' (*C*, 1007). This monstrous form of his own labour confronts the worker 'as something not merely alien, but hostile and antagonistic, when it appears before him objectified and personified in capital' (*C*, 1025). And this relationship appears moreover as a trap which the worker is condemned to reproduce: 'Previously, the conditions of production confronted the worker as capital only in the sense that he *found* them existing as *autonomous* beings opposed to himself. What he now finds so opposed to him is the product of his own labour. What had been the premiss is now the result of the process of production.' (*C*, 1061.) Not only, then, do 'the visible products of labour take on the appearance of its masters' (*C*, 1055), but they must continue to do so as long as labour continues to replenish their alien power.

The earlier chapters of *Capital* present the same picture. Just as 'man' is governed, in religion, by the products of his own brain, so, Marx writes, 'in capitalist production he is governed by the product of his own hand' (*C*, 772). This product, in the form of machinery, is 'a mechanical monster' of 'demonic power', which again appears as an 'animated monster' working as if consumed by love (*C*, 503, 302).

Marx's comparison of alienation in the productive process with alienation in religion is both a mark of the concept's origin in the left-Hegelian critique of Christianity and a reminder of its wide scope in Marx's later writings as well. In a world produced and reproduced under conditions of alienated labour, a mystifying and inverted world over which humanity has lost its control, alien powers appear outside the factory gates too: in the money-relation between people, in social institutions, and in the state. In the money-relation, 'The social character of activity, as well as the social form of the product, and the share of the individual in production here appear as something alien and objective, confronting the individuals, not as their relation to one another, but as their subordination to relations which subsist independently of them' (*G*, 157). Just as they do in production, so in economic exchange and circulation too, people's 'own collisions with one another produce an *alien* social power standing above them, produce their mutual interaction as a process and power independent of them' (*G*, 197). This phenomenon Marx and Engels had traced, in *The German Ideology*, back to the 'natural'—that is, the accidental rather than consensual or voluntary—division of labour which gives rise to the property relation. Under such a division of labour, 'man's own deed becomes an alien power opposed to him, which enslaves him instead of being controlled by him'. Marx and Engels go on to expand upon the significance of this problem:

This fixation of social activity, this consolidation of what we ourselves produce into an objective power above us, growing out of our control, thwarting our expectations, bringing to naught our calculations, is one of the chief factors in historical development up till now. The social power, i.e. the multiplied productive force, which arises through the cooperation of different individuals as it is determined by the division of labour, appears to these individuals, since their cooperation is not voluntary but has come about naturally, not as their own united power, but as an alien force existing outside them, of the origin and goal of which they are ignorant, which they thus cannot control . . .[14]

In the capitalist mode of production, these 'natural' conditions are reproduced in the sense that association remains involuntary for the producers, and the social nature of their productive powers remains obscured from them.

The same kind of alienation is projected into the institution of the state, likewise a creation of society which becomes autonomous from it and turns upon it to become its master. In *The Civil War in France* Marx seizes the opportunity offered by the Commune and its dissolution of alienated state forms to point out this monstrous character of the state, in contrast to which the Commune appears as

the reabsorption of the state power by society as its own living forces instead of as forces controlling and subduing it, by the popular masses themselves, forming their own force instead of the organized force of their suppression— the political force of their social emancipation, instead of the artificial force (appropriated by their oppressors) (their own force opposed to and organized against them) of society wielded for their oppression by their enemies. (*FI*, 250)

[14] Karl Marx and Frederick Engels, *The German Ideology, Part One*, ed. C. J. Arthur (London, 1974), 54.

For Marx the state is a 'supernaturalist abortion of society' which
by turning its begetter's own strength against it becomes 'the state
monster' (*FI*, 249, 253).

These more extensive analyses of alienation originate in the young
Marx's participation in the left-Hegelians' critique of religion. So in
*On the Jewish Question* Marx tackles the nature of money through
the medium of an analysis of fetishism: 'Money is the estranged
essence of man's work and existence: this alien essence dominates
him and he worships it.' (*EW*, 239.) In the same work Marx argues
again that 'Selling is the practice of alienation. As long as man is
restrained by religion he can objectify his essence only by making
it into an *alien*, fantastic being.' (*EW*, 241.) But as Marx distances
himself from the idealism of the Young Hegelian group, the routine
attribution of all ills to religious *ideas* becomes the target of his
sharpest sarcasm in the Preface to *The German Ideology*.

Hitherto men have constantly made up for themselves false conceptions
about themselves . . . The phantoms of their own brains have got out of
their hands. They, the creators, have bowed down before their creations.
Let us liberate them from the chimeras, the ideas, dogmas, imaginary beings,
under the yoke of which they are pining away.[15]

As the new Marxist Marx saw it, the problem was no longer that
men and women had become the slaves of their own false ideas (and
could therefore be set free by correct ones), but that their practical
conditions of life were monstrously out of control. The creations
which had come to dominate their creators were those of material
production, not primarily those of philosophy and religion. In other
words, Marx retained the structure of his diagnosis of fetishism, but
with a new content: it was not so much religion as the alienated practical
life of men and women in class society that was phantasmagoric.[16]
Feuerbach had already pointed out that 'man' creates a God after

[15] Ibid., 37.
[16] The best commentary on this continuity between the religious and social senses
of alienation appears in Engels's *Anti-Dühring*: 'But it is not long before, side by side
with the forces of nature, social forces begin to be active—forces which confront
man as equally alien and at first equally inexplicable, dominating him with the same
apparent natural necessity as the forces of nature themselves. . . . At a still further
stage of evolution, all the natural and social attributes of the numerous gods are
transferred to *one* almighty god, who is but a reflection of the natural man. . . . In
this convenient, handy and universally adaptable form, religion can continue to exist
as the immediate, that is, the sentimental form of men's relation to the alien natural
and social forces which dominate them, so long as men remain under the control

his own image; the modern problem, however, is that the bourgeoisie in particular 'creates a world after its own image' (*RE*, 71). The fullest account of this new practical form of fetishism is to be found, again, in *Capital*. Here Marx traces the process by which money appears to acquire a magical value of its own, independent from the social relations which make it a universal equivalent.

What appears to happen is not that a particular commodity becomes money because all other commodities express their values in it, but, on the contrary, that all other commodities universally express their values in a particular commodity because it is money. The movement through which this process has been mediated vanishes in its own result, leaving no trace behind. . . . Hence the magic of money. Men are henceforth related to each other in their social relations of production in a purely atomistic way. Their own relations of production therefore assume a material shape which is independent of their control and their conscious individual action. (*C*, 187)

Such loss of control is not merely a matter of 'things' rebelling against people, but of the social *relations* between people vanishing behind their results so as to assume the appearance of a material fetish—money, or the commodity; human labour disappearing into the form of its product. This 'riddle of the money fetish' (*C*, 187) has its source in the deeper paradox of the commodity. 'The objective conditions essential to the realization of labour are *alienated* from the worker and become manifest as *fetishes* endowed with a will and a soul of their own. *Commodities*, in short, appear as the purchasers of *persons*.' (*C*, 1003.) The initial expropriation of the direct producer endows the alienated means of production and the commodities produced from them with the power of human labour and organization—a power now separated from the producers and turned against them in magnified, hostile forms.

In the first chapter of *Capital* the closing section on commodity fetishism explains this process by analogy with religion, to account for the social relations between people assuming 'the fantastic form of a relation between things' (*C*, 165). In the misty realms of religion, 'the products of the human brain appear as autonomous figures

of these forces. However, we have seen repeatedly that in existing bourgeois society men are dominated by the economic conditions created by themselves, by the means of production which they themselves have produced, as if by an alien force. The actual basis of the reflexive activity that gives rise to religion therefore continues to exist, and with it the religious reflection itself.' K. Marx and F. Engels, *On Religion* (Moscow, 1957), 131–2.

endowed with a life of their own . . . So it is in the world of commodities with the products of men's hands.' (*C*, 165.) As Marx goes on to develop the analogy in his unpublished seventh chapter, the capitalists begin to appear as denizens and victims of a completely alienated world, and the workers as the lever standing partly outside it all the better to shake it from its axis.

> Hence the rule of the capitalist over the worker is the rule of things over men, of dead labour over living, of the product over the producer. . . . Thus at the level of material production, of the life-process in the realm of the social—for that is what the process of production is—we find the *same* situation that we find in *religion* at the ideological level, namely the inversion of subject into object and *vice versa*. . . . What we are confronted by here is the *alienation* of man from his own labour. To that extent the worker stands on a higher plane than the capitalist from the outset, since the latter has his roots in the process of alienation and finds absolute satisfaction in it whereas right from the start the worker is a victim who confronts it as a rebel and experiences it as a process of enslavement. (*C*, 990)

The worker appears as Prometheus again, but here less as Prometheus *plasticator*, giver of the spark of life and shaper of human clay, than as the rebel Prometheus of Aeschylus and Percy Shelley, vindicating in his rebellion his superiority over Zeus, his resistance exposing the limits of divine power. Capital as a fetish is as vulnerable to iconoclasm as the gods: if men and women can reclaim their human powers from the fantastic projections of religion, so too can they recover control over their social production from the equally fantastic material world of the commodity—that inverted world characterized by 'the personification of things and the reification of persons' (*C*, 1054).

In such a fetishized world it is hard to recognize that behind the production of 'things' lies the much more important production of people and of their social relations, which, far from being naturally fixed, are constantly made and remade in processes which appear as the production only of objects. Marx is as conscious as Carlyle of the radically fictile and plastic nature of the modern world and its reshaped humanity. The basic elements of class society—the state and the division of labour—have produced new kinds of people: the division of labour 'makes man, as far as is possible, an abstract being, a lathe etc., and transforms him into a spiritual and physical abortion' (*EW*, 269); while the state replaces the 'actual man' with the abstract citizen or political man, who is 'simply abstract, artificial man, man as an *allegorical, moral* person' (*EW*, 234). The real products of the advanced division of labour in capitalist production are 'the stunted monsters produced by overwork in the mechanical monotony of the factories!' (*EW*, 406). The development of capitalist manufacture 'converts the worker into a crippled monstrosity' by confining his activity to a single operation; by such a process 'the individual himself is divided up, and transformed into the automatic motor of a detail operation, thus realizing the absurd fable of Menenius Agrippa, which presents man as a mere fragment of his own body' (*C*, 481–2). Broken down in this way and then reassembled, the human capacities of the workers reappear in monstrous form as a purely artificial being, effectively as a machine: 'The collective worker, formed out of the combination of a number of individual specialized workers, is the item of machinery specifically characteristic of the manufacturing period.' (*C*, 468.) Even the process by which the fragments come into being is an artificial one, as Marx implies in his early comments on the German proletariat: 'For the proletariat is not formed by *natural* poverty but by *artificially produced* poverty; it is formed not from the mass of people mechanically oppressed by the weight of society but from the mass of people issuing from society's *acute disintegration* and in particular from the dissolution of the middle class.' (*EW*, 256.)

The working class, then, is both, at the level of the labour process, a combination of fragmented operations into the collective worker, and, at the level of social class-formation, a reassembly of fragments from a decayed social order. In this light Franco Moretti seems fully justified in equating the Frankenstein monster with the bourgeoisie's alarmed vision of the proletariat—that artificial and powerful new aggregation by which capitalists were threatened the more they depended upon it. Yet the senses in which the capitalist world is a Frankensteinian one go further in Marx's writings than the kind of fearful proletarian monster we meet in the cartoons or in Gaskell's nightmares. Marx's dialectical inversions restore the double-edged character of the Frankenstein myth, recognizing maker and monster as the twin faces of a Janus-headed problem. Marx insists that the 'monster' condemned by bourgeois society is the true maker of it, while the maker of this monstrous outcast is itself the true monster. Capital and labour continually produce and reproduce not just goods but one another and the relation between them:

. . . the result of the process of production and realization is, above all, the reproduction and new production of the *relation of capital and labour itself*, of *capitalist and worker*. This social relation, production relation, appears in fact as an even more important result of the process than its material results. And more particularly, the worker reproduces himself as labour capacity, as well as the capitalist confronting him, while at the same time the capitalist produces himself as capital as well as the living labour capacity confronting him. Each reproduces itself, by reproducing its other, its negation. The capitalist produces labour as alien; labour produces the product as alien. The capitalist produces the worker, and the worker the capitalist . . . ( *G*, 458 (cf. *C*, 716, 1061–2))

In the world Marx describes, which is above all a humanly produced world, the monster is not a stable or unchangeable figure, since the category of the 'alien' can be produced only as a *relation*.

The result of this kind of insistence in terms of Marx's reversals of myths is that the Frankensteinian vision of the nineteenth century is given another dimension: not only is capital necessarily driven to produce the dispossessed alien 'collective worker' as an assembly of human fragments summoned into threateningly autonomous life; but equally, from the other side, labour's Promethean activity produces the world of capital as the corpse of past labour continually revived to feed on the living. This relation becomes a Titanic cycle of torture, a Promethean condition in which enormous powers are just as enormously frustrated. Productive forces emerge as destructive forces; and the greater the creative power of human beings, the more certainly does this power turn against them. As Marx puts it in his notes on James Mill's *Elements of Political Economy*,

[man's] own creation confronts him as an alien power, his wealth appears as poverty, the essential bond joining him to other men appears inessential, in fact separation from other men appears to be his true existence, his life appears as the sacrifice of his life . . . his production is the production of nothing, his power over objects appears as the power of objects over him; in short he, the lord of creation, appears as the servant of that creation. ( *EW*, 266)

In the topsy-turvy world of private property relations, it is not the heir who comes into possession of the land but the land which comes into possession of the heir—'it inherits him' ( *EW*, 318).

Marx argues, in a similar vein, that with the increase of productive forces for dominating nature, the established social relations throw this apparent progress into reverse, ensuring that men and women are all the more dominated themselves. There is a paradox here of 'ecological' proportions, adumbrated by Marx in his *Economic and Philosophical Manuscripts*: 'And what a paradox it would be if the more man subjugates nature through his labour and the more divine miracles are made superfluous by the miracles of industry, the more he is forced to forgo the joy of production and the enjoyment of the product out of deference to these powers.' (*EW*, 330.) The same problem is there in Marx's discussion of the role of machinery under capitalism in *Capital*: machinery 'in itself . . . is a victory of man over the forces of nature', he writes, 'but in the hands of capital it makes man the slave of those forces' (*C*, 569). What Marx is summing up in such formulae is the great problem of the uncontrolled productive expansion which the nineteenth century had to face in its most alarming forms—an extension of industrial force which was at the same time a diminution of human control. Marx's most impressive survey of this Frankensteinian world comes in his speech on the anniversary of the *People's Paper* in 1856:

There is one great fact, characteristic of this our nineteenth century, a fact which no party dares deny. On the one hand there have started into life industrial and scientific forces which no epoch of former human history had ever suspected. On the other hand, there exist symptoms of decay, far surpassing the horrors recorded of the latter times of the Roman empire. In our times everything seems pregnant with its contrary. Machinery, gifted with the wonderful power of shortening and fructifying human labour, we behold starving and overworking it. The new-fangled sources of wealth, by some strange weird spell, are turned into sources of want. The victories of art seem bought by the loss of character. At the same pace that mankind masters nature, man seems to become enslaved to other men or to his own infamy. Even the pure light of science seems unable to shine but on the dark background of ignorance. All our invention and progress seem to result in endowing material forces with intellectual life, and in stultifying human life into a material force. (*SE*, 299–300)

In this knot of ominous historical contradictions, the myth of Frankenstein has become the great fact of nineteenth-century life.

# 7

## *Dangerous Discoveries and Mad Scientists: Some Late-Victorian Horrors*

There is no surer testimony to the Frankenstein story's assured place in the public imagination—albeit in sharply simplified form—than the ease with which a knowledge of the tale is taken as read in debased comic versions. Just as the burlesque stage versions of *Frankenstein* pay implicit tribute to the popularity of the earliest dramatizations, so too do comic prose adaptations testify to the wide currency of Mary Shelley's story, whether at first or at second hand.

A striking example is the rather inept story which appeared anonymously in *Fraser's Magazine* in 1838 under the title 'The New Frankenstein'. What is 'new' about the monster of this tale is really only the established pattern of the stage versions: that it is mute and that its problem is largely one of possessing no soul. The freedom of the prose medium is not, in this case, used to redress the simplifications of the dramatic presentations of monstrosity but is directed instead to an aimless and inconclusive slapstick tour of European Romanticism. The narrator claims to be an associate of E. T. A. Hoffmann (whose stock-in-trade reappears in an interpolated tale about a haunted violin-maker), a student of anatomy who discovers galvanism at Paris and later reads Mary Shelley's *Frankenstein*, taking it for literal truth. And so—up to a point—it turns out to be, as his former anatomy tutor appears with the very monster itself, which is, to the narrator's disappointment, only a mindless automaton barely capable of co-ordinated movement. Our narrator resolves to complete Frankenstein's unfinished labour by endowing this creature with a mind, to which end he resorts to his own discovery of brain gas or 'afflatus'. He manages to extract samples of this precious substance from the heads of Goethe, Percy Shelley, and Coleridge, pumping them into the monster's skull. The monster refuses, of course, to worship his painstaking benefactor, and regards him with hatred; moreover, the experiment has failed in that the monster's speech is only a scrambled

confusion of languages and ideas. The clumsy joke here is supposed
to be at the expense of Romantic abstraction and metaphysics, but
it inadvertently endorses the basis of Romantic psychology and
aesthetics: in Coleridge's terms, the monster's mind is held together
only in the associative mode of Fancy, and lacks the unifying basis
of Imagination. The disgruntled narrator's diagnosis, though, is that
his creature lacks a soul, and so he goes to the Egyptian Necropolis
to steal one, whereupon the indignant dead awake to repel the
intruder. The narrator wakes up to find that the whole incident has
been a dream.

It is certainly an unimpressive piece of fictional hack-work, but
'The New Frankenstein' tells us something of the extent to which
the Frankenstein story has been assimilated and accepted not just
as the contemporary form of the Faust myth but as a common
imaginative property susceptible to endless experiment and revision.
The cliché of the Mad Scientist was taking shape. After *Frankenstein*,
the figure of the scientist in fiction has, almost as a rule, to be that
of an aspiring young medical student who dabbles in galvanism, and
whose long hours in the seclusion of the laboratory engender or
reinforce a misanthropic, or at best insensitive, disregard for his social
bonds and duties. So entrenched is this cliché that we find authors
of far greater powers than those shown in 'The New Frankenstein'
resorting to it even when their tales seem not to require its services.

A redundant stereotype of this kind can be found in George Eliot's
uncharacteristic foray into the supernaturally fabulous, 'The Lifted
Veil' (1859). The aim of this fable is to demonstrate that the supposed
'gifts' of privileged knowledge beyond natural limits would in practice
turn out to be curses. The protagonist, Latimer, becomes mysteriously
endowed with capacities both of telepathy and of prevision; he can
therefore see the worst, both of what others think of him and of
what is to befall him in the future. Latimer starts his narrative by
predicting the exact moment of his death, and spends much of it
in a state of misanthropic revulsion against what he sees as the
meanness and egoism of other people's thoughts. The most prominent
victim of this curse is his now hated brother Alfred, whose fiancée,
Bertha, Latimer covets despite a clear premonition of an unhappy
marriage with her. After Alfred's accidental death Latimer does
overcome 'this double consciousness'[1] of desire and premonition in

---

[1] George Eliot, *The Lifted Veil* (London, 1985), 32.

his attitude to Bertha, largely because she is—again inexplicably—immune from his telepathic scrutiny; and he marries her. As Bertha's immunity fades, Latimer sees in (or reads into) her mind too the signs of vanity, selfishness, and pettiness, from which he recoils, finally separating from her and living the life of an embittered recluse to the end.

A surprising feature in Eliot's construction of this story is her insistence upon making Latimer a poetical young man who is obliged by his father to pursue a scientific education for the good of the family business. Latimer studies the secrets of magnetism and electricity, completing his education at Frankenstein's home town, Geneva, before his premonitory gifts come to him in the wake of a serious illness. No causal link, however, is established between Latimer's scientific pursuits and his mysterious powers. Later in the tale, this unnecessary element is compounded by the reappearance of Latimer's former student friend Meunier, whose anatomical experiments have almost reached the point of successfully reviving corpses by transferring blood. Eliot goes well out of her way to give Meunier his opportunity, by arranging a temporary suspension of Latimer's telepathic powers while he is still living with Bertha. Latimer suspects that Bertha is hiding something from him, although her servant, Mrs Archer, is in on the secret. When Mrs Archer dies, Meunier is able to revive her, and she accuses Bertha of plotting to poison Latimer. This whole side of the story is a noticeable oddity, an extraneous complication which can hardly be justified on the grounds of introducing some event which can at last surprise the protagonist: Latimer is at this stage too morally numbed by his 'curse of insight'[2] to register any significant response. It seems rather that Eliot has attempted to ground her rather abstract fable of knowledge and its limits within a more popularly recognizable convention of scientific transgression, of a Frankensteinian or Hawthornian type; but, perhaps worried by the anti-scientific conservatism of the convention, has stepped back from establishing any causal link between Latimer's studies and his curse. What remains, like a half-built bridge, is the implication in the corpse-reviving episode that the telepathic access which Latimer has to other people's secrets is as flatly contrary to nature (and therefore, thankfully, as impossible) as the reanimation and interrogation of dead servants. In the temporary absence of the one method of

---

[2] Ibid., 66.

revealing secrets he has to resort to the other, and the two knowledges are thus equated as deathly, just as Latimer's access to the future also resolves itself into a vision of his own death.

Eliot's stereotypical meddling scientist is used, then, merely as a visible figure to help flesh out her more abstract moral theme. In a number of the better 'supernatural' tales of the late Victorian period we will find that this helpfully recognizable convention of laboratory horrors serves much the same purpose—to illustrate what Eliot saw as the underlying moral economy of the given world, from which any release promised by exceptional gifts will turn out to be delusive and imprisoning. As in *Frankenstein*, the vehicle of the scientific experiment carries within it other implications about the remaking of people in the modern world.

This is clearly true of the most successful and memorable of these tales, R. L. Stevenson's *Dr Jekyll and Mr Hyde* (1886)—a story sharing with Frankenstein's a number of features which help to make it another modern myth. Like *Frankenstein* (and like Stevenson's other fictional 'crawler', 'The Body Snatchers'), *Dr Jekyll and Mr Hyde* is set in a noticeably male world of isolation and guilty privacy, thus highlighting and condensing the theme of irresponsible secrecy which runs through the nineteenth-century tradition of Romantic transgression. Jekyll's mysterious seclusion within the study which had once been used as a dissecting room is itself a primary evil which is projected and reproduced in the name of his *alter ego*, as Utterson's pun reminds us: 'If he be Mr Hyde . . . I shall be Mr Seek.'[3] Jekyll harbours what Lanyon calls 'scientific heresies', and in the isolated world of the study his concentrated energies convert these into those dangerous 'scientific passions' which Utterson cannot comprehend (*JH*, 43, 37). Jekyll is an aspiring figure, like Frankenstein, and what in his 'Full Statement of the Case' he describes as 'the exacting nature of my aspirations' (*JH*, 81) is in the first place a striving for ethical purity. It is this impulse—evidently based on the Calvinism of Stevenson's own background—which, as Jekyll explains, drives open the widening gulf within himself between his public good works and his concealed pleasures, and which inspires his project of jettisoning his shameful side by completing the division.

[3] Robert Louis Stevenson, *The Strange Case of Dr Jekyll and Mr Hyde, and Other Stories*, ed. Jenni Calder (Harmondsworth, 1979), 38. Subsequent page references in the text are to this edition, abbreviated as *JH*.

Jekyll's experiment is primarily an ethical one conducted, apparently, for the best of reasons, but it has unacknowledged motives which the tale exposes metaphorically in the shape of Hyde. The creature who emerges from Jekyll's study is a monster in the classical sense, demonstrating visibly the ugliness of the hidden: just as the hideousness of Frankenstein's monster is a figure for the unhealthy secretive conditions of its creation, so Hyde is the emblem of the need to hide. The inexplicable loathing felt by those who encounter Hyde in the streets is the shock of witnessing a publication of the very soul of concealment. Both Victor Frankenstein and Jekyll begin with good intentions, but their projects are internally contradictory: Frankenstein tries to become the benefactor of his race by turning his back on it, while Jekyll wishes to rid himself of shameful secrecy by secret means. Their creations therefore mock them by appearing in the shape of the conditions in which they were brought forth, rather than the ends for which they were conceived. Jekyll begins to understand this logic when he reflects on his error: 'Had I approached my discovery in a more noble spirit, had I risked the experiment while under the empire of generous or pious aspirations, all must have been otherwise, and from these agonies of death and birth I had come forth an angel instead of a fiend.' (*JH*, 85.) Jekyll still believes here that purer aspirations alone would have prevented the disaster, but since the 'empire' under which he is reborn is that of the locked study and the scientific secret, he is *already* cast in the mould of Hyde before he takes his potion. Secrecy and shame merely fuel one another, and Jekyll behaves towards his friends in the same guilty fashion as Frankenstein does towards Clerval after the monster's escape.

The place of Stevenson's story in the Frankenstein tradition is established less by the twitching and hideous appearance of Hyde alone, or by his 'monstrous' pleasures (*JH*, 86), than by the manner in which Hyde figures forth the discrepancy between Jekyll's aspiration and the conditions of its execution. The abortive attempt to re-create himself leads Jekyll inevitably into subjection to his own creature—which, in a climax more clearly cathartic than Mary Shelley's, kills itself and its creator at exactly the same time. As Jekyll foresees the culmination of this process, he translates his sense of horror into Frankensteinian terms.

He had now seen the full deformity of that creature that shared with him some of the phenomena of consciousness, and was co-heir with him to death:

and . . . he thought of Hyde, for all his energy of life, as of something not only hellish but inorganic. This was the shocking thing; that the slime of the pit seemed to utter cries and voices; that the amorphous dust gesticulated and sinned; that what was dead, and had no shape, should usurp the offices of life. (*JH*, 95)

That sense of usurpation, of human life dominated by its own disastrous animation of the inorganic, which we find in so many nineteenth-century uses of the Frankenstein myth, is given here a disturbing new immediacy which gets literally under the skin: the one person Jekyll can no longer hide from is Hyde, who is already within him. The insurgency of Jekyll's monster is of a kind that can obliterate what remains of Jekyll's already fragile identity. What may look like a simple dramatization of Calvinist dualism reaches well beyond that. To the ostensible moral of the tale, 'that man is not truly one but two' (*JH*, 82), Jekyll is made to append an unusual postscript:

I say two, because the state of my own knowledge does not pass beyond that point. Others will follow, others will outstrip me on the same lines; and I hazard the guess that man will be ultimately known for a mere polity of multifarious, incongruous and independent denizens. (*JH*, 82)

Inverting the usual direction of the body politic metaphor, Stevenson suggests, as Dickens had imagined before him, that human identity is merely an assemblage of ill-fitting fragments; that what we please to call the 'individual' is in fact endlessly divisible.

   *Dr Jekyll and Mr Hyde* stands as the clearest presentation of Victorian writers' concern with the 'divided self'. But there are other prominent works within the late-Victorian revival of Gothic fantasy which display the same interest, in less obviously Frankensteinian forms. Reverting from the secular, laboratory-based 'science fiction' of Mary Shelley and R. L. Stevenson, they adopt shamelessly supernatural devices to represent a similar fragmenting of identity, a similar loss of control to the forces of unreason.

   After *Frankenstein* and *Dr Jekyll and Mr Hyde*, the third nineteenth-century horror story of mythic proportions, Bram Stoker's *Dracula* (1897), is again a tale of an overreacher who seeks both immortality and exemption from the moral responsibilities of ordinary mortals. Like Frankenstein, he attempts to reproduce himself by resurrecting the dead rather than by sexual generation. As Van Helsing explains, 'He is experimenting, and doing it well; and if it had not been that we have crossed his path he would be yet—he may be yet if we fail—the father or furtherer of a new order of beings, whose road must lead through Death, not Life.'[4] Count Dracula's dubious gift of immortality—it is at the same time a curse of isolation and secrecy—tempts him, like Hyde and like the Frankenstein monster, to indulge in an immunity from the consequences of criminal action: in an early episode in Transylvania he commits one of his murders dressed in Harker's clothes, and he is later able to assume more impenetrable disguises. The vampires, having evaded the limits of life and death, must be hunted down and finally staked into stability, and the Count himself pursued to his lair. By an unwitting irony, though, the chief vampire-hunter Van Helsing becomes, in Stoker's hands, the 'double' of Dracula himself. Like Conan Doyle's contemporaneous antagonists Holmes and Moriarty, the pair of obsessive old men dodge and chase one another from London across Europe to their fateful encounter, their identities mirrored in proud mutual respect. They are the twin halves of a single, perversely sexualized Frankensteinian transgressor; blood-brothers by proxy, the one draws blood out of women while the other pumps blood into them.

Although Dracula seeks to produce a new order of beings by means not directly sexual, he is identified throughout with the dangerous awakening of female sexual pleasure; and it is Van Helsing who comes to re-enact Frankenstein's tearing up of the female monster, as he organizes the posthumous, and patently sexual, staking of Lucy Westenra. His ostensible reason is the same—to prevent her propagating her monstrous kind. The fear of sexuality (in this case, of Lucy's polyandrous desires) echoes the righteous mutilation of the female in *Frankenstein*; here, however, it is intensified to a hysterical degree of obsessive misogyny which goes unchallenged from within the novel. *Dracula*'s conservatism is held in place by a narrative form (derived from Wilkie Collins's *The Woman in White*) which appears to offer several points of view after the manner of *Frankenstein*; but these turn out to corroborate rather than to question or to challenge one another as the narrative voices of *Frankenstein* do. The collated diaries and phonograph records dovetail into a consistent body of 'evidence' which both confirms the incredible events and justifies Van Helsing in his housebreaking, bribery, and desecration of graves. There is no view or voice within the novel which can contradict the

[4] Bram Stoker, *Dracula*, ed. A. N. Wilson (Oxford, 1983), 302.

militant xenophobia of Van Helsing and his associates, and so *Dracula* proceeds instead to drown out all its teeming symbolic suggestions and to enact a single-minded rite of exorcism. Although there are in this novel hints, as Moretti has shown,[5] of late-Victorian anxieties about the economic power of foreign monopoly as a revival of feudal tyrannies, *Dracula* is finally concerned more with the overlapping of sexual and religious terrors than with the monstrous creations and disobedient powers of the modern world. In that sense, it turns away from the tradition of *Frankenstein* towards an older kind of Gothic novel in which the bourgeoisie flirtatiously replays its victory over the baronial despot: Dracula is feudalism's death warmed up.

The Decadent literature of the 1890s was able, however, to revive Gothic fantasies in forms more intelligently challenging than Stoker's, and more directly concerned with Frankensteinian transgression. Oscar Wilde's *The Picture of Dorian Gray* (1891) is in many ways the aesthete's version of *Dr Jekyll and Mr Hyde*—a story which Vivian in Wilde's 'The Decay of Lying' had complained was too lifelike: 'the transformation of Dr Jekyll reads dangerously like an experiment out of the *Lancet*', and is therefore, according to Wilde's paradoxical aesthetic, too realistic to be believed.[6] The transformation of Dorian Gray (or rather of his portrait) on the other hand, reads quite deliberately like a fairy tale, and his crimes like a cheap melodrama. Dorian simply makes an impossible wish, and it comes true without any effort at explanation being made, nor any supernatural atmosphere created to cover the intrusion of this Hawthornian miracle into a sunny and cheerful modern setting.

At first sight, it would appear that, by dispensing with the mad scientist cliché, Wilde has forsaken the Frankenstein myth in favour of a much simpler moral fable of Good and Evil. Clearly, the story of Dorian's fateful wish is a version of the Faust myth which is cast in terms reminiscent of Hawthorne's allegories: the painting is explicitly offered as 'the visible emblem of conscience', as 'a visible symbol of the degradation of sin',[7] and the tale depends entirely on the allegorical equation which Basil explains to Dorian: 'Sin is a thing that writes itself across a man's face. It cannot be concealed. People

[5] Moretti, *Signs Taken for Wonders*, 90–8.

[6] Oscar Wilde, *De Profundis and Other Writings* (Harmondsworth, 1973), 61.

[7] Oscar Wilde, *The Picture of Dorian Gray* (Harmondsworth, 1949), 105, 109. Subsequent page references in the text are to this edition, abbreviated as *DG*.

talk sometimes of secret vices. There are no such things. If a wretched man has a vice, it shows itself in the lines of his mouth, the droop of his eyelids, the moulding of his hands even.' (*DG*, 166.) By founding itself upon this premiss, Wilde's story condemns itself to a two-dimensional existence, because its tale of concealment can work only on the understanding that concealment is ultimately impossible. The result, though, is far from being a simple story, or a fable that wears its moral on its sleeve. Although Dorian is plainly guilty of pride in aspiring beyond what would be called natural limits of physical decay, and is therefore recognizable as a traditional transgressor, there is a complication in that Wilde's world has little that can be transgressed against: the standard of 'Nature' has been abolished by Wilde's insistence that this world is a thoroughly artificial one. Given the attractions of the ostensible villain, Henry Wootton, no safe moral conclusion is really available here. His witticisms constantly remind us that the novel is less about the 'nature' of Good or Evil than about the artificial manufacture of human personality.

What appears to be the novel's simplest device—the doubling of Dorian Gray and his portrait—is in fact extended in quite complex ways. It is itself redoubled in the patterning of characters: *The Picture of Dorian Gray* takes a Frankensteinian creator and his monstrous creation, and subjects them to a further split, thus producing two creators—Wootton and Basil Hallward—and two monsters— Dorian and the picture. To be a Frankenstein, neither of the creators needs to be a scientist. Victor Frankenstein himself antedates the word and the concept; he is, in Mary Shelley's version, an 'artist', and so too are Basil and—less obviously—Henry Wootton. Basil creates what is clearly a monstrous work of art which he has animated with too much of his own life and therefore wishes to conceal in secrecy. Since meeting Dorian, he says, 'I can now re-create life in a way that was hidden from me before' (*DG*, 16). But the life he has re-created asserts its independence from him, and finally its original (and double), Dorian himself, turns upon and kills him.

Ironically reversing the scientist-creator cliché, Wilde brings in (unnecessarily, as in 'The Lifted Veil') a medical experimenter towards the end of his tale, not to revive Hallward's body but to eliminate it completely. Alan Campbell is an obviously Frankensteinian type: a chemist who locks himself away from his mother in his laboratory, and who has become absorbed in 'certain curious experiments' in biology (*DG*, 184). According to Dorian, he dissects human bodies without questioning their origin, as his aim is 'benefitting the human race . . . or gratifying intellectual curiosity' (*DG*, 188). But Campbell's ideals crumble under the pressure of Dorian's mysterious blackmail; the scientist is obliged to eliminate the corpse of the artist and then commit suicide. His scientific ardour proves to be weaker than his enslavement to secrecy, an enslavement which parallels that of Dorian and Basil (as of Frankenstein and Jekyll before them). As Basil has explained to Henry, about his desire to conceal Dorian's identity, 'I have grown to love secrecy. It seems to be the one thing that can make modern life mysterious or marvellous to us. The commonest thing is delightful if one only hides it.' (*DG*, 10.) By making this admission, Basil introduces us to the fatal error which damns both him and Dorian: the seductive appeal of the mysterious or marvellous third dimension which concealment can give to the 'mere surface' of things. Henry Wootton eludes this trap because he remains consistently committed to surfaces. Although he lies to his wife as a matter of course, there is no real concealment involved, because she already sees through his excuses. At a more general level, Wootton is immune to the seduction of hidden mysteries because his entire attitude to life disdains profundities. In one of his most celebrated and most challenging paradoxes Wootton proclaims that 'It is only shallow people who do not judge by appearances. The true mystery of the world is the visible, not the invisible.' (*DS*, 29.) Dorian, though, is from the start Basil's secret, and the picture therefore duplicates this function: it is Basil's 'Hyde' as it later becomes Dorian's own, serving the need both feel for something to be hidden. Dominated by this Hyde compulsion, Dorian plummets to the status of one who, like Hyde, slinks in disguise through the opium-dens and brothels of London.

Wootton, although immune to the consequences, is implicated in the destructive cycle of the tale as a second creator, his creation being Dorian himself. Wootton is described in ways which are there to remind us of his status as a fabricator of human character, a superior analyst who, like Faust, is bored by the everyday topics of scientific investigation:

He had always been enthralled by the methods of natural science, but the ordinary subject-matter of that science had seemed to him trivial and of no import. And so he had begun by vivisecting himself, as he had ended by vivisecting others. Human life—that appeared to him the one thing worth investigating. (*DG*, 66)

Of Henry the vivisector, Dorian complains that he is apt to 'cut life to pieces' with his epigrams (*DG*, 110). But Wootton can also move from analysis to synthesis, assembling life in new forms and interesting combinations. Dorian, of course, is the product of his scientific experiments with human character: Wootton sees Dorian, after first meeting him, as a chance to 'project one's soul into some gracious form', as a perfect material to be 'fashioned into a marvellous type . . . There was nothing that one could not do with him. He could be made a Titan or a toy.' (*DG*, 44.) Later, Wootton reviews his success in this enterprise: 'To a large extent the lad was his own creation. He had made him premature.' (*DG*, 67.)

Henry Wootton's Promethean meditations serve to complicate the doubling of the portrait and the young man. It is no longer simply that the picture mirrors an 'original' in nature, or merely that it symbolizes Dorian's soul. In Wilde's world it is not Art that imitates Nature but Nature that imitates Art, and accordingly Dorian is shown to be Wootton's own *chef d'œuvre*. But, as Dorian comes to reflect, 'Art, like Nature, has her monsters' (*DG*, 150), and although he does not see the relevance of this observation to himself, he is evidently one of these monsters of Art. The term 'monstrous' recurs in the novel with extraordinary frequency, as if to remind us of Dorian's status. His wish for the portrait to age and his own youth to be preserved is made in 'a monstrous moment of pride and passion' (*DG*, 244); it seems monstrous both to him and to Basil that it should come true (*DG*, 103, 173); the portrait lives a 'monstrous soul-life' which Dorian takes 'a monstrous and terrible delight' in examining (*DG*, 247, 173); and to Alan Campbell, Dorian's admission that he killed Basil is a 'monstrous confession' (*DG*, 187). Beyond these perhaps predictable indications of the breach in natural and criminal law, though, there is an unusual extension of the monstrous atmosphere throughout Dorian's world. In 'this grey monstrous London of ours' (*DG*, 57), drunkards in the streets look 'like monstrous apes' (*DG*, 101), and the shadows of people in lighted windows move like 'monstrous marionettes' (*DG*, 205). Dorian regards the Jewish theatre manager as a monster, and after his murder of Basil, the sky too appears to him to be 'like a monstrous peacock's tail' (*DG*, 57, 177).

If everything around Dorian looks ˌmonstrous, this is clearly because he is monstrous himself. His dim perception of this condition — the corollary of the artificiality in which he delights — brings with it a reflection upon the individual's multiformity which resembles strikingly Dr Jekyll's thoughts about the polity of warring factions that constitutes human identity:

Is insincerity such a terrible thing? I think not. It is merely a method by which we can multiply our personalities.
    Such, at any rate, was Dorian Gray's opinion. He used to wonder at the shallow psychology of those who conceive the Ego in man as a thing simple, permanent, reliable, and of one essence. To him, man was a being with myriad lives and myriad sensations, a complex multiform creature that bore within itself strange legacies of thought and passion, and whose very flesh was tainted with the monstrous maladies of the dead. (*DG*, 158–9)

As Dorian ponders the many personalities of which he is composed, he studies the family portraits in his picture-gallery, scrutinizing those ancestors whose different traits have been combined to make him. Just as his own portrait is made from himself, so he in turn appears here to have been assembled from parts of portraits, his life monstrously produced from multitudes of the dead.

    Perhaps more powerful as a meditation on the monstrous, though, is Henry Wootton's speech on the poisonous effects of self-denial:

We are punished for our refusals. Every impulse that we strive to strangle broods in the mind, and poisons us. . . . The only way to get rid of a temptation is to yield to it. Resist it, and your soul grows sick with longing for the things it has forbidden to itself, with desire for what its monstrous laws have made monstrous and unlawful. (*DG*, 25–6)

It is this speech which first draws Dorian under Henry's influence and awakens him to the life of sensation. In his more polished paradoxes Wootton has rephrased William Blake's Proverbs of Hell: 'Sooner murder an infant in its cradle than nurse unacted desires', and 'Prisons are built with stones of Law, brothels with bricks of Religion'.[8] Within the logic of what we now call repression, the true monstrosity of unlicenced desires resides not in the desire itself nor in its object but in the repressive law. The 'monstrous', Wilde understands, is the image of the prohibition which excludes it, and of the hypocritical moral code which recoils from its own creations.

    While Wilde deliberately raised his parable from the realm of medical explicitness for which he criticized *Dr Jekyll and Mr Hyde*

---

[8] William Blake, *The Marriage of Heaven and Hell* (London, 1793), Plates 10 and 8.

into a more elevated sphere of allegorical ideality and abstraction, there were other writers at work on the Frankenstein theme who were to move in quite the other direction, highlighting the story's tendency to mock ideal visions with the botched and hideous corporeality of the miscreated. William Morrow's tale 'The Monster-Maker' is possibly the crudest of late-Victorian efforts in this physiological vein. Its protagonist is an old surgeon suspected of vivisectionist vices, who is provided—by a young man seeking voluntary euthanasia—with an ideal opportunity to put into practice his dream of creating a humanoid with a purely artificial brain. His wife becomes suspicious of his secret activities in the laboratory, and alerts the police, who arrive too late to save her from the monster's crushing embrace. The surgeon attempts to grapple with his creature, and in the ensuing struggle a lamp is overturned which sets fire to both of them, along with the laboratory. The monster itself is glimpsed briefly by the police: 'They saw what appeared to be a man, yet evidently was not a man; huge, awkward, shapeless; a squirming, lurching, stumbling mass, completely naked. It raised its broad shoulders. *It had no head*, but instead of it a small metallic ball surmounting its neck.'[9] The surgeon's error (and the author's) lies, it seems, in the crudity of his conception: the artificial brain contains a cerebrum but no cerebellum, and is therefore an unthinking vehicle of destructive instinct and reflex.

Just as repulsive in its physiological bias, but a great deal more reflective in its imaginative recasting of the Frankenstein myth's larger issues, is H. G. Wells's romance, *The Island of Doctor Moreau* (1896). Wells acknowledged in 1933 that his 'scientific romances', as he called them, were based, unlike those of Jules Verne, upon impossibilities. 'They belong', he wrote, 'to a class of writing which includes the *Golden Ass* of Apuleius, the *True Histories of Lucius*, *Peter Schlemil* and the story of *Frankenstein*.'[10] As we shall see, their relationship to *Frankenstein* is closer than mere membership of the same general class. To begin with, *Moreau* succeeded in becoming the first member of this class to stir the same outrage and

---

[9] William C. Morrow, *The Ape, The Idiot, and Other People* (London, 1898), 273.
[10] *The Scientific Romances of H. G. Wells* (London, 1933), vii. Wells claimed mistakenly in the preface to this collection that his tales were novel in their rejection of magical intrusions: 'Frankenstein even, used some jiggery-pokery magic to animate his artificial monster. There was trouble about the thing's soul.' (viii.) Wells here recalls later elements in the myth rather than Mary Shelley's distinctly unmagical novel itself.

disgust among its first readers that *Frankenstein* provoked. Wells was justified, though, in feeling disappointed at this work being received as 'a mere shocker',[11] for behind the distressing emphasis on physical pain in this story lurk much larger issues. The *Guardian* reviewer, more perceptive than the others, asked whether *Moreau* was meant to 'rebuke the presumption of science' or to parody God's creation of man.[12] This is precisely the difficulty that readers of *Frankenstein* have had in trying to place it either as a conservative moral fable or as an impious Romantic travesty of God's providence. Moreau is certainly more than just a man who aspires to usurp divine powers. Within his island world he is regarded as a god; he is, as Bernard Bergonzi points out, a 'perverted image of Prospero',[13] with his creatures cast as Calibans (his assistant Montgomery, by giving brandy to M'ling, recalls the similar tormenting of Caliban by Trinculo and Stephano). These Beast Folk appear to worship Moreau in their chanting of the chorus '*His* is the hand that makes', and in their tenuous adherence to 'the law', a parody of the Mosaic Decalogue.[14] Prendick's speech to the Beast Folk, denying that Moreau is dead, is again a mischievous echo of the Christian resurrection.

That it should be animals rather than corpses that Moreau uses as his raw materials is a clear reflection of Wells's Darwinian interests: Moreau is used as a model of a cruelly indifferent and bungling 'God' of the evolutionary process, the implication being that *homo sapiens* is a freak or an abortive creature of chance, in the same way that the Beast Folk are products of trial and error—mainly error. As Bergonzi recognizes, Moreau represents not just unethical scientific conduct, but the arbitrariness of natural selection: 'He is Frankenstein— the would-be creator of life—in a post-Darwinian guise.'[15]

For all his more extensive and, at first, more successful endeavours in what he calls 'man-making' (*DM*, 105), Moreau's career follows the same pattern as Frankenstein's. A bachelor, he falls under 'the overmastering spell of research' and is gripped by an 'intellectual

[11] Cited by Bernard Bergonzi, *The Early H. G. Wells: A Study of the Scientific Romances* (Manchester, 1961), 98.
[12] Ibid., 98.
[13] Ibid., 110.
[14] H. G. Wells, *The Island of Doctor Moreau* (Harmondsworth, 1946), 86. Subsequent page references in the text are to this edition, abbreviated as *DM*.
[15] Bergonzi, *Early H. G. Wells*, 108.

passion' for vivisection and ultimately for the manufacture of humanoids from animal parts (*DM*, 49, 105). Seeking seclusion for his research, he hides away from his fellow-creatures on his own island, an outcast driven away by public opinion after his first experiments. Finally, one of his half-created monsters—a humanized she-puma—breaks loose from the laboratory, turns upon Moreau, and kills him. The essential poetic justice of Moreau's fate again follows the example of Frankenstein's, hinging as it does on his neglect of his own creatures. The pitiful Beast Folk wandering the island are all Moreau's rejects who have failed to become fully human, and are relapsing into their original forms. His assistant Montgomery takes some interest in them but, Moreau insists, 'It's his business, not mine. They only sicken me with a sense of failure. I take no interest in them.' (*DM*, 113.) The narrative form of *Moreau* does not allow us, as in *Frankenstein*, to register the full weight of injustice and misery this imposes upon the monsters, but the narrator Prendick does reflect on it all the same, once he has partly overcome his initial disgust at these creatures.

Poor brutes! I began to see the viler aspect of Moreau's cruelty. I had not thought before of the pain and trouble that came to these poor victims after they had passed from Moreau's hands. . . . Before, they had been beasts, their instincts fitly adapted to their surroundings, and happy as living things may be. Now they stumbled in the shackles of humanity, lived in a fear that never died, fretted by a law they could not understand; their mock-human existence began in an agony, was one long internal struggle, one long dread of Moreau—and for what? It was the wantonness that stirred me. . . . I could have forgiven him a little even had his motive been hate. But he was so irresponsible, so utterly careless. His curiosity, his mad, aimless investigations, drove him on, and the things were thrown out to live a year or so, to struggle, and blunder, and suffer; at last to die painfully. (*DM*, 138)

Moreau's indifference leaves his creatures with the worst of both worlds: they are driven by animal instinct to struggle with one another, but are held back by human law from arriving at any decisive resolution of that struggle.

This whole series of reflections on the dilemma of the Beast Folk is a thinly-veiled allegory of human existence itself; in case Wells's impious indictment of his Darwinian 'God' escapes us, he has Prendick preface these thoughts with the realization that on Moreau's island 'I had here before me the whole balance of human life in miniature, the whole interplay of instinct, reason, and fate, in its simplest form' (*DM*, 138). As Prendick acclimatizes himself to these extraordinary conditions, he comes to see that they are, after all, not so unlike those of the human world from whose own cannibalistic strife he has—by pure chance—been rescued. Montgomery also finds, on his infrequent trips to Africa for new animal stock, that the sailors he travels with seem just as strange to him as the Beast Folk do to Prendick. This disturbance of human norms finally stays with Prendick upon his return to London, where he feels a Swiftian estrangement from his fellows: 'I could not persuade myself that the men and women I met were not also another, still passably human, Beast People, animals half-wrought into the outward image of human souls, and that they would presently begin to revert, to show first this bestial mark and then that.' (*DM*, 189.) When Prendick sees 'weary pale workers go coughing by . . . with tired eyes and eager paces like wounded deer dripping blood' (*DM*, 191), he is clearly reinterpreting the struggle for existence in the capitalist metropolis as, only too literally, the law of the jungle. Wells suggests, through his hero's apparent delusion, that such a competitive struggle of each against all is the sign of a reversion to the bestial. *The Island of Doctor Moreau* is not just a travesty of religion's conflict with instinct, or of divine creation and its cruel injustice; it is also a fable which directs its painful probings at the contemporary miscreation of the world that we call human.

If Moreau appears to telescope the arbitrary processes of Darwinian natural selection into the single moment of his experiment, other Victorian representations of the monstrous are content to prognosticate the future emergence of man-made monsters from the more gradual fruition of trends already observable, but extrapolated fictionally into the distant future. This is clearly the method of Wells's own *The Time Machine*. Before examining this work, it will be worth noticing an important precedent for its concerns in Samuel Butler's *Erewhon*, in which the satirical speculations of the 'Book of the Machines' foresee the evolution of machines into a master-race subduing a servile humanity. More important, perhaps, than this in itself implausible vision is the degree to which, in this work, people can already be represented as machines and as machine-products. As Carlyle had feared, it had now become possible to speak of human identity as if its mechanical nature were taken for granted. So even the counter-argument which Butler's narrator offers against the prognosis of the 'Book of the Machines' rests on the equation of human limbs with machines: 'a leg', he claims, 'is only a much better wooden leg than anyone can manufacture'.[16] The Book itself argues more directly that 'Man's very soul is due to the machines; it is a machine-made thing: he thinks as he thinks, and feels as he feels, through the work that machines have wrought upon him.' (*E*, 207.)

Butler's point is not that people are literally machine-made, of course, but that the essential conditions of their lives are moulded by their reliance upon mechanical power. And it is from this creeping state of dependence, reaching into the heart of the modern personality, that the author of the 'Book of the Machines' draws his machine-breaking conclusions:

. . . it is the machines which act upon man and make him man, as much as man who has acted upon and made the machine; but we must choose between the alternative of undergoing much present suffering, or seeing ourselves gradually superseded by our own creatures, till we rank no higher in comparison with them, than the beasts of the field with ourselves. (*E*, 221)

Our habitual view of machines as servants is comforting but, this author insists, delusive, a product of the machines' cunning: 'they serve that they may rule', encouraging human dependence upon them so that 'the servant glides by imperceptible approaches into the master' (*E*, 207, 206). The grievance which these machines are said to hold against their creators is, like that of Frankenstein's monster, a feeling of neglect. As a penance for this, human beings will be condemned to act out the assembling role of Victor Frankenstein in their new servitude, helping the machines 'in either burying their dead or working up their deceased members into new forms of mechanical existence' (*E*, 221).

Behind the anxieties provisionally entertained in the shadow of the narrator's—and Butler's—scepticism, there lies a more pressing problem of nineteenth-century life: it is not difficult to find in the 'Book of the Machines' an expression of bourgeois forebodings, less about machines themselves than, more literally, about the servants becoming masters. The most distressing of the questions posed in the Book carries no direct reference to machines: 'Are we not ourselves creating our successors in the supremacy of the earth? daily adding to the beauty and delicacy of their organisation, daily

---

[16] Samuel Butler, *Erewhon*, ed. Peter Mudford (Harmondsworth, 1970), 223. Subsequent page references in the text are to this edition, abbreviated as *E*.

giving them greater skill and supplying more and more of that self-regulating self-acting power which will be better than any intellect?' (*E*, 209.) The terms of this question seem to apply more to the refashioned people of the working class in the new age of mass education and advanced technical skills, than to machines alone. Growing industrialization only increases the power, skill, and self-organization of this class; while on a wider scale, colonial expansion helps to prepare other peoples for 'the supremacy of the earth'.[17]

It is to issues like these that Wells's *The Time Machine* more openly addresses itself, forecasting a sinister reversal of mastery and servitude brought about by mechanical technology. Wells's tale of time-travel manages at the same time to translate the dualities of *Dr Jekyll and Mr Hyde* back into terms of social development and class struggle, through the fictional device of evolutionary prophecy. Time and natural selection between them bring about the transformation that once had to be concocted in the laboratory, producing in the Eloi and the Morlocks the Jekylls and Hydes of historical development.

Wells astutely attributes to the Time Traveller a sense of complacency in the apparently idyllic world of the Eloi, which turns sour with his discovery of a hidden underworld of pallid monsters. Now forced to revise his attitudes, he attempts to account for the existence of an artificial underworld by proposing a 'splitting of the human race' which directly implicates the Victorian capitalist class structure:

At first, proceeding from the problems of our own age, it seemed as clear as daylight to me that the gradual widening of the present merely temporary and social difference between the Capitalist and the Labourer, was the key to the whole position. No doubt it will seem grotesque enough to you — and wildly incredible! — and yet even now there are existing circumstances to point that way. . . . Even now, does not an East-end worker live in such artificial conditions as practically to be cut off from the natural surface of the earth?[18]

---

[17] *Erewhon* is set in New Zealand — more exactly, in a colony which the narrator refuses to name lest this information give his readers a commercial advantage in its exploitation.

[18] H. G. Wells, *The Time Machine* (London, 1935), 55–6. Subsequent page references in the text are to this edition, abbreviated as *TM*. Wells's Morlocks are anticipated by the sinister subterranean figure of Jeanlin, who hides down a disused coal-mine in Émile Zola's *Germinal* (1885). '[Etienne] felt strangely troubled as he contemplated this child who, with his pointed muzzle, green eyes, long ears, resembled some degenerate with the instinctive intelligence and craftiness of a savage, gradually reverting to man's origins. The pit had made him what he was . . .' Foreshadowing

If the Morlocks are an extrapolation of Victorian Labour buried away in underground works, then the Eloi are just as clearly the remote offspring of West-End decadence and corrupting comfort, the upper world produced by the labour of the lower. Each race is very much the creature of artificial conditions, but the Eloi— presumably because they have exempted themselves from the invigorating Darwinian exigencies of struggle—have lost their predominance and are now little more than the decorative domesticated livestock of their former servants, who now keep them for meat. Wells points up the moral unmistakably: 'The Nemesis of the delicate ones was creeping on apace. Ages ago, thousands of generations ago, man had thrust his brother man out of the ease and the sunshine. And now that brother was coming back—changed!' (*TM*, 66.)

Despite this recognition of the poetic justice at work in the evolutionary development, the Time Traveller is none the less committed to defending the childlike Eloi against the violent Morlocks. He is incapable of translating his grasp of historical trends into an immediate considered partisanship. 'Since the Morlocks on one level stand for the nineteenth-century proletariat,' writes Bergonzi, 'the Traveller's attitude towards them symbolizes a contemporary bourgeois fear of the working class, and it is not too fanciful to impute something of this attitude to Wells himself.'[19] The Time Traveller is indeed meant to be close, in his attitudes, both to Wells and to an assumed bourgeois reading public. Unlike many other scientists in this tradition, he is no Frankensteinian transgressor, but a helpless witness, an amiable and gregarious bourgeois, as Bergonzi points out. Even his vestigial Prometheanism is of a casually bungling sort: he brings fire (in the form of a box of matches in his pocket) into a world which has forgotten it, but can find little to do with it except to entertain the Eloi, until he sees its usefulness as a weapon against the Morlocks—at which point he manages to start a forest fire in which his pet nymph Weena is killed. Thanks to the dangerous gift of fire, the Traveller thus kills the very thing he loves (or at least that he fondles: Weena's sentimental status is an embarrassing weakness of the tale). This movement whereby the

---

the Morlocks again, Etienne later regards the class struggle in Darwinian terms, asking himself 'if one class had to be devoured, surely the people, vigorous and young, must devour the effete and luxury-loving bourgeoisie?' *Germinal*, trans. L. W. Tancock (Harmondsworth, 1954), 265, 496.

[19] Bergonzi, *Early H. G. Wells*, 56.

discoveries of human ingenuity—from the domestication of fire to the building of underground factories—recoil upon those who vainly imagine that they are in control of them, is reinforced in the story's epilogue, where the Traveller, despite his disappearance, has the last word through the narrator's recollection of his pessimistic views: 'He, I know—for the question had been discussed among us long before the Time Machine was made—thought but cheerlessly of the Advancement of Mankind, and saw in the growing pile of civilization only a foolish heaping that must inevitably fall back upon and destroy its makers in the end.' (*TM*, 105.)

Wells has too often been regarded as the smug prophet of technological progress and Utopian complacencies, but his most powerful fictional work is in fact far less sanguine about the prospects of amelioration through scientific discoveries. Repeatedly, Wells's stories turn on the failure of the best-laid scientific plans to overcome the pettiest everyday problems and popular prejudices. The seemingly all-powerful Martians in *The War of the Worlds* are defeated by the common cold, while the protagonist of the celebrated short story 'The Country of the Blind' has to abandon his dreams of power in the face of unforeseen practical difficulties which transform him from would-be king to terrified pariah. In his short stories Wells often follows the pattern of Eliot's 'The Lifted Veil', using the 'dangerous gifts' plot to show that what at first seems a miraculous blessing is, in the workaday world, a curse. Like Eliot again, he resorts to the laboratory setting even when the tale ('A Slip Under the Microscope' or 'The Reconciliation', for instance) does not really require it. Wells's scientists tend to come from Gower Street rather than central Europe, and they are short-sighted bunglers rather than world-conquering maniacs. The zealous young physicist in 'Filmer' invents a flying machine, but is trapped between a desire to show off the invention and an equally strong fear of heights, ending as a suicide. Likewise, the secretive and ambitious protagonist of 'The Diamond Maker' discovers a technique for making gems of a quality and value beyond even the dreams of the alchemists, but is foiled by the practical social problem of selling his fabulous products without being suspected of theft.

In all these tales the ordinary world of social expectations and suspicions proves to be a more powerful force than the brilliance of the inventor, reducing him to the position of an outcast. Wells's most extended exercise in this vein is *The Invisible Man* (1897), a study in failed scientific ambition which could be taken as a slapstick version of *Frankenstein*: the novel echoes Mary Shelley's narrative form by embedding Griffin's own account of his experiment in the central chapters; and it includes, like *Moreau*, deliberately impious allusions to God's creation when Griffin manifests himself to the tramp Marvel as 'The Voice', choosing him as his earthly representative. Griffin shows prominent Frankensteinian traits of secluded ambition, which seem now to have hardened into the cliché of the Mad Scientist. He hides his researches from his professor, determined to 'become famous at a blow',[20] and is too busy with this secret even to clear his ruined father's name after bringing about his suicide. Increasingly detached from family and public life, he regards his former girlfriend as 'very ordinary' (*IM*, 116), and devotes himself instead to his true love—his chemical apparatus. Once his experiment in invisibility succeeds, though, Griffin is forced to confront the petty problems of the ordinary world which his grandiose ambition has so scornfully ignored. He may have conquered the mysteries of chemistry, but he is helpless before snow, muddy footprints, prying landladies, and his own digestive system.

Griffin's decline from the sublimity of scientific achievement to the ridiculous sporting of a false nose turns out, however, to be no real transformation at all. He is shown to have been, all along, as petty as the village yokels he despises, since his invisibility can have no useful function other than to help him in petty thieving and in schoolboy pranks like the debagging of the vicar. Frankenstein's tragedy is repeated as farce, although the conclusions to be drawn are similar in Griffin's confession of failure:

The more I thought it over, Kemp, the more I realised what a helpless absurdity an Invisible Man was—in a cold and dirty climate and a crowded, civilised city. Before I made this mad experiment I had dreamt of a thousand advantages. That afternoon it seemed all disappointment. I went over the heads of the things a man reckons desirable. No doubt invisibility made it possible to get them, but it made it impossible to enjoy them when they are got. Ambition—what is the good of pride of place when you cannot appear there? What is the good of the love of women when her name must needs be Delilah? I have no taste for politics, for the blackguardisms of fame, for philanthropy, for sport. What was I to do? And for this I had become a wrapped up mystery, a swathed and bandaged caricature of a man. (*IM*, 148)

---

[20] H. G. Wells, *The Invisible Man* (Harmondsworth, 1938), 112. Subsequent page references in the text are to this edition, abbreviated as *IM*.

Griffin's search for invisibility is, like Jekyll's experiment, an attempt to escape that world of personal responsibilities which only reappears in more humiliating forms the more one tries to evade it. Like Jekyll, Griffin becomes both Frankenstein and the monster at once; the continuity between the secrecy of the self-exiled scientist and the loneliness of the hunted outcast is not impeded in this story by the creation of any 'second self'. Although the comic pranks, and Griffin's inexplicable urge to establish a 'reign of terror', are glaring weaknesses in the novel, the imaginative logic of irresponsibility turning into monstrosity remains convincing; it is summed up in the death sentence pronounced by Kemp: 'He has cut himself off from his kind. His blood be upon his own head.' (*IM*, 157.)

Of *The Invisible Man* Bernard Bergonzi remarks that 'Griffin is not only Wells's last version of the romantic scientist of the Frankenstein type, but also his most fully realised'.[21] More obviously even than Moreau, Griffin pays the price for his irresponsible Frankensteinian withdrawal from social ties. He undergoes at humiliating length the ordeal of many other Wellsian scientists, defeated by the unshakeable resistance of petty material obstacles to his idealist dream of power and fame. That this should be Wells's last exercise in the Frankensteinian mode—and so early in his writing career—is a sign that his very success with it had worn the convention thin; the ponderous element of slapstick, along with Griffin's unaccountable ambitions of world conquest, seem to indicate an exhaustion of this Frankensteinian vein in Victorian fiction, as Wells allows it to lapse into the predictable forms of the Mad Scientist cliché.

[21] Bergonzi, *Early H. G. Wells*, 120.

# 8

## Monsters of Empire:
## Conrad and Lawrence

> The need of a constantly expanding market for its
> products chases the bourgeoisie over the whole surface
> of the globe.
>
> Marx and Engels, *The Communist Manifesto*

Wells may have brought the Frankenstein myth's fictional exploitation
to one kind of dead end in *The Invisible Man*, but in *The Island
of Doctor Moreau* he had opened it out in another direction already
foreshadowed by the colonial setting of Butler's *Erewhon*. Moreau's
island settlement, like Prospero's before it, is a colony, and his efforts
to 'raise' his Beast Folk to his own condition reflect in macabre form
the cruelties and dangers of late-Victorian imperialism and its
'civilizing mission'. In English fiction the most powerfully imaginative
extension of the Frankenstein myth to this imperialist period and
to the forces at work in it, which would spill out of control in the
wars and revolutions of 1914–18, are to be found in the work of
Joseph Conrad and D. H. Lawrence.

Conrad had read *The Time Machine* and *The Island of Doctor
Moreau* in the mid-1890s, and it seems quite possible that he lifted
the narrative frame of his *Heart of Darkness* from Wells's use
of a group of anonymous professionals sitting in darkness listening
to the Time Traveller. Conrad was repeatedly concerned, too,
with the theme of transgression, especially in the form of 'that
immoral detachment from mankind . . . fostered by the unhealthy
conditions of solitude' which the Editor in 'The Planter of Malata'
condemns.[1] But the solitaries and transgressors in his fiction are
not scientists or inventors; these latter meddlers he held responsible
for unforgiveable destruction to the ships and men of his own beloved
profession, and he dismissed them with harsh sarcasm. On the
inventors of modern armaments he wrote, in his memoir *The Mirror
of the Sea*,

---

[1] Joseph Conrad, *Within the Tides* (Harmondsworth, 1978), 33–4.

The learned vigils and labours of a certain class of inventors should have been rewarded with honourable liberality as justice demanded; and the bodies of the inventors should have been blown to pieces by means of their own perfected explosives and improved weapons with extreme publicity as the commonest prudence dictated. By this method the ardour of research in that direction would have been restrained without infringing the sacred privileges of science.[2]

Conrad's most memorable transgressors go to their remote hideouts not to invent or experiment like Moreau, but to exploit raw materials and cheap labour. They seek gold, silver, or ivory, not in the alchemist's crucible but by means of colonial pillage.

The remaining link in Conrad's fiction between the quest for heroic discoveries and the sordid scramble for raw materials is that they are both conducted by deluded men who imagine themselves to be benefactors of the human race. Charles Gould in *Nostromo* disobeys his father's instruction not to reopen the 'cursed' San Tomé silver-mine (which has afflicted him with dreams of vampires), in the belief that the weight of 'material interests' will stabilize the chaotic state of Costaguana. At first, this civilizing ideal appears to have been realized, but by the end of the novel we are obliged to conclude with Dr Monygham that 'There is no peace and no rest in the development of material interests. They have their law, and their justice. But it is founded on expediency, and is inhuman.'[3] The inhuman logic of the silver-mine and the railway (and by extension, that of capitalist development in general) will come, Monygham predicts, to oppress the people of Costaguana as heavily as the barbaric misrule from which Gould has intended his enterprise to liberate them. An imperialist Adam, Gould has literally undermined the 'paradise of snakes' at Sulaco, setting in motion an inhuman logic beyond his control, which in true Frankensteinian fashion separates him and his obsession from his wife.

Mrs Gould continued along the corridor away from her husband's room. The fate of the San Tomé mine was lying heavy upon her heart. It was a long time now since she had begun to fear it. It had been an idea. She had watched it with misgivings turning into a fetish, and now the fetish had grown into a monstrous and crushing weight. It was as if the inspiration of their

     [2] Joseph Conrad, *The Mirror of the Sea; with A Personal Record* (London, 1947), 150. Subsequent page references in the text are to this edition, abbreviated as *MS*.
     [3] Joseph Conrad, *Nostromo: A Tale of the Seaboard*, ed. Martin Seymour-Smith (Harmondsworth, 1983), 423.

early years had left her heart to turn into a work of silver-bricks, erected by the
silent work of evil spirits, between her and her husband. He seemed to dwell
alone within a circumvallation of precious metal, leaving her outside . . .[4]

The corrupting lure of the silver-mine here is in part a more restrained
version of Hoffmann's 'The Mines at Falun', a fable of industrial
transgression presented as a Fall from the Paradise of snakes into
unwitting idolatry, which leaves Gould and Nostromo morally
compromised and Martin Decoud, like Judas, fatally weighed down
by his pieces of silver. The pacific ideal of material progress has
engendered an industrial monster which crushes it under the full
weight of commodity fetishism.

Similar ideals are overtaken by their own creatures in *Heart of
Darkness*, a novella which bears a number of uncanny resemblances
to the design of *Frankenstein*. The equatorial equivalent of Walton's
voyage, Marlow's expedition to the Congo is likewise a young man's
quest for the limits of the known world, which becomes, in his
encounter with the central transgressor-figure, a revelation of moral
chaos and uncertainty. Like *Frankenstein*, and like *Moby Dick*
too,[5] *Heart of Darkness* takes the path of masculine adventure and
exploration to its self-destructive terminus, self-consciously excluding
the world of women ('We must help them to stay in that beautiful
world of their own', Marlow insists[6]), to whom the true story
cannot even be told. In the narrative structure of *Heart of Darkness*
we have another case of that concentric design favoured by high
Romantic fiction: Kurtz's vision of horror is distanced by a third-
hand account, as if it were too scorching to be met directly, while
at the same time some of its implications can be brought home
through the conduit of Marlow to disturb his civilized auditors in
London, thus bringing the Heart of Empire into correspondence,
complicity, even equivalence, with the Heart of Darkness.

Kurtz is unmistakably the typical Transgressor. The wilderness
has 'beguiled his unlawful soul beyond the bounds of permitted

[4] Ibid., 204–5.
[5] Conrad dismissed *Moby Dick* as a strained and wholly insincere work (letter
to Humphrey Milford, 15 Jan. 1907, cited by Harold Beaver in *Moby Dick*, 20).
None the less, *Heart of Darkness* is his version of Melville's tale, just as *The Shadow-
Line* is his version of 'The Rime of the Ancient Mariner'.
[6] Joseph Conrad, *Heart of Darkness*, ed. Paul O'Prey (Harmondsworth, 1983).
Subsequent page references in the text are to this edition, abbreviated as *HD*. The
function of women in Conrad's fiction is very often to be told soothing lies.

aspirations' (*HD*, 107), but the apparent point of divergence from the Frankenstein tradition is that neither Marlow nor Kurtz creates anything: Kurtz is nearer to Captain Ahab, in that he is both an ungodly-godlike transgressor and a factitious and miscreated agent of civilized trade who runs destructively out of his masters' control. Like Ahab, he does his job too well, too single-mindedly and obsessively for the comfort of his Starbucks and Pelegs; his ghastly surplus of ivory exposing too openly the barbaric nature of the pillage they have undertaken. The excess of his productivity in looting ivory is the mocking counterpart to that excess of idealism over mere trade which Kurtz has brought to Africa, and which distinguishes Gould and Ahab too. Kurtz at first tells the other managers that 'Each station should be like a beacon on the road towards better things, a centre for trade of course, but also for humanizing, improving, instructing' (*HD*, 65). But it is just this surplus of civilizing zeal which is the real danger in Kurtz, since it already gives him a role he imagines to be that of a god; that he should come to be worshipped idolatrously is the fulfilment of his missionary presumption. For all his high ideals, he is reduced to the position of a 'pitiful Jupiter' (*HD*, 100), a mere 'voice', a hollow mouthpiece for the existing fetishism of ivory.

Kurtz is a factitious 'god', made up of bits of European civilization, like the harlequin suit of his Russian follower, or like the multicoloured map over which Marlow pores. 'His mother was half-English, his father was half-French. All Europe contributed to the making of Kurtz.' (*HD*, 86.) And Kurtz eventually returns to confront his creators in Marlow's narrative. Marlow's function—like Walton's—is to hear the dying words of the transgressor and report them back to the heart of civilization, his own early zeal for exploration now chastened (as a boy, Marlow has a passion for exploring the map's blank spaces at the North Pole and the Equator). Moreover, he is able to bring home from the Congo, like some contaminated cargo, an unsettling acknowledgement of kinship with the monstrous. The connection stretches from the untamed nature of the jungle—'monstrous and free', as Marlow describes it—through the natives ('what thrilled you', he explains, 'was just the thought of their humanity—like yours—the thought of your remote kinship with this wild and passionate uproar' (*HD*, 69)), via Kurtz and Marlow in a chain of such recognitions which ends with the Accountant, the Lawyer, the Director of Companies, and finally the reader. As Frankenstein's monster demands acknowledgement of kinship from his creator, who is in turn recognised as a brother by Walton in his letters home to his sister, so the impossibility of disavowing the monstrous consequences of imperialism is brought home to the metropolis itself, to London, 'the monstrous town' (*HD*, 29).

It is in this London that Alvan Hervey, the protagonist of Conrad's tale 'The Return', has a vision of monstrosity beginning with the shock of his wife's desertion and spreading to embrace the whole of that civilized urban life of which he is the polished representative.

The contamination of her crime spread out, tainted the universe, tainted himself; woke up all the dormant infamies of the world; caused a ghastly kind of clairvoyance in which he could see the towns and fields of the earth, its sacred places, its temples and its houses, peopled by monsters—by monsters of duplicity, lust, and murder. She was a monster—he himself was thinking monstrous thoughts . . . and yet he was like other people.[7]

Monstrosity is again brought home from the 'criminal' fringe, and revealed in the ordinary, the quotidian, and the domestic. Conrad himself shows just such a 'ghastly kind of clairvoyance' in his fiction, stripping away his characters' illusions with his acid scepticism, to expose them as disconnected jumbles of monstrous impulses.

Like Dickens, Conrad peoples his novels with characters who have hardened into corpse-like automata. He sets *The Secret Agent* in a darker and more artificial version of Dickens's London, 'a monstrous town more populous than some continents and in its man-made might as if indifferent to heaven's frowns and smiles'.[8] This London is itself a man-made monster set apart from any natural morality. Its own mad scientist, the Professor, directs his 'frenzied puritanism of ambition' (*SA*, 102) towards the perfecting of an explosive charge which will reduce himself and all those around him to fragments. In the same novel Mr Verloc—another agent who has gone blunderingly and destructively beyond his masters' intentions—is presented as an absurd monstrosity: 'Mr Verloc [moved] woodenly, stony-eyed, and like an automaton whose face has been painted red. And this resemblance to a mechanical figure went so far that he had an

---

[7] Joseph Conrad, *Tales of Unrest* (Harmondsworth, 1977), 126.
[8] Joseph Conrad, *The Secret Agent: A Simple Tale*, ed. Martin Seymour-Smith (Harmondsworth, 1984), 40–1 (Author's Note). Subsequent page references in the text are to this edition, abbreviated as *SA*.

automaton's absurd air of being aware of the machinery inside of him.' (*SA*, 186.) Verloc belongs to a large family of such Dickensian effigies in Conrad's works: Kayerts and Carlier in 'An Outpost of Progress' are puppets of Society's routines, who 'could only live on condition of being machines',[9] while in *Victory* Wang has an 'unreal cardboard face' which we see 'grimacing artificially', and Morrison too moves 'like an automaton'.[10] In the same novel Mrs Schonberg is described repeatedly as a mechanism, automaton, or dummy capable only of nodding its head, and Heyst sees the people around him as 'figures cut out of cork' (*V*, 150). His antagonist, Jones, is constantly referred to as a spectre (accompanying the 'tame monster' Pedro), his appearance being 'gruesomely malevolent, as of a wicked and pitiless corpse' (*V*, 306). The first mate Burns in *The Shadow-Line* looks like a scarecrow or an 'animated skeleton', while in *The Nigger of the 'Narcissus'* James Wait 'looked as ridiculously lamentable as a doll that had lost half its sawdust'.[11]

Several other Conrad characters have this appearance of being dolls — Babalatchi in *An Outcast of the Islands*, Laspara's daughters in *Under Western Eyes*, and Heemskirk's warrant officer in 'Freya of the Seven Isles', who appears, like Wait, to have been stuffed. It is the idea of losing one's stuffing that gives a clue to the function of these Conradian marionettes. Conrad's use of monstrosity follows a traditional moral convention, as we shall see below, and in the case of his dolls and automata, the lack of an organic interior figuratively presents a moral evacuation: lacking any coherent moral purpose or ideal around which their actions can be organized, these people are hollowed out into a crustacean stupidity, their lives reduced to a repertoire of meaningless gestures. The horror of which Kurtz speaks is already hinted at and given disturbing concreteness by Marlow when he describes the company agent at Central Station as a 'papier-mâché Mephistopheles'. As Marlow tells us, 'it seemed to me that if I tried I could poke my forefinger through him, and would find nothing inside but a little loose dirt, maybe.' (*HD*, 56.) This character is a mere social machine, like his counterparts Kayerts

⁹ Conrad, *Tales of Unrest*, 87.
¹⁰ Joseph Conrad, *Victory: An Island Tale* (Harmondsworth, 1963), 278, 25. Subsequent page references in the text are to this edition, abbreviated as *V*.
¹¹ Joseph Conrad, *The Shadow-Line: A Confession*, ed. Jeremy Hawthorn (Oxford, 1985), 86; *The Nigger of the 'Narcissus', Typhoon, and Other Stories* (Harmondsworth, 1963), 67.

and Carlier—all of them as brittle as the ivory they worship, all
hollow men.

It is the hollow women, though, who are more alarming still in
Conrad's eyes. In the short story 'Because of the Dollars', the wild
laughter of the former prostitute Anne startles Captain Davidson 'like
a galvanic shock to a corpse'; while the irresistible flesh of Hermann's
niece in 'Falk' provokes the narrator to describe her with a nervous
jocularity as if she were a ship: 'All I know is that she was built on
a magnificent scale. Built is the only word. She was constructed, she
was erected, as it were, with regal lavishness.'[12] A more macabre
(and again nameless) female construction, bearing some resemblance
to Mrs Skewton in *Dombey and Son*, is Madame de S—— in
*Under Western Eyes*. Conrad's intense discomfort with women and
with democratic politics expresses itself here (under the guise of
Razumov's revulsion) in repeated violent dismemberments of this
character.

> At that moment he hated Madame de S——. But it was not exactly hate.
> It was more like the abhorrence that may be caused by a wooden or plaster
> figure of a repulsive kind. She moved no more than if she were such a figure;
> even her eyes, whose unwinking stare plunged into his own, though shining,
> were lifeless, as though they were as artificial as her teeth.[13]

In Razumov's vividly disordered perception, this salon anarchist
confronts him as a 'grinning skull', a 'painted mummy', and worse
still, 'like a galvanised corpse out of some Hoffmann's Tale' ( *WE*,
182). As she speaks of extirpating the Czar and his family, she is
again presented as a hardened type of inauthenticity: 'Her rigidity
was frightful, like the rigour of a corpse galvanised into harsh speech
and glittering stare by the force of murderous hate.' ( *WE*, 187.) The
force of hatred here is more likely to be Razumov's, the rigidity that
of Conrad's resistance to democratic 'fanaticism', above all in women.
When other writers want to scare themselves and their readers, they
introduce a ghost; Conrad brings in a woman, for him the most
fearful figure of ghastly artificiality.

Conrad's monstrosities are, clearly enough, traditionally allegorical
representatives of inner moral faults, projected in the form of physical
deformity and horror. The clearest such case, and one which carries

---

[12] Conrad, *Within the Tides*, 159; *Nigger*, 263.
[13] Joseph Conrad, *Under Western Eyes* (Harmondsworth, 1957), 190. Subsequent
page references in the text are to this edition, abbreviated as *WE*.

some echoes of Mary Shelley's description of her monster in
*Frankenstein*, is the account of Cesar, a treacherous villain involved
in one of Conrad's first smuggling voyages as recalled in his *Mirror
of the Sea*:

His parchment skin, showing dead white on his cranium, seemed to be glued
directly and tightly upon his big bones. Without being in any way deformed,
he was the nearest approach which I have ever seen or could imagine to
what is commonly understood by the word 'monster'. That the source of
the effect produced was really moral I have no doubt. An utterly, hopelessly
depraved nature was expressed in physical terms, that each taken separately
had nothing positively startling. You imagined him clammily cold to the
touch, like a snake. (*MS*, 165–6.)

This clammy and rather artificial-looking person advertises in his
bodily appearance the fact that he is morally a monster of disloyalty
who betrays his fellow-sailors. This is a straightforward and
recognizable use of the idea of monstrosity; but what is more curious
in Conrad is that, while he readily attributes monstrosity to depraved
human hearts and to nature itself (as in *Heart of Darkness*), he will
not extend it to human artefacts in the way that Carlyle, Dickens,
and so many other writers did in the nineteenth century. On the
contrary, while Conrad makes some familiar observations on the
subordination of people to their products, his reflections on this
problem are quite at odds with that tradition. He writes in *Mirror
of the Sea* that 'we men are, in fact, the servants of our creations.
We remain in everlasting bondage to the productions of our brain
and to the work of our hands.' (*MS*, 25.) To Carlyle or Emerson
this state of affairs was cause for lamentation and protest, but for
Conrad it is a basis—perhaps the only basis—for hope: his pessimism
about human behaviour, almost pretentiously cosmic in its scope,
attributes a limitless depravity to all human action and a boundless
capacity for self-deception to all human thought, but it exempts our
artefacts from blame. It is we who are the monsters; our innocent
creatures are our betters, particularly if they be ships, and certainly
if they be sailing ships. As Conrad explains, 'a ship is a creature which
we have brought into the world, as it were on purpose to keep us
up to the mark.' (*MS*, 28.) Men have betrayed their ships, but
no ship can betray a man—it can only offer him the chance of
redemption, calling on his capacities for loyalty and duty to test
themselves in its service. If we do not serve the productions of our

hands and brains, Conrad suggests, then we would only revert to serving our vain and egotistical selves; only our works can call us out of our inner moral chaos towards some higher purpose.[14] There are common features in Conrad's attitudes to seamanship and to art which endorse this ideology of service, just as there is an equivalence between the workmanlike truthfulness of Marlow's navigation and that of his narration—both of them leading him out of the temptation represented by Kurtz.

The irony of all this is that the writer who so powerfully presented and condemned imperialism's commodity fetishism in the ivory-looting of *Heart of Darkness* should have done so from within an ideological position which is itself deeply fetishistic in conception. With Conrad's ideology of service, as with the Carlylean gospel of Work which prefigures it, there are serious problems. A code of duty to the task at hand and of unswerving loyalty to the collective yet hierarchical effort against the sea's perils is, by its unquestioning and immediately demanding nature, a palliative to certain kinds of cosmic scepticism; yet it only raises, beyond its immediate imperatives, the uncomfortable question, what further end does such maritime service itself serve? The depressing answer, and one which drags down (often literally) the basis of the sailor's enviable ethical certainties, is that the beloved creatures of which Conrad writes too often serve the contaminating greed and violence of the landlubber: murderous warfare, unscrupulous trade, and imperialist plunder. As surely as the old sailing craft of the Indian ocean succumbed to steam and the Suez Canal, so the clear moral directives of seamanship are sullied by piracy in its various forms, the pure ideals of maritime service being mocked by the unclean idols which call upon its devotion: ivory, silver, potatoes, rotten hippopotamus-meat, the dangerously smouldering coal in *Youth*, the dollar-crazed Chinamen in *Typhoon*. By serving that floating creature which Conrad casts as his better angel, the sailor becomes at the same time the servant of those fetishized 'material interests' which drag him back towards the bestial, and towards the monstrosity of imperialism's organized greed. Describing the imperialism of 'our modern Conquistadores' to his friend R. B. Cunninghame Graham, Conrad wrote that 'Their achievement is monstrous enough in all conscience—but not as a

---

[14] Conrad transfers to ships the role allotted by many Victorian writers to women: that of inspiring men to overcome their baser selves through a pure devotion.

great human force let loose, but rather like that of a gigantic and obscene beast.'[15] From this enormous monster the ideology of service was hardly likely to offer any escape.

The equivalent devotion and selflessness of the artist was unstable, too: Conrad was slow to come to writing, but then quick to discover that alarming sense of the printed word's alien and independent life which had disturbed Mary Shelley. The first time he saw his words in print—on receiving the proofs of *Almayer's Folly*—he was 'horrified by the thing in print', and disconcerted by a 'fear of the ghosts which one evokes oneself and which often refuse to obey the brain that has created them'.[16] Conrad felt the Frankensteinian problem as an artist confronted by his own products, and he gave us, in *Nostromo* and *Heart of Darkness*, powerful images of Frankensteinian transgression; but he was too complicit with prevailing forms of fetishism to have recognized, behind his conveniently isolated maritime model of 'service', the greater problem of who was serving what. In this sense, his attention to the unleashing of monstrous forces in the modern world is damagingly distracted, compromised in ways which make it far inferior to that of D. H. Lawrence.

Poles—not the Joseph Conrad sort, of course, but the magnetic, geographical, and conceptual—were as important to the thinking of D. H. Lawrence as they were to the dreams and ambitions of Mary Shelley's Walton. In Lawrence's formative years as a writer, Polar exploration again captured the world's attention as the old hopes of reaching the North and South Poles were at last realized by Peary in 1909 and Amundsen in 1911. Of this achievement Lawrence observed that 'the supreme little ego in man hates an unconquered universe. We shall never rest till we have heaped tin cans on the North Pole and South Pole, and put up barb-wire fences on the moon. Barb-wire fences are our sign of conquest. We have wreathed the world with them.'[17] Writing in 1915, Lawrence could see in retrospect the connection between the barbed-wire wreaths of the Great War and

[15] *Joseph Conrad's Letters to R. B. Cunninghame Graham*, ed. C. T. Watts (Cambridge, 1969), 148–9 (26 Dec. 1903).

[16] *The Collected Letters of Joseph Conrad, Volume 1: 1861–97*, ed. Frederick R. Karl and Laurence Davies (Cambridge, 1983), 425 (20 Dec. 1897).

[17] D. H. Lawrence, *Phoenix II: Uncollected, Unpublished and Other Prose Works*, ed. Warren Roberts and Harry T. Moore (London, 1968), 391.

the preceding scramble for territorial conquest symbolized by these Polar expeditions. In 1912, when Lawrence himself was exploring the North/South contrasts of European culture on his route from Germany to Italy, the British Empire suffered two humiliating and instantly legendary disasters, both of them inflicted by ice and cold: the death of Captain Scott's Antarctic team, and the sinking by an iceberg of the 'unsinkable' liner *Titanic* with the loss of more than 1,500 lives. In the enormous public impact of these events one can detect, so to speak, a new 'ice age' of the imagination threatening the expansive certainties of the great industrial empire. To the superstitious (among them Thomas Hardy in his poem 'The Convergence of the Twain'), the *Titanic* disaster revived familiar conservative warnings about tempting fate or titanically transgressing the limits to human control over the elements. The exertion of the human will (specifically, of the British will) had been humbled in an exemplary symbolic spectacle.

Out of this symbolic ice age of British imperial decline emerges Lawrence's most ambitiously representative fictional character, Gerald Crich in *Women in Love*. Gerald embodies the world-conquering will of the British industrial bourgeoisie, depicted in its agony of disorientation and self-destruction, drifting to an appropriately icy death. Our first ominous sight of Gerald Crich, through the eyes of Gudrun Brangwen in the opening chapter of the novel, fixes him inescapably in his polar identity: 'There was something northern about him which magnetized her. In his clear northern flesh and his fair hair was a glisten like cold sunshine through crystals of ice. And he looked so new, unbroached, pure as an arctic thing.'[18] Gerald is, as we shall see, a creature of northern mechanical will-power, and his trajectory in the novel is an almost exact reversal of the career of Frankenstein's monster: the latter is unleashed in the Alps and finally wanders off to the North Pole to kill himself, while Gerald makes his first appearance as an 'arctic thing' and dies after walking off into the snows of the Alps. It is quite possible that this design was not directly or consciously adapted by Lawrence from Mary Shelley, but it is clear that Lawrence is employing a Romantic vocabulary of geographical symbols derived from the Shelley–Byron circle's Alpine obsessions, and that

---

[18] D. H. Lawrence, *Women in Love*, ed. Charles L. Ross (Harmondsworth, 1982), 61. Subsequent page references in the text are to this edition, abbreviated as *WL*.

his equation of Alpine and Arctic zones parallels Mary Shelley's in reinforcing the symbolic impact of ice: for both novelists, these zones represent the dangers of unfeeling isolation which are courted by the mentality of challenge, aspiration, and the conquering will. To be born from one and to die in the other is to bind (even to define) the intervening north-European world in an embrace of death, wherein ashes return to ashes, ice to ice.

Gerald's 'arctic' nature and Alpine fate function partly to enhance his representative status as Northern Man, although Gudrun's very sudden recognition of this is well in advance of the reader's in the opening chapter. Only later does Lawrence's symbolic design emerge; while the world of *The Rainbow* is built with geometric and architectural figures (arches, columns, circles, portals), that of *Women in Love* is charged with electrical and magnetic imagery. Gudrun, as we have seen, is magnetized by Gerald, while Birkin's notorious loins of darkness are 'electric' in their power, and Lawrence even goes to the trouble of making Gudrun's previous lover an electrician. At a deeper level, Lawrence is working with an idea of magnetic attraction and repulsion, of basic polarity, which works through to his characters from the very sources of life itself. The cosmology which he had evolved in *The Study of Thomas Hardy* and *The Crown* in 1914 and 1915 had been built upon polarities of female and male, dark and light, power and love, flesh and spirit, which in their necessary opposition correspond broadly with the polarity of North and South in *Women in Love*.

There is some possible confusion in that now, the polar opposite of the Arctic is the Equatorial or African, not the Antarctic (Lawrence's horizons had not yet stretched as far as the antipodean *Kangaroo*); but the exposition of this polarity in Chapter XIX still clarifies considerably the initial mystery of Gerald's arctic attributes. As Birkin meditates on the African statuette he has seen at Halliday's flat, he sees the impending collapse of civilization as a fission in which the vital polar opposition of northern (male/rational/light) and southern (female/instinctual/dark) principles falls apart into separate processes of decomposition, one of which has already run its course in Africa:

There remained this way, this awful African process, to be fulfilled. It would be done differently by the white races. The white races, having the arctic north behind them, the vast abstraction of ice and snow, would fulfil a mystery of ice-destructive knowledge, snow-abstract annihilation. Whereas the West Africans, controlled by the burning death-abstraction of the

Sahara, had been fulfilled in sun-destruction, the putrescent mystery
of sun-rays. . . .

Birkin thought of Gerald. He was one of these strange white wonderful
demons from the north, fulfilled in the destructive frost-mystery. And was
he fated to pass away in this knowledge, this one process of frost-knowledge,
death by perfect cold? Was he a messenger, an omen of the universal
dissolution into whiteness and snow? ( *WL*, 331)

The polar extremes, Arctic and African, figure forth the destinations
allotted to the dissevered halves of European civilization as they burst
apart in the self-destruction of the Great War. Gerald as the harbinger
of the northern process of dissolution is made to return to his chosen
element, in that Alpine territory which Gudrun recognizes as 'the
centre, the knot, the navel of the world' ( *WL*, 492), as if to deliver
at this central junction of Latin and Germanic cultures his prophecy
of Europe's conquest by ice.

As a messenger of northern abstraction and destructive knowledge,
Gerald represents a process which is no longer a term in a vital
polarity, but a sheer negation of life. As William Blake had insisted,
there is a difference between contraries which are necessary to life,
and negations which are flatly opposed to it; the qualities embodied
in Gerald 'the denier' are terms in this latter kind of opposition, best
formulated in Lawrence's description of his industrial modernization
as 'the substitution of the mechanical principle for the organic' ( *WL*,
305). This pair of opposites stand, of course, as the central terms
of the Romantic critique of modern society since Schiller, Coleridge,
and Carlyle, and they are drawn into even more violent and repeated
confrontations throughout Lawrence's work. Gerald is the champion
and avatar of the mechanical principle in its insistent subordination
of the organic, not just in his industrial aims, but in his very
person. Like Kurtz, and like Captain Ahab (another 'northern
monomaniac'[19]), he resembles both Victor Frankenstein in the
enormity of his transgression and the monster in his artificially
assembled nature. He confesses that his life has no centre but is
'artificially held together by the social mechanism', he feels emptily
inert 'like a machine that is without power'; and the repetitive
rhythms of 'his clenched, mechanical body' finally repel Gudrun, who

---

[19] D. H. Lawrence, *Studies in Classic American Literature* (Harmondsworth,
1971), 166. Subsequent page references in the text are to this edition, abbreviated
as *SCAL*.

likens them to the clockwork regimentation of modern society: 'He, his body, his motion, his life—it was the same ticking, the same twitching across the dial, a horrible mechanical twitching forward over the face of the hours.' ( *WL*, 109, 344, 554, 564.) Gudrun recognizes here the same mechanical motion which she had felt, upon her return to Beldover, in the 'half-automated colliers' whose voices had sounded to her like strange machines ( *WL*, 174). She is reminded of its power when listening to Loerke (himself a kind of Morlock or 'obscene monster of the darkness' born from 'the underworld of life' ( *WL*, 522)) as he explains the fairground design on his frieze as an interpretation of modern industry. 'What is man doing,' asks Loerke, 'when he is at a fair like this? He is fulfilling the counterpart of labour—the machine works him instead of he the machine.' ( *WL*, 519.) This inversion certainly applies to Gerald, who is the God of the Machine, and at the same time its creature and victim.

Gerald's automatism is echoed in the repeated mechanical images applied to people in Lawrence's other early works. Lawrence's own first direct experience of modern industry was, unusually for the son of a mining village, not down t'pit but in a factory which made—of all things—artificial limbs. In *Sons and Lovers* he makes Paul Morel undergo the same initiation into monstrosity: 'It seemed monstrous', to Paul, 'that a business could be run on wooden legs.'[20] While the colliery, as Lawrence believed, still allowed some physical integrity to the miners, this kind of 'light' industry seemed more directly and visibly to subordinate human life to the mechanical principle. As Paul watches Clara Dawes working at her spinning jenny, 'her arm move[s] mechanically, that should never have been subdued to a machine' ( *SL*, 321). The same principle extends beyond the industrial to the military mechanism, when Mrs Morel defines a soldier as 'nothing but a body that makes movements when it hears a shout' ( *SL*, 234), and to the education system in *The Rainbow*, where Ursula sees the other teachers at Brinsley Street School as machines. Applying this diagnosis more widely, Lawrence has Ursula look down on her fellow-citizens from her new-found position of dark fecundity, seeing the passengers in the trains and trams as 'only dummies exposed . . . And all their talk and all their behaviour was sham, they were dressed-up creatures. She was reminded of the

[20] D. H. Lawrence, *Sons and Lovers*, ed. Keith Sagar (Harmondsworth, 1981), 133. Subsequent page references in the text are to this edition, abbreviated as *SL*.

Invisible Man, who was a piece of darkness made visible only by his clothes.'[21] Her lover Anton similarly despises the people around him as 'so many performing puppets, all wood and rag', equipped with 'man's legs, but man's legs become rigid and deformed, mechanical' (*R*, 500). At the centre of this pervasive mechanizing of human life is the colliery which Ursula sees on her visit to Uncle Tom in Wiggiston. The pit has become the governing principle of this town, reducing all life outside it to a mere side-show, 'human bodies and lives subjected in slavery to that symmetric monster of the colliery' (*R*, 397). To Ursula's horror, Winifred and Uncle Tom worship this 'impure abstraction', feeling happy and free only in its service, hypnotized by the power of 'the monstrous mechanism that held all matter, living or dead, in its service' (*R*, 397–8).

At this inclusive level of his social criticism, Lawrence assails modern industrial society as a monstrous machine, or as a huge deformed body devoted and enslaved to the machines it has created. America, he writes in *Studies in Classic American Literature*, has been 'mastered by her own machines' (*SCAL*, 27); and in earlier drafts of the same work he defines the organizing principle of American society as 'the perfect mechanical concord, the concord of a number of parts to a vast whole, a stupendous productive mechanism'.[22] Lawrence is referring not simply to the new assembly-line factory systems, but to the fearsome political monster of democracy itself. 'This thing, this mechanical democracy, new and monstrous on the face of the earth' (*SM*, 28) is for Lawrence a new Burkean nightmare of popular self-assertion, now equipped with overwhelming industrial power. Europe's domination was now, as Lawrence and many others saw, giving way to that of its American child, this 'monstrous reflection of Europe', this 'mechanical monstrosity of the west' (*SM*, 28, 29).

Confronted by the enormous body politic of modern democracy, Lawrence is driven to account for the existence of such a monster. From his standpoint of radical individualism, a human collectivity is a contradiction in terms: Ursula is terrified of her class of schoolchildren in *The Rainbow* 'because they were not individual

---

[21] D. H. Lawrence, *The Rainbow*, ed. John Worthen (Harmondsworth, 1981), 498. Subsequent page references in the text are to this edition, abbreviated as *R*.
[22] D. H. Lawrence, *The Symbolic Meaning: The Uncollected Versions of 'Studies in Classic American Literature'*, ed. Armin. Arnold (Arundel, 1962), 27. Subsequent page references in the text are to this edition, abbreviated as *SM*.

children, they were a collective, inhuman thing' (*R*, 426). Larger and more powerful industrial collectives are still more inhuman, drawing their power from the masses' blasphemous and self-destructive longing to become superhuman. Gerald's miners commit this sacrilege by accepting the new order of their 'high priest':

The men were satisfied to belong to the great and wonderful machine, even while it destroyed them. It was what they wanted. It was the highest that man had produced, the most wonderful and superhuman. They were exalted by belonging to this great and superhuman system which was beyond feeling or reason, something really godlike. (*WL*, 304)

Gerald's modernized industry can proceed only on the basis of this perverse submission to an inhuman mechanical collectivity which seems godlike, but to Lawrence is monstrous.

The miners willingly make (in a sense, make up) the very power which outgrows and dominates them, in a Frankensteinian process that recurs often in Lawrence's writings on democracy and modern civilization. In *The Rainbow* Will Brangwen feels awed and threatened by the massive artificial superstructure that is London: 'The works of man were more terrible than man himself, almost monstrous.' (*R*, 235.) And in a letter to Lady Cynthia Asquith in 1915 Lawrence remarks that 'we have created a great, almost overwhelming incubus of falsity and ugliness on top of us, so that we are almost crushed to death'.[23] Again, Lawrence's reference is less to the physical bulk of industrial technology in itself than to the concomitant worship of an abstract democratic deity, whom he analyses in his essay on 'Democracy' as the Average Man. 'The average human being: put him on the table, the little monster, and let us see what his works are like. He is just a little monster. . . . What a loathsome little beast he is, this Average, this unit, this Homunculus.'[24] Horrified at the creation of a democratic prodigy which would challenge his own natural superiority over the herd of other people, Lawrence is driven straight back into the arms of Edmund Burke, denouncing democracy as a monstrous and mechanical threat to the organically-given hierarchy of human life.

Lawrence blames the existence of a monstrous democracy upon the subordination of instinctual life to a false ideality — above all,

[23] *The Letters of D. H. Lawrence, Volume 2: June 1913–October 1916*, ed. George J. Zytaruk and James T. Boulton (Cambridge, 1981), 379 (16 Aug. 1915).
[24] *Phoenix: The Posthumous Papers of D. H. Lawrence*, ed. Edward D. McDonald (London, 1936), 699.

to the predominance of *will* (Lawrence frequently italicizes the word, mimetically). Attempting to account for the modern disease which has led to war, Lawrence claims in his 1917 article, 'The Reality of Peace', that 'we have been filled with a frenzy of compulsion, our insistent will has co-ordinated into a monstrous engine of compulsion and death'.[25] The monstrous mechanism of modern society originates in this insistent will, in the subordination of the individual's real self to an ideal self, 'that fancy little homunculus he has fathered in his own brain.'[26] The will forces the instinctual life relentlessly into the service of mechanically-conceived ideals, just as Gerald forces his mare to confront the speeding train in *Women in Love*. As in so many other respects, Gerald embodies the northern disease in this mono-maniac wilfulness too. Lawrence's analysis of Gerald in his capacity as Industrial Magnate insists monotonously upon his obsession with the power of his will. Gerald glories in the fact that the miners are instruments subordinated to his will, and in his subjection of nature to human control. Ultimately, his motive in the mining enterprise is not money, Lawrence claims, but purely the fulfilment of his own will; the transforming of people into pure instrumentality. Living under this obsession, Gerald himself becomes a creature of the process he has willed. Gudrun recognizes that he is 'a pure, inhuman, almost superhuman instrument' ( *WL*, 511).

The will-driven Gerald resembles not just Ahab, in his lust for conquest over nature, but Frankenstein too. In a series of essays written in 1918 and later revised for *Studies in Classic American Literature*, Lawrence devoted one essay to Benjamin Franklin, in which he fulminated against the predominance of the will in the 'self-made' American. After inaccurately presenting William Godwin's supposed doctrine of perfectibility as the recipe for a 'perfect' man, Lawrence holds up Franklin as the image of what such a creature would be like. 'He was, perhaps, the most admirable little automaton the world has ever seen, the invention of the human will, working according to good principles. So far as affairs went, he was admirable. As far as life goes, he is monstrous.' ( *SM*, 46.) Franklin is monstrous, of course, because his life is the pure product of an imposed will, not an organic growth from instinctual sources. 'This deliberate entity, this self-determined man, is the very Son of Man, man made

[25] Ibid., 674.
[26] Ibid., 712.

by the power of the human will, a virtuous Frankenstein monster.'
(*SM*, 43.) Franklin is interpreted as a mock Saviour, made not
begotten, consubstantial with the godlike idealism and rationality
of the Enlightenment, yet truly an Antichrist in the pride and conceit
of his self-making.

Lawrence's commentary upon *Frankenstein* in the Benjamin
Franklin essay is subsumed into his larger warnings against the
tyranny of the will:

The magicians knew, at least imaginatively, what it was to create a being
out of the intense *will* of the soul. And Mary Shelley, in the midst of the
idealists, gives the dark side to the ideal being, showing us Frankenstein's
monster.

The ideal being was man created by man. And so was the supreme
monster. (*SM*, 36)

Recent interpretations of *Frankenstein* which read it as a covert
critique of Godwinian idealism are foreshadowed here, although
Lawrence's use of the story is barely an interpretation, more a
polemical appropriation of the idea of the monster to emphasize his
point about the imposition of human will on nature. The picture
of Frankenstein's creature as 'the supreme monster', for example,
does not faithfully reflect the suffering and initially benevolent being
whose story appears in Mary Shelley's novel. There are several more
frightening, and certainly more inhuman monsters in ancient
mythology who could contend for the monstrous supremacy of which
Lawrence writes, but only Frankenstein's, mild as it is, will fit
Lawrence's diatribe against deliberate efforts to remake the human
world from a conscious design.

It is something of an irony that a writer who has long been
regarded not just as an example but as the great modern champion
of human creativity actually argued himself into a position from
which that same creativity is denied as a monstrous blasphemy:

This has been the fallacy of our age — the assumption that we . . . can create
the perfect being and the perfect age. . . . But we can *create* nothing. And
the thing we can make of our own natures, by our own will, is at the most
a pure mechanism, an automaton. So that if on the one hand Benjamin
Franklin is the perfect human being of Godwin, on the other hand he is
a monster, not exactly as the monster in *Frankenstein*, but for the same
reason, viz., that he is the production or fabrication of the human will, which
projects itself upon a living being, and automatises that being according to
a given precept. (*SM*, 37)

Lawrence understands the monstrous quality of Frankenstein's creature not as the result of a noble aspiration gone disastrously wrong, but as the sign of an inherent perversion in the aspiration itself, in the assertion of will. It is the same sin with which Lawrence charges Ahab when he interprets the voyage of the *Pequod* as the 'ideal will' of the white race rushing to self-destruction. This northern racial will 'sank in the war,' Lawrence writes, 'and we are all flotsam' (*SCAL*, 169).

Lawrence's belief that a life lived from the ideal will rather than from the blood and the body is only a mockery of life helps to account for his use of the Frankenstein monster in the Benjamin Franklin essay, as it does for the frequent resort to Gothic or ghostly images in his early works. The life of the ideal will which is maintained by strangling the life of the body is the life of ghosts, vampires, and the walking dead. In a letter to Henry Savage in 1913, Lawrence wrote that 'all Englishmen are swathed in restraint and puritanism and anti-emotion, till they are walking mummies'.[27] In *The Study of Thomas Hardy*, a year later, Lawrence characterized the excessively spiritual relationship between Jude Fawley and Sue Bridehead as 'a *frisson* of sacrilege, like the Frenchman who lay with a corpse'.[28] Over this necrophilic world of the mechanical will broods the shade of Edgar Allan Poe, whose vampires Lawrence had also interpreted as monomaniacs of the spirit (Poe's Raven makes unexpected appearances in both *The White Peacock* and *Sons and Lovers*). It is a world in which the dead 'cling to the living, and won't let go', as Birkin puts it in *Women in Love* (*WL*, 253). Gerald comes to Gudrun's bedroom at night with the clay of his father's grave still clinging to his feet (and, Lawrence adds, 'on his heart' (*WL*, 424)); his need to draw sustenance from Gudrun is distinctly vampiric, and, not surprisingly, he confronts her and Loerke in his final scene 'like a ghost' (*WL*, 571). The will-driven and hyperconscious Hermione is described insistently as a ghost, a corpse, a ghoul, a *revenant*, or as sepulchral, and she is only one among many. Ursula and Birkin meet whole crowds of 'spectral people' (*WL*, 480) at Ostend and Ghent, who correspond to the spectral colliers Ursula sees at Wiggiston in *The Rainbow*, and to the 'corpse-like inanation' of Anton Skrebensky, who feels 'like a corpse that is inhabited with

---

[27] Lawrence, *Letters II*, 102 (15? Nov. 1913).
[28] Lawrence, *Phoenix*, 505.

just enough life to make it appear as any other of the spectral, unliving beings which we call people in our dead language' ( *R*, 501, 508). Ursula's task in seeking her independence is to fight clear of the clammy embrace of corpses: her disobedient pupil Vernon Williams has a 'half transparent unwholesomeness, rather like a corpse', while Winifred Inger and Uncle Tom seem to her to be 'ghoulish' in their worship of the monstrous colliery ( *R*, 452, 397).

It is worth noticing in connection with this last attribution of ghoulishness to Tom and Winifred that these characters are scientists. In describing Ursula's lesbian affair with her teacher, Lawrence has taken care to inform us that 'Winifred had had a scientific education', and he tells us that Tom Brangwen has converted the front room of his house into a laboratory which looks out over the 'abstraction' of the town to 'the great mathematical colliery' beyond ( *R*, 388, 394). The ghoulishness and the scientific abstraction in the relation of this couple to the industrial system merge together, Lawrence's purpose being to force the laboratory and the tomb, the scientist and the graverobber, into the kind of equivalence they have in *Frankenstein*. It is no accident that at the training college (itself a 'laboratory for the factory' ( *R*, 485)), Ursula's physics teacher is called Dr Frankstone; she refuses to acknowledge any special mystery in life, regarding it only as a complex of physical and chemical processes. Ursula, who prefers botany, clings to the mystical and religious conception of life as she watches it gleaming under the microscope, and dismisses Dr Frankstone's view as a reduction of this supreme mystery to the merely mechanical.

Science is always portrayed in Lawrence's work as a reductive, corrosively impersonal dismantling of life into mechanical components, always substituting the mechanical principle for the organic. In this, Lawrence is of course restating some long-standing Romantic anxieties in even more harshly polarized terms, and appealing, through echoes of *Frankenstein*, to the received reduction of all scientific rationality to anatomical dissection. In an often-quoted distillation of Romantic arguments Lawrence claimed that 'Analysis presupposes a corpse', recalling Wordsworth's line, 'We murder to dissect'.[29] Lawrence's Romantic proverb is literally true only in so far as the rapid advances in medicine in the preceding century could

---

[29] Lawrence, *Phoenix II*, 391; William Wordsworth, 'The Tables Turned', *Lyrical Ballads* 1798.

not have been achieved without examining cadavers; but by including all Analysis—chemical, physical, philosophical, cultural—Lawrence makes an absurd reduction which implies further that analysis and organic life are incompatible. As a matter of fact, physicians of all kinds spend much of their daily practice in analysing living beings— often without that religious veneration for life which Lawrence would demand, it is true, but also without resorting to murder. Lawrence's attempt to equate all scientific enquiry with ghoulishness is a version of the Mad Scientist stereotype (albeit in rather different terms than H. G. Wells's), pushing our attitude to the scientist back through the Frankenstein myth all the way to Edmund Burke. Every scientist— and Lawrence would add, every democrat too—is an anatomist who hacks her or his parent in pieces just for the sake of the experiment.

If Lawrence's attitudes to science look back across a century to Anti-Jacobinism and the Gothic novel, his vision of modern civilization's self-destructive capacities appears to look forward prophetically, with Gudrun and Loerke in *Women in Love*:

> As for the future, that they never mentioned except one laughed out some mocking dream of the destruction of the world by a ridiculous catastrophe of man's invention: a man invented such a perfect explosive that it blew the earth in two, and the two halves set off in different directions through space . . . ( *WL*, 551)

If this looks like prophecy, it is not because of any uncanny powers of Lawrence's—he was writing about the world of 1916—but because Lawrence's nightmare is one that we still inhabit.

# 9

## Realism and the Aspiring Anatomist

> Will felt inexpressibly mournful, and said nothing. . . .
> it seemed to him as if he were beholding in a magic
> panorama a future where he himself was sliding into
> that pleasureless yielding to the small solicitations of
> circumstance, which is a commoner history of perdition
> than any single momentous bargain.
>
> George Eliot, *Middlemarch*

The cold-hearted naval surgeon Dr Cuticle, who has a 'peculiar love'
for morbid anatomy and experimental dismemberment, is in his
rooms aboard the *Neversink* at midnight, alone with his strange
bottled specimens. A cabin-boy enters to find the rooms full of blue
smoke and smelling of brimstone. Rushing out with a wild cry, he
alerts the other officers of the ship, who discover that 'the vapor
proceeded from smoldering bunches of Lucifer matches, which had
become ignited through the carelessness of the surgeon'.[1] In this
little episode from *White-Jacket*, Melville slyly teases his readers by
dangling before them a conventional Faustian laboratory setting but
snatching away its expected transgressive action. Hints of the
surgeon's ambitious and fanatical design splutter out into mere
clumsy accident; if we anticipated devilry, all we are given is an
infernally bad pun.

A similar prank at the reader's expense is played by Wilkie Collins
in *The Woman in White*. While we are congratulating ourselves on
not being taken in by the smooth-talking Italian aristocrat Count
Fosco, we little suspect that Collins has laid a false trail for us: the
first description we have of the corpulent villain credits him with
being 'one of the first experimental chemists living'[2]—which is
almost enough for us to condemn him in advance as a murderer.
When Marian Halcombe collapses with fever, and Fosco substitutes

---

[1] Melville, *White-Jacket*, 246–8 (ch. 61).
[2] Wilkie Collins, *The Woman in White*, ed. Julian Symons (Harmondsworth,
1974), 243. Subsequent page references in the text are to this edition, abbreviated
as *WW*.

himself for the doctor attending her, we fear the worst, especially because Fosco is now boasting again of his 'vast knowledge of chemistry, and . . . luminous experience of the more subtle resources which medical and magnetic science have placed at the disposal of mankind' (*WW*, 359). A man of such sinister learning—and an Italian to boot—can hardly fail now to do away with our plucky heroine. Fortunately, though, Fosco prefers to ogle Marian rather than to poison her, and his ingenious plot—far more complex than our expectations credit—does not require her murder; on the contrary, his skills have indeed cured her, and his manœuvring has saved her from an incompetent physician.

In his final confession Fosco protests at the 'odious insinuations' that he had planned to use his chemical knowledge against Marian or against Anne Catherick; he has in fact employed only two harmless sleeping draughts in the execution of his designs. Fosco prides himself on possessing immensely powerful knowledge and on *not* using it when he can get by with cunning alone. He maintains that chemists could be 'the most omnipotent of all potentates', that they might sway the destinies of humanity, but that this power is frittered away by mediocrities:

On my sacred word of honour it is lucky for Society that modern chemists are, by incomprehensible good fortune, the most harmless of mankind. The mass are worthy fathers of families, who keep shops. The few are philosophers besotted with admiration for the sound of their own lecturing voices, visionaries who waste their lives on fantastic impossibilities, or quacks whose ambition soars no higher than our corns. Thus Society escapes, and the illimitable power of Chemistry remains the slave of the most superficial and the most insignificant ends. (*WW*, 622)

Like Melville, Collins has whetted our appetite for medical villainy, only to dispel the experimenter's Gothic allure by reminding us of the real mundane fallibility of chemists and doctors: accident, incompetence, timidity, and the paltry distractions of worldly existence all bar the physician's path to heroic transgression. Like Catherine Morland, whose Gothic parchment in *Northanger Abbey* turns out to be a recent laundry-list, we are shamed into a disenchanted recognition of the ordinary, our disappointment exposing the inappropriate fantasies we have entertained.

Traps of this kind are a typical parodic ploy of literary realism. From *Don Quixote* to *Ulysses* and beyond, the tradition of the novel has relied heavily upon bathetic deflation of romance or sentimentality, but in the nineteenth century this tendency flourished to the point at which it became a dominant novelistic ethic. Always more than a set of narrative techniques, nineteenth-century realism encoded a new grasp of complexities in social intercourse and social structure, and with it an ironic dampening of individual aspirations: the protagonist's youthful ardour would typically have to be shown chastened, compromised, or even broken by the material weight of complex social circumstances. Among the more promising candidates for this ritual sacrifice of the Romantic ego to the Reality Principle was the figure of the aspiring doctor, anatomist, or chemist. Inheriting the Frankensteinian or Faustian experimenter from Romantic tales of the earlier nineteenth century, realism plucked him from the darkness of his sulphurous laboratory to show how the common light of day would transform him, under its ironic glare, from a modern Titan to a pitiable mortal. Because he was still a central Romantic figure of Promethean transgression, the medical experimenter thus stood as a salient target for realism's assault upon the delusions of romance. And so in two of the finest products of literary realism—Gustave Flaubert's *Madame Bovary* and George Eliot's *Middlemarch*—we find doctors in positions of unusual prominence, and unusual similarity too. In deliberate contrast with the scientific overreachers of Romanticism, whose researches cost them their women, Bovary and Lydgate are underachievers who find that their women cost them their researches; their fall comes about through no heroic transgression, but because they have failing practices and spendthrift wives.

Flaubert, usually so scrupulous with his figures of speech, does at one point liken Emma Bovary to a galvanized corpse as she writhes in pain on her death-bed, but all other traces of the Gothic medical fantasy are ruthlessly expunged in *Madame Bovary*, leaving us only with a pair of provincial mediocrities: Charles Bovary and the druggist Homais. Charles is so far from being the errant chemical genius that he fails the medical examinations on his first attempt, and makes his one experiment—the bungled operation on Hippolyte's club foot—only because he is harried into it by Homais. The pharmacist has perhaps the makings of a godless anti-hero, but his Voltaireanism is too inconsistent, and both his transgressions (he dispenses without a licence) and his aspirations are far too banal. The romantic aspirations in the story are allotted instead, of course, to the sorry figure of Emma, whose deluded thirst for romance only highlights the sluggish mediocrity of her husband. George Eliot's Lydgate (of whom more below) is no bovine dullard—indeed, he aspires to make through his anatomical and galvanic researches some famous medical discovery; yet he is dragged down to Bovary's level, entangled in parochial backbiting, maligned by the entrenched pharmaceutical interest, and financially compromised by a wife he has failed to satisfy. Realism tells us that although Titanic transgressions may be possible among Alpine crags and glaciers, there is no danger of any Frankenstein emerging from Normandy or Warwickshire. Monstrous crimes, as Jane Austen insisted, are not to be looked for in the midland counties of England; here, the most ardent aspiration could never break through the enveloping provincial dullness, because country doctors are only human.

Literary realism would appear to be telling us a story very different from those we have reviewed in previous chapters. Yet in one respect at least it agrees with the Romantic or symbolic novelist: both kinds of fiction question the value of aspiration, chastising the misguided individualist who would renounce the claims of human solidarity. The difference is that Romanticism usually conducts its critique negatively or by subtraction, illustrating the self-inflicted torments of the solitary (and at its Byronic extremes, indulging in them), while realism adds to the portrait of its aspiring protagonist a set of social constraints which can subdue and reclaim the potential exile. Differing widely as they do in the directions from which they approach the problem of the 'isolato', however, they usually find a consensus at the level of ethical intention. From this slender connecting link between the two great tendencies of nineteenth-century fiction, George Levine has elaborated in his book *The Realistic Imagination* a provocative revision of literary history, arguing that *Frankenstein* is a forerunner not just of the Romantic, symbolic, or melodramatic line in subsequent English fiction, but of the Victorian realist tradition as well.[3]

Perverse though his assertion may seem, Levine's thesis has at least two credible premises: first, that realist fiction shares with *Frankenstein* a common critique of individual aspiration (or more exactly, a simultaneous reverence for and distrust of heroic ambitions);

---

[3] George Levine, *The Realistic Imagination: English Fiction from Frankenstein to Lady Chatterley*, (Chicago, 1981).

and secondly, that *Frankenstein* inhabits the distinctly secular, disenchanted world characteristic of realism, a world in which people damn themselves not by Mephistophelean contract but by the consequences of their own worldly actions. The first proposition is clearly true, but only in such a general way as to be limited in its value, since a distrust for heroic aspiration can be found in different forms in just about every period and national tradition in world literature. To say that *Frankenstein* and the Victorian realist novel share in this distrust is hardly more significant than to notice that they both use the same alphabet, unless one goes on to specify the particular kinds of anti-heroic fiction in question — at which point the major differences of approach between Romantic and realist novels reassert themselves. In other words, Levine's first proposition risks reducing realism to an anti-heroic outlook and forgetting its distinct kinds of subject-matter and narrative convention. This danger is partly averted, however, by the second proposition, which does put us back on the firmer ground of realism's peculiar features. To recognize the radically secular cast of Mary Shelley's novel (as Levine has led the way in doing) is, at the very least, to dislodge it from the Gothic canon and to reveal an element in its anti-heroic meaning which relates it to realist modes of disenchantment.

Levine rightly claims that there is a kinship with realism in *Frankenstein*'s tracing of natural causes and consequences and its rejection of supernatural interventions; it is this secular logic which distinguishes Victor Frankenstein's tragedy from the spirituality of the Faust myth. Realism prides itself on its exclusive adherence to observable causes and effects, on its detailed connections between individual acts and social consequences; and in this important sense it can claim *Frankenstein* as a not-too-distant cousin, its consanguinity leading through the Godwinian line from *Caleb Williams*. One could go further, and argue that realism's presentation of characters as creatures of circumstance, and its examination of the determining conditions of human action, bring it back frequently to the problems of *Frankenstein*. From the other side too, the Frankensteinian writings reviewed in the preceding chapters are just as concerned with creatures of circumstance as realist novels are; as I have occasionally emphasized, their critiques of heroic transgression can best be understood in terms of the *conditions* under which an otherwise admirable ambition is pursued, and in this light their narrative logic seems less fantastic and more congruent with realism than might at first appear.

It should be possible, once these links are recognized, to reach some definition of the relation in which *Frankenstein* and its analogues stand towards the tradition of literary realism—but not without parting company with George Levine at this point. His *The Realistic Imagination* looks beyond the propositions we have examined, to formulate a relationship between the Frankensteinian and the realistic which is characterized chiefly by realism's repression, domestication, or exorcism of 'the monstrous'. In this account, the insights of *Frankenstein* are the skeletons in realism's cupboard, straining to burst out and disrupt its safe domestic world of order and compromise. The argument relies on certain Romantic-Modernist and Deconstructionist critiques of realism which regard the realistic mode of fiction as an inherently repressive and ideologically numbing opiate, or as a kind of cultural patriarch against whose tyranny any formal disruption counts as a liberation. Although Levine sets out to qualify the most condescending caricatures in Deconstruction's critique of realism, he ends by adopting that school's fundamental myth of a cosmic struggle between Desire and Order, translating it as the warfare between 'the monstrous' on one side and the repressive compromises of realism on the other. The monstrous is, Levine argues, a truth which realism continually screens or evades, and only its irruption rescues realistic works from fatal blindness and complacency. As the 'domestic compromise' of realism finally breaks down in the early twentieth century, we find that D. H. Lawrence 'rejects the realists to embrace the monster they feared'.[4]

A major weakness in this argument is that 'the monster' which realism is supposed to dread bears scarcely any resemblance to the monsters of the literary tradition, nor to Frankenstein's monster in particular. When, for example, Levine claims that in Thomas Hardy's works, 'the monster stalks freely and visibly again',[5] the monster he is referring to turns out to be something as unspecific as non-human reality or 'the unnameable'. Monstrosity in Levine's account is defined not by reference to its actual meanings in the literary tradition, but by a very broad nature/culture opposition which allows Levine to call anything undomesticated, instinctual, or non-human 'the monstrous'. With such a blunt instrument of analysis, one cannot expect to establish convincingly the relationship between realism and

---

[4] Ibid., 328.
[5] Ibid., 238.

the Frankenstein myth. To do that, one would need to accept that realist writers are quite capable of using and examining monstrosity without necessarily being thrown into ideological panic.

Realist novelists—including those who might regard themselves as 'naturalists'—carry on, as we have noticed, that Godwinian revision of 'monstrous' criminality which shows how society engenders its own felons and miscreants. Like Dickens, the more consistently realist novelist George Gissing insists on showing those outcasts from whom middle-class opinion recoils to be products of social ills. In *The Nether World* Gissing explains how Bob Hewett turns to forgery, not because he has an evil nature but because he is too weak, under the pressure of poverty, to resist the temptation. 'Society produces many a monster,' Gissing observes, 'but the mass of those whom, after creating them, it pronounces bad are merely bad from the conventional point of view; they are guilty of weakness, not of crimes.'[6] The allusion to *Frankenstein* is obvious enough; but more important is the continuity of argument from Mary Shelley's and William Godwin's redefinition of monstrosity as a product, to this Dickensian kind of commentary in a realistic novel of slum life. This very continuity in the social criticism the two kinds of novel can make reveals more clearly the difference in the scope and method of its application: while a Mary Shelley or, say, a Nathaniel Hawthorne can show us an isolated transgressor or a lone pitiful monster in more or less allegorical form, a novelist like Gissing who depicts a complex urban society in some intricacy will be able to expose more fully that interlocking of causes and of personal circumstances which constitutes the social production of monstrosity. Realism, in short, can flesh out and provide detailed evidence of those monstrous processes which in a symbolic or Romantic mode of fiction usually appear only as mythic patterns.

While it is often true that literary realism distrusts the ambitious heroine or hero, and thus echoes the ostensible moral of *Frankenstein* and other tales of trangression, only the crudest account of realistic fiction could maintain that its attitude to individual aspirations is simply prohibitive: the vague yearnings of an Emma Bovary or a Maggie Tulliver may be criticized, but they are not offered for our condemnation. If one believes that realism is essentially a strategy to repress Desire, then one is perhaps likely to regard such cases of

[6] George Gissing, *The Nether World* (London, 1973), 218.

sympathy towards the protagonists' romanticism as an insurgence
into the realistic of extraneous liberating energies; but it would be
wiser to acknowledge that disruptive ambitions and desires (rather
than Desire as such) are quite at home among the familiar tensions
with which realism works. Realist writers set out not so much to
suffocate or disable their aspiring characters as to play them off against
their milieux in ways which ask us to question both the aspirants'
misdirected energies and the social constrictions which wastefully
frustrate them. Some 'romantic' sympathy for the ambitions of the
protagonist is presupposed in every realist fiction of any vitality or
significance. Unlike most Romantic fables, a realist novel has the
capacity not just to dramatize a distrust for transgressive heroism,
but also to distrust that very distrust; to apply its debunking irony,
in other words, to the anti-heroic as much as to the heroic. We can
see how it does this by examining briefly four realist accounts of
allegedly transgressing doctors.

   George Eliot's *Middlemarch* offers us not just an implied criticism
of earlier fables of medical transgression, but a reversal of their
normal pattern. Scorning melodramatic simplicities of character,
George Eliot mixes Tertius Lydgate's passion for anatomy with 'a
flesh and blood sense of fellowship which withstood all the abstractions
of special study'.[7] He is too healthily balanced a man to succumb
to Casaubon's kind of monastic seclusion; unlike the physicians of
Romantic fable, he actually goes about curing people of diseases, and
even enjoys the human contact which his practice brings him. The
introduction to Lydgate's ambitions in Chapter 15 of *Middlemarch*
begins by offering us an almost Gothic account of the young doctor's
'intellectual passion' for anatomy and his longing to become an
'immortal discoverer' (*M*, 173, 178). But in Eliot's realist world,
all things have their disappointing impurities, so the idealism of
Lydgate's scientific ardour has to cohabit with a certain 'commonness'
in his attitudes to women. To illustrate this fateful weakness, Eliot
interpolates an unusually melodramatic tale of Lydgate's student days
in Paris, where he has worshipped an actress from afar 'without
prejudice to his galvanism' (*M*, 180)—or so he believes; this illusion
that his relations with women will leave his experimental career
unaffected is of course to be shattered by his experiences in

   [7] George Eliot, *Middlemarch*, ed. W. J. Harvey (Harmondsworth, 1965), 174.
Subsequent page references in the text are to this edition, abbreviated as *M*.

Middlemarch. The object of his infatuation in Paris, Mme Laure, stabs her actor husband on stage, and Lydgate defends her from suspicions of murder, assuming romantically that beauty in distress must be innocent and that the killing was accidental. Pursuing the actress to the South, he proposes to her, but withdraws in horror when she tells him that she did indeed intend to kill her husband. Lydgate is alarmed to find that he has 'two selves within him', one rational and the other infatuated, and he resolves henceforth 'to take a strictly scientific view of woman' (*M*, 182, 183).

As an omen of the doctor's coming troubles, the tale is ingeniously contrived, its very melodramatic absurdity corresponding to Lydgate's own failure to look beyond the trite and the sentimental in his view of women. It neatly reverses the cliché in which students of galvanism and anatomy are distracted from women by the lure of research; here, it is the woman who distracts the student away from his laboratory. The story of Lydgate's marriage unfolds the same pattern at greater length and in realist detail. During his courtship with Rosamond Vincy he still feels that it is his research which is truly 'his fair unknown' (*M*, 305), but once he is engaged to her, his laboratory falls into neglect and disarray. Lydgate likes a woman 'to adore a man's pre-eminence without too precise a knowledge of what it consisted in' (*M*, 301), and he believes that Rosamond will respect this strict separation of marriage and work by not interfering with his ambitions. If he will not choose a wife who can collaborate with him, though, he can only expect the wife he has to compete with his researches. Rosamond starts by complaining that Lydgate neglects her for his phials and microscopes, and then reveals her distance from her husband's ambitions when he enthuses about the pioneers of anatomy:

'I am thinking of a great fellow, who was about as old as I am three hundred years ago, and had already begun a new era in anatomy. . . . His name was Vesalius. And the only way he could get to know anatomy as he did, was by going to snatch bodies at night, from graveyards and places of execution.'

'Oh!' said Rosamond, with a look of disgust on her pretty face, 'I am very glad you are not Vesalius. I should have thought he might find some less horrible way than that.'

'No, he couldn't,' said Lydgate, going on too earnestly to take much notice of her answer. 'He could only get a complete skeleton by snatching the whitened bones of a criminal from the gallows, and burying them, and fetching them away by bits secretly, in the dead of night.'

'I hope he is not one of your great heroes,' said Rosamond, half-playfully, half-anxiously, 'else I shall have you getting up in the night to go to St Peter's churchyard. . . .' (*M*, 497)

To Rosamond, her husband's preoccupation seems 'almost like a morbid vampire's taste' (*M*, 711), and is merely a distasteful and incomprehensible embarrassment. From Lydgate's point of view, however, it is Rosamond who is the real ghoul: he ends by likening her to the basil plant which feeds upon a dead man's brains in Boccaccio's tale (*M*, 893).

Lydgate's final inversion of the normal Gothic contrast between murdered bride and ghoulish groom sums up a series of such reversals in the novel, which challenge the anti-scientific drift of popular fable. George Eliot is concerned ultimately with the same problem as Mary Shelley or Hoffmann or Hawthorne—that dangerously exclusive sexual division of labour which separates marriage from work and keeps women from knowledge. But she shows the destructive price of this division being paid less in terms of terrible scientific inventions than in anti-scientific prejudice and ignorance. As in the fables of transgression, where the figure of the fiancée represents social and familial anxieties about the inventor's secrecy, Rosamond comes to stand for the Middlemarchers' collective resistance to scientific innovation. Her objection to her husband's research is that it damages the social status of his practice, and her revulsion from anatomy echoes the parochial superstition and gossip which hold Lydgate guilty of murdering to dissect. The whispering campaign in Middlemarch against Lydgate's enlightened medical reforms starts with the claims made by the landlady of the Tankard pub, that the doctor's dissecting habits resemble the case of Burke and Hare,[8] and it culminates in the rumours of his complicity in the poisoning of Raffles. Lydgate may have asked for it—like Silas Marner, whose neighbours believe him to be in league with the devil—but we are invited to feel also the injustice of this Gothic innuendo. George Eliot thus reworks the problem of scientific pride and irresponsibility, but in such a way as to make the reactionary prejudices fomented by the Mad Scientist cliché a more dangerous problem than any outlandish invention a

---

[8] *M*, 481–2, 494–5. *Middlemarch* is set, of course, in the four years leading up to the Reform Act of 1832. For the purposes of Lydgate's story, though, the significant dates are those of the Burke and Hare murder trial (1829) and the less celebrated reforms embodied in the Anatomy Act (1832), which legalized and regulated the use of criminals' corpses by medical schools.

country doctor is likely to perpetrate. As in Flaubert's novel, it is stupidity rather than scientific genius which triumphs.

A similar deflection of scientific ambition by parochial obstacles can be seen in Thomas Hardy's *The Woodlanders*. Despite its relatively happy ending, this novel aligns itself clearly with realism's critique of individual aspiration, its heroine and anti-hero both being afflicted with yearnings for higher things beyond the hamlet of Little Hintock. The young Doctor Fitzpiers burns the midnight oil in his laboratory, combining an 'anatomical ardour'[9] with studies in poetry, alchemy, and German metaphysics. The woodlanders regard him suspiciously and assume that he has dealings with the devil, especially when he offers ten pounds to Grammer Oliver for the use of her brain after her death—'as a natomy', she explains to her neighbours ( *W*, 91). It is this old woman's fear of being used for godless experiments which throws Grace Melbury into Fitzpiers's path, when Grammer Oliver asks her to 'save a poor old woman's skellington from a heathen's chopper' by pleading with the doctor for a cancellation of their ghoulish bargain ( *W*, 170).

Although Fitzpiers does at one point drunkenly compare himself with Prometheus, Grace's forebodings about visiting such a sinister anatomist turn out to be misplaced. 'Miss Melbury's view of the doctor as a merciless, unwavering, irresistible scientist was', Hardy explains, 'not quite in accordance with fact. The real Dr Fitzpiers was a man of too many hobbies to show likelihood of rising to any great eminence in the profession he had chosen.' ( *W*, 171.) Fitzpiers lacks the single-minded devotion of a great scientific transgressor, and once he has met Grace, he begins to replace his medical ambitions with the dream of accepting 'quiet domesticity' with her ( *W*, 189).

Why should he go further into the world than where he was? The secret of happiness lay in limiting the aspirations; these men's thoughts were coterminous with the margin of the Hintock woodlands, and why should not his be likewise limited—a small practice among the people around him being the bound of his desires? ( *W*, 185)

Fitzpiers is distracted from the idealism of the laboratory by the promise of a woman's domesticity, saved from scientific abstraction by his readiness to compromise with the woodland community's real limits. Grace finally tells him 'to give up those strange studies' of his

⁹ Thomas Hardy, *The Woodlanders*, ed. James Gibson (Harmondsworth, 1981), 172. Subsequent page references in the text are to this edition, abbreviated as *W*.

( *W*, 414), and they start a new life in that classically realist province, the midland counties of England.

A more consistently ardent and more admirable scientific researcher is the eponymous hero of *Le Docteur Pascal*, the concluding novel in Émile Zola's Rougon-Macquart saga. This aged doctor has retired from full-time medical practice, living in provincial seclusion and attending only a few patients, because his time is devoted to anatomical experiments and to the perfecting of his theories of heredity. He dreams of regenerating humanity through a miracle cure, an injection which he half-jokingly describes as an elixir to resurrect the dead. The more suspicious among the townsfolk whisper that he is pounding up dead men's bones in the blood of babies, and his mother, Félicité Rougon, resents the secrecy of his godless experiments. She is supported by his pious servant Martine and, at first, by his young niece Clotilde; and the three women plot to prevent his damnation by destroying his scientific papers. Pascal breaks this female conspiracy by converting his niece from religious delusion to the cause of science. Thus the familiar division between women and science is partly breached, as Pascal at last opens up his dark cupboard of secrets to Clotilde.

Zola's novel follows a basic pattern in which this antagonism is overcome from both sides, and a triumphant synthesis achieved: Pascal's seclusion in his laboratory and Clotilde's mystical reveries are shown to have been the symptoms of parallel refusals of vital energy. Both of these misdirected pursuits give way to the power of the sexual love between uncle and niece, so that Clotilde gives up her religion to become a disciple of Science, while Pascal abandons his more unrealizable medical ambitions, confining himself more sanely to the relief of pain and the gradual accumulation of knowledge. Through Clotilde, he has made his peace with nature, and he no longer dreams of subduing it.

Correct nature, interfere, modify it and venture to distort its balance, — can one justify such an objective? Cure, retard death at one's own whim, prolong life at the expense of damaging the species, no doubt, is that not undoing what nature wants to do? And have we any right to dream about making humanity healthier, stronger, modelled according to our idea of health and strength? . . . I am full of doubts, I tremble at the idea of my twentieth-century alchemy. I am beginning to think that it would be better and far wiser to allow evolution to go its own way.[10]

[10] Émile Zola, *Doctor Pascal*, trans. Vladimir Kean (London, 1957), 166–7.

Although Pascal's wildest dreams are moderated in a symmetrical realist compromise, there can be no mistaking his status as a heroic figure, and as an idealized representative of Zola's own scientific rationalism. The real blessings which his medical skills bring to suffering neighbours (they revere him as a god capable of reviving the dead), and his stoicism in the face of death mark him out as an admirable champion of the scientific attitude, whose only transgression in Zola's eyes has been to offend nature temporarily by failing to procreate. Certainly, his virtues contrast sharply with the meanness and scheming bigotry of his mother, who succeeds finally in destroying his life's work. Like George Eliot and Thomas Hardy, but more vehemently — given the fiercer contest in France between Faith and Science — Zola defends the anatomist against his superstitious neighbours, seeking only to moderate the researcher's impossible dreams, allowing him to be reclaimed by women.

Realism's sympathy for the doctor, and its firm rejection of Gothic enchantments, appear particularly starkly, even cruelly, in Stephen Crane's story 'The Monster', which is a calculated travesty of the Frankenstein myth. Here it is the doctor, more than the monster, who is cast out by a callous community, all the more unjustly because he has, unlike Victor Frankenstein, accepted full responsibility for the 'monster' he has produced and cared for. The events of the tale gather hardly the slightest Gothic atmosphere: a fire breaks out at the home of Doctor Trescott, whose infant son is rescued from the flames by the black servant Henry Johnson; but while trying to escape with the boy, Johnson collapses in Trescott's laboratory, where a bottle bursts and spills its contents on his face. Trescott brings his son's rescuer back from the brink of death, but only in a brain-damaged and hideously deformed condition. Johnson has to be hidden away from the public eye, so Trescott pays a local family to look after him. Trescott's friends and neighbours are revolted by the presence of this 'monster', and they boycott his practice and even his wife's tea-parties.

Emphasizing the Frankensteinian dimension of the tale, Trescott's friend Judge Hagenthorpe warns him before the operation on Johnson that 'He will be your creation, you understand. He is purely your creation. Nature has very evidently given him up. He is dead. You are restoring him to life. You are making him, and he will be a monster, with no mind.'[11] Trescott needs little reminding of his

---

[11]  *The Portable Stephen Crane*, ed. Joseph Katz (New York, 1969), 473.

sole responsibility for Johnson's new life, and he has no intention of evading it, unlike the other experimenters in the tradition we have reviewed. A further difference from *Frankenstein* emerges in the meaning of monstrosity used here. In Hagenthorpe's speech, Crane has evacuated the concept of any traditional moral content and reduced it to a matter of physical abnormality, thus making Trescott's neighbours guilty of a cruelly bigotted response to a human being (not coincidentally black) who has neither rebelled nor turned against them. Like the monster in *Frankenstein*, who is shot at despite having just saved a child's life, the black 'monster' of Crane's tale is spurned despite his bravery in rescuing Trescott's son; and the doctor is, in turn, punished for the very responsibility he has shown in rescuing Johnson from death. By any moral standard, it is the offended citizens of Trescott's neighbourhood who are the real monsters.

In these four realist tales, the authors are willing to question, in their own ways, the scientist's evasion of social controls, even to criticize the specifically masculine exclusiveness of his ambition; but they see the disaster which the doctor brings upon himself as a product not of scientific experiment itself, but of an irrationally superstitious popular reaction. It is not just that these writers, in the wake of the nineteenth century's wars and cholera epidemics, had more tangible evidence of the benefits brought to the suffering by a Lister or a Pasteur. They refuse to gothicize the medical experiment also because they know it to be a symbol of wider social and political innovation. Like Mary Wollstonecraft, they are impatient with the superstitious, reactionary fables of Pandora and other mythical transgressors, and so they set out to challenge the anti-scientific prejudices fomented by the Gothic tradition of Romantic conservatism in fiction since *Frankenstein*. Their disenchanted travesties of the Frankenstein myth dispel the conventional Gothic atmosphere which had gathered around it in conservative revisions, and restore the balance—or rather the productive equivocation—of Mary Shelley's own novel.

Despite the strong temptation in current criticism to impeach realism for crimes of ideological tyranny, or even to hack this aged parent in pieces, it needs to be remembered that the realistic strategy of parody and disenchantment can be, on due occasion, as liberating as those fables and fabulations which today's very selective critical Formalism celebrates as 'the literature of subversion'.[12] The body of fictional work whose Frankensteinian filiations I have traced in this book cannot seriously be offered as a rival tradition to contend with that of realism, which remains the highest achievement of nineteenth-century fiction. At the same time, this monstrously symbolic mode of writing does retain an important and enduring claim upon our attention, one which a purely realistic mode would forbid itself from offering. Realism's paradoxical disillusioning illusionism 'shows' us the world as it is before our eyes, stripped of dreams and fancies, but this world typically turns out to be (and in realism's chosen focus on details, perhaps has to be) a sleepy provincial town undisturbed except by a soon-forgotten scandal. While realism can depict small disturbances to an ordered community, the larger turmoils and metamorphoses of the modern world elude its normal perspective, and can be grasped only by figurative representations of history's 'invisible' workings — of those alarming and uncontrolled processes going on 'behind our backs', as Marx habitually put it.

To show the modern world fully, writers need, so to speak, eyes at the back of their heads; they have to shift to a non-realistic register which can apprehend the monstrous dynamics of the modern as well as its visible phenomena. It is this which the Frankenstein myth and its variants can provide. When Zola, for instance, has accumulated the most thoroughly-researched facts and descriptions of the railways and the mining industry in *La Bête humaine* and *Germinal*, he has still to show us the governing (yet ungoverned) tendencies underlying them, and for this he has to resort to the monstrous. To symbolize the controlled power of industrial development in *La Bête humaine*, he uses the memorable closing image of the driverless train hurtling onward as an 'escaping monster';[13] and in *Germinal* the Le Voreux colliery appears repeatedly as a flesh-eating idol gorged on the miners it swallows, while behind it stands Capital itself, an even larger artificial monster which cannibalistically devours smaller capitals. In such Frankensteinian departures from realistic or naturalistic convention, Zola, along with the boldest writers of his age, gains access to what Marx called the 'one great fact' of the nineteenth century.

[12] See, for example, Rosemary Jackson, *Fantasy: The Literature of Subversion* (London, 1981).

[13] Émile Zola, *La Bête humaine*, trans. Leonard Tancock (Harmondsworth, 1977), 366.

# Appendix

## The Plot of Frankenstein Summarized

(This summary follows the first edition of 1818; significant changes to the story in the 1831 edition are noted in square brackets.)

In the year 17— Robert Walton writes home to his sister Mrs Margaret Saville in England, from St Petersburg, then from Archangel, reporting on his expedition to reach the North Pole. He recruits a crew from whaling ships, finding a lieutenant who has renounced his claim to the hand of a young Russian woman and given his money to his impoverished rival in order to ensure her happiness. Walton's fourth letter records a sighting, while his ship is icebound and far from land, of a large man in a dog-sledge travelling northwards ahead of the ship. The next day, another man is found drifting on an iceberg, and is brought aboard. Walton nurses the stranger back to health and begins to love him as a brother, admiring his cultivation and discernment. After some hesitation, the stranger decides to tell Walton his story, upon hearing that his rescuer is a seeker after knowledge.

Victor Frankenstein (for it is he) relates his tale, while Walton transcribes it: he is the eldest son of Alphonse Frankenstein, a syndic of the Genevese republic who, late in life, had married a deceased friend's daughter, Caroline Beaufort. Four years after Victor's birth, Alphonse and Caroline had adopted their orphaned niece, Elizabeth Lavenza, bringing her up as Victor's 'sister' and future wife. [1831: Elizabeth is no longer Victor's cousin, but an orphan adopted by the Frankensteins while on an Italian holiday.] At school Victor befriends a merchant's son, Henry Clerval. One rainy day, Victor begins reading Cornelius Agrippa, and his father's brusque dismissal of the alchemists only encourages him to go on to read Paracelsus and Albertus Magnus; and he learns [not in 1831] of the principles of electricity from his father.

When Victor reaches the age of seventeen, his parents decide to send him to Ingolstadt university, but Elizabeth catches scarlet fever. Victor's mother insists on nursing her, and is fatally infected, although Elizabeth recovers. His mother's dying wish is for Victor to marry Elizabeth. Henry Clerval is prevented by his father from joining Victor at university. At Ingolstadt, Victor is repelled by Professor Krempe, who scorns alchemy, but he falls under the sway of the chemistry professor, M. Waldman.

After two years studying chemistry, Victor decides to go on to study physiology and anatomy rather than return home. From his study of corpses he arrives at the discovery of 'the cause of generation and life', and is even able to animate dead tissue. (At this point he warns Walton that he will never disclose this secret.) Victor decides to make a human being eight feet tall, and spends some months collecting materials for it from charnel-houses and dissecting-rooms. Obsessed by his work, he forgets his family and friend, and does not reply to his father's letters.

One November night, his work is completed: Victor infuses the spark of life in the lifeless body, and it breathes, opening its yellow eye. Suddenly disgusted by the ugly result of his labours, Victor rushes from the room and attempts to get some sleep, only to be disturbed by a nightmare in which, as he kisses Elizabeth, she changes into the corpse of his mother. Starting from his sleep, he sees the monster entering the bedroom, and flees the house; whereupon he meets Henry, who has at last been allowed to come to university. Victor makes no mention of the monster to Henry, and is relieved to find that it has disappeared when they reach his rooms; but his exhaustion and terror bring on a nervous fever through which Henry nurses him for several months, concealing Victor's condition from the Frankenstein family.

When Victor has recovered, Henry gives him a letter from Elizabeth, which brings news of Victor's younger brothers Ernest and William, and of the Catholic servant-girl Justine Moritz — a favourite of Victor's late mother who has returned to the Frankenstein household after her own mother's death. Victor at last writes home to relieve his family's anxieties. Unable to bear the sight of a chemical apparatus, Victor joins Henry in the study of Oriental languages, while Henry helps to revive his love of nature and of his fellow-creatures. Just as Victor has overcome his morbid memories, a letter from his father arrives, telling him that little William has been murdered while wearing a valuable miniature of his mother, which is accepted as the explanation of the killer's motive; Elizabeth blames herself for letting him wear it. Victor now returns to Geneva after six years' absence. Outside the city, he visits Plainpalais, the scene of the crime, during a thunderstorm which illuminates the passing figure of the monster. Victor suspects that his creature is the murderer, but decides to say nothing, convinced that his explanation would be regarded as evidence of lunacy. Upon his arrival at home, Victor is told by Ernest that Justine has been arrested for William's murder, the miniature having been found on her; she will be tried the next day. Victor declares her innocent, without explaining himself, and assumes that the evidence will be too circumstantial to secure her conviction. Elizabeth too refuses to believe that Justine could be guilty, and is told by Alphonse Frankenstein to rely on the justice of Genevese law.

Victor attends the trial, where Justine is unable to account for her possession of the miniature. Even Elizabeth's speech defending Justine's good character fails to impress the judge, and Victor flees the courtroom in an agony of guilt. The next day, he is shocked to learn that Justine has been condemned on the basis of her own confession. When he and Elizabeth visit her, Justine explains that she confessed falsely because her priest had threatened her with excommunication. She is hanged, while Victor is plunged into a hell of remorse, restrained from suicide only by thoughts of Elizabeth and the urge for vengeance against the monster.

Two months later, while on a walking trip by the Mer de Glace near Chamonix, he again sees the monster, whom he addresses with vengeful hatred and attempts vainly to attack. The monster appeals to Victor to be calm and to recognize his responsibilities towards him: it is misery and rejection which have made him fiendish; happiness will make him virtuous again. Victor agrees to listen while the monster tells his story:

The monster's first sensations upon escaping Victor's room (with some of his clothes) are confused, but he lives off berries in the forest near Ingolstadt and becomes accustomed to the world around him. Finding a fire left by vagrants, he learns how to control it and cook food. Beyond the forest he finds a shepherd's hut, whose occupant runs away screaming, leaving the monster to eat his breakfast. At the next village he is driven off by a volley of stones and takes shelter in a hovel adjoining a cottage, where he watches the cottagers through a chink in the wall and becomes enchanted by their music. Through the winter he helps them secretly by collecting firewood at night, meanwhile slowly picking up their language (French), and learning their names: Agatha and Felix are brother and sister, supporting their aged and blind father, De Lacey. He sympathizes with these poor folk and admires their beauty and gentleness, but is horrified by his own reflection in a pond.

The De Laceys are gladdened by the arrival of Safie, a Turkish girl, whom they instruct in written French, thus teaching the peeping monster the elements of reading and history. He is horrified to learn from Volney's *Ruins* about human crime, tyranny, and the division of property. The more he learns of human society and its familial bonds, the more he feels his exclusion from it. He discovers the reason for Safie's presence as the De Laceys' history unfolds: they are exiles from France, punished for contriving the escape from prison of a Turkish merchant (Safie's father) who has been persecuted by the French government. Felix and Safie have fallen in love, and her father has at first promised to allow their marriage, but has then treacherously planned to take her off to Turkey instead. Safie, however, inspired by the ideals of female independence instilled in her by her deceased Christian mother, has escaped him to return to Felix.

The monster's self-education develops further as he finds some books in the wood: Goethe's *Sorrows of Werter*, Milton's *Paradise Lost*, and Plutarch's *Lives*. Of these, *Paradise Lost* affects him most deeply, as he compares his own situation with Adam's and then with Satan's. His other reading-matter, discovered in the coat he had taken at the time of his escape, is Victor's journal describing his creation; reading this, he curses his maker. After a year in the hovel, he at last summons the courage to introduce himself to the cottagers, carefully choosing a day when all but the blind father are absent. Before he can fully explain his predicament to the sympathetic old man, the others return. Agatha faints at the sight of him, Safie flees, and Felix strikes him before he escapes. Bitterly dejected, he decides to wage war against humanity in general and Frankenstein in particular. After the De Laceys have abandoned their cottage, he burns it down, and then heads for Geneva to demand just treatment from Victor.

On the way, he saves a girl from drowning but is still shot at by her guardian. Later, near Geneva, he meets a young boy and tries to befriend him, but is rejected rudely. When the boy (i.e. William) discloses that his father is M. Frankenstein, the monster begins his revenge upon Victor by strangling him. Seeing a young woman (i.e. Justine) passing by, he plants in her dress the miniature he has taken from William's neck. [1831: While hiding, he finds her asleep in a barn and plants the miniature on her then.] Here the monster concludes his narrative, and demands that Victor create a female companion for him.

Victor refuses at first, but when the monster promises to live with his mate away from human habitation in the wastes of South America, he agrees to his creature's demand. He forgets this promise for some time, but when his father presses him to marry Elizabeth, he decides that he must conclude this business first. To make a female, Victor needs advice from English experts, so he sets out with Henry on what is ostensibly a pre-marital vacation, first to London and then to Scotland. Victor leaves Henry at Perth and goes to a remote Orkney island to work on his next creation. As he works, he reflects upon the possible danger to the human race if his monsters breed. The monster has followed Victor and now arrives to check on his progress, but Victor tears to pieces the half-finished female, vowing never to resume this work. The monster swears revenge, threatening to appear on Victor's wedding night, and departs. Victor disposes of the female remains at sea, then falls asleep and wakes to find himself adrift in his small boat.

Victor lands at an Irish harbour to a hostile reception from the townsfolk, who accuse him of a murder committed the previous day by a man in a boat. When he is shown the body—that of Henry Clerval—he collapses into a prolonged fever. Evidence at last arrives of Victor's presence in the Orkneys at the time of the murder, and he is handed over to his father, who has come to collect him. On their way home, a letter reaches him from Elizabeth, in which she asks whether he loves another. He writes to reassure her, but warns that he has a dreadful secret which he will disclose the day after their wedding.

Victor and Elizabeth marry and set off for their honeymoon, staying for a night at an inn near Evian. While Victor goes out in search of the monster, whose threat he recalls, a scream is heard from the bedchamber: Elizabeth has been strangled. The monster grins through the window, then eludes Victor's gunfire and the innkeeper's search-party. Alphonse Frankenstein dies broken-hearted at this news, and Victor goes mad for a while. Upon recovering, he applies unsuccessfully to a Genevese magistrate to have the monster apprehended, then leaves Geneva to devote his life to vengeance against his creature. He pursues the monster—who deliberately leaves traces for him to follow—across Russia, and finds food and taunting messages left for him as his quarry heads north. The monster steals a sledge with dogs and sets off across the Arctic ice. Victor follows suit, but just as he is closing on the monster a crack in the ice separates them and he is set adrift to be found by Walton, whom he now instructs to kill the monster if he, Victor, should die.

As Walton resumes his own narrative, the ship is in danger of being crushed by ice, and he fears a mutiny by the crew whose lives he has endangered. The crew demand that they sail southward if the ice permits, but Frankenstein, although weakened by fever, reminds them of the heroic honour and glory of the expedition, and accuses them of cowardice. Walton reluctantly agrees to the crew's proposal; when Victor learns of this, he attempts to leave his sickbed, but collapses. After making a speech justifying his treatment of the monster, he dies. Later, Walton finds the monster himself by Victor's death-bed, asking pardon of his late creator. The monster explains the misery which his vengeance has brought upon him. Loathing himself, he now seeks only his own death, and sets off for the North Pole to build and ignite his funeral pyre.

# Index

Frankenstein discovered that I made notes concerning his history: he asked to see them, and then himself corrected and augmented them in many places; but principally in giving the life and spirit to the conversations he held with his enemy. 'Since you have preserved my narration,' said he, 'I would not that a mutilated one should go down to posterity.'

Walton, in Mary Shelley's *Frankenstein*

What his feelings were whom I pursued, I cannot know. Sometimes, indeed, he left marks in writing on the barks of the trees, or cut in stone, that guided me, and instigated my fury. 'My reign is not yet over . . .'

Victor, in Mary Shelley's *Frankenstein*